Comparative Government and Politics

Harper's Comparative Government Series

Michael Curtis, Editor

COMPARATIVE GOVERNMENT AND POLITICS

An Introductory Essay in Political Science

Second Edition

MICHAEL CURTIS

Rutgers University

Harper & Row, Publishers

New York   Hagerstown   San Francisco   London

To Mike and Tony, two beyond compare

Sponsoring Editor: Dale Tharp
Project Editor: Brigitte Pelner
Production Supervisor: Marion A. Palen
Compositor: P & M Typesetting, Incorporated

Library of Congress Cataloging in Publication Data

Curtis, Michael, Date
 Comparative government and politics.

Bibliography: p.
 Includes index.
 1. Comparative government. I. Title.
JF51.C85 1978 320.3 77–25060
ISBN 0–06–041462–6

Contents

Preface

This book is the core volume in the series of books that I have edited on individual countries and areas. It seeks to introduce students to the subject of comparative politics through both an analytical and institutional approach. A wise bird uses both wings to fly. There is no incompatibility in using a variety of approaches or techniques in the search for meaningful illumination of comparative politics.

A book of this length can only touch on a number of issues that might profitably be given more space. One of these is the large number of approaches and principles of methodology used in the study of the subject. But students approaching the subject of comparative politics for the first time need not be as concerned with the discussion of methodology or approaches as those more professionally interested in the subject. Most of the book is therefore concerned with comparative analysis of processes, ideas, and institutions. Believing that their use in the text will normally be immediately comprehensible, I have not dwelled upon the elucidation of such terms as "power" or "legitimacy," which have preoccupied students of politics for centuries.

In an era when the international political arena contains over 140 nation-states and when students pay greater attention to the influence of nongovernmental bodies and personnel on politics and society, few political analysts can claim to have achieved a total mastery or understanding of more than a limited number of systems or cultures. The great diversity of these systems and the political behavior within them and the rapidity of political change make general principles difficult to frame or to sustain.

Nevertheless, the study of comparative politics is at the heart of contemporary political science, and the need to classify regimes and political behavior remains. So does the need to compare those norms and values that underlie political behavior. This book, therefore, compares the bases on which regimes rest—the norms and rules supporting ordered society, and the different processes of citizen participation, group behavior, and party activity, as well as the major institutional activities of government. Examples have been drawn from a wide range of political regimes, institutions, and forms of political behavior, with an emphasis on the political experience of the developed countries, which is no doubt most familiar to beginning students.

Above all I have tried to avoid unnecessary jargon, unfamiliar terms, and unduly complex classificatory devices in the belief that "except ye utter by the tongue words easy to be understood, how shall it be known what is spoken?"

Among the colleagues and friends who have kindly shared their time and views with me, I particularly want to thank Bernard Brown, Harry Eckstein, Mark Roelofs, and Herbert Rowen.

MICHAEL CURTIS

Comparative Government and Politics

Chapter One

The Study
of Comparative Government
and Politics

Comparative politics is concerned with behavior, institutions, processes, ideas, and values present in more than one country. It searches for those regularities and patterns, those similarities and differences between more than one nation-state that help clarify the basic nature, working, and beliefs of regimes. It attempts to find either the common or the distinctive element in the political phenomena studied. The study involves comparison of both entire nation-states or political systems and partial systems or particular processes or institutional activity. It ranges over both time and space. Thus, comparative politics can study the political significance of Venice in the fifteenth century as compared with that of New York today[1] or look for similarities and differences between current democratic and communist regimes.

Since comparison rests on data, the study of comparative politics is empirical: it searches for and accumulates exact information through observation, experiments when possible, and uses a variety of research techniques. But it is also theoretical: it formulates propositions and explanatory hypotheses, and categorizes, classifies, or finds patterns that can order the data collected. Explanations in politics, however, do not spring automatically from observation of data; as in physics, they result from "ingenuity, tenacity, imagination and conceptual boldness."[2]

Comparative politics is also necessarily concerned with the norms, basic beliefs, and values underlying political activity. Some political theorists, such as Plato, believe the two are connected because the analysis of political patterns is valuable in the search for the good life and the good society. Others would explain the connection by saying that one cannot understand the operations of systems and political behavior without a knowledge of people's beliefs and values.

Why should political scientists seek out comparisons? A short answer might be that it aids understanding of a particular system or activity: Who really knows his own system who knows only that system? But the real reason is that comparison allows systematic empirical testing of generalizations used to order diverse data. By comparison, one can see patterns of activity taken by different regimes, analyze differing ideologies and processes of decision making, and examine propositions about both the importance of certain characteristics under study and the relationships between classes of data.

Comparative politics is scientific in method, but that does not mean its theories are certain, final, and unchangeable. For one thing, formulating hypotheses requires a selection from among data. The art of theorizing, as Michael Balfour has said, largely consists of knowing what to omit.[3] In other investigations, with other purposes or methods, different data may be selected as significant. Thus, the systems, classifications, and categories of comparative politics are always tentative, not final. Nor is the study reducible to mathematical formulas. Sometimes the most significant political phenomena are those changes in the mood of the times that are impossible to quantify.

Comparative politics in recent years has been greatly influenced by *behavioralism*. The motives behind the modern search for conceptual frameworks, the more rigorous approach to the search for data, the emphasis on careful precision, and statistical accuracy are beneficial. The behavioral approach, "is an attempt to improve our understanding of politics by seeking to explain the empirical aspects of political life by means of methods, theories, and criteria of proof that are acceptable according to the canons, conventions, and assumptions of modern empirical science."[4] Too often, however, this approach has become obsessed with the scientific method and technical jargon. The result has been studies whose rigor has come to seem like rigor mortis. Moreover the enthusiasm of some investigators which has led them to suggest that political studies are meaningful only when capable of quantitative analysis has led some to illustrate the obvious with the enthusiasm of shortsighted detectives.

There is now a lively and healthy ferment in the field of comparative politics on the nature of the subject and the manner in which it should be studied. A profusion of concepts, theories, models, classifications, and ideal types have been proposed as the basis of analysis.

At the heart of this ongoing discussion is a concept of politics itself. *Politics* is organized dispute about power and its use, involving choice among competing values, ideas, persons, interests, and demands. The study of politics is concerned with the description and analysis of the manner in which power is obtained, exercised, and controlled, the purposes for which it is used, the manner in which decisions are made, the factors that influence the making of those decisions, and the context in which those decisions take place.

Politics is a continuous and timeless process but an ever-changing one. The purposes, the contexts, the manner, the personnel, the arena of politics are always in flux. Since the selection of the significant and relevant subject matter of politics depends on changing goals and interests, the proper subjects for its study—whether institutions, behavior, power, decisions, or interests—always require personal interpretation.

The essence of political activity—command or influence over the action of people and over the disposition of things—is present in human behavior and social relations of many kinds: in the selection of a university president or departmental chairman, in the internal struggles among the various schools of psychoanalysis and followers of Sigmund Freud, Carl Jung, and Alfred Adler, in the struggle for leadership of the women's liberation movement, in the decision of a television network to show a comedy program rather than a Senate committee hearing. But these actions, and countless other human conflicts and decisions, are largely concerned with private rather than public affairs; they are not central to the operation of government, the activities of nation-states, and the exercise of political power. The student of politics is normally concerned with matters of public concern, with the behavior and acts that may concern the whole society or that may ultimately be resolved by the exercise of legitimate coercion.

Approaches and Techniques

Since Aristotle, students of comparative politics have analyzed the nature and quality of political regimes, the behavior of rulers and their relationship with the ruled, the manner in which rules are determined, made, and executed, the way in which conflicts are decided or arbitrated, the conditions of political stability and the causes of change, the factors affecting political decisions, and the values held by political communities. Until recently the area of comparative politics was limited largely to those few countries in Europe and the English-speaking world with highly developed or long-lived political institutions. In the post–World War II period efforts have been made to include the newer nation-states within the scope of universal or broad generalizations. Moreover, no modern student of politics is content merely with descriptions of legal processes, institutions, and constitutional arrangements in states. More attention is now paid to nongovernmental and social groups, to the political processes and the political behavior of individuals and groups. In the attempt to embrace a larger geographical area and a wider spectrum of human experience, to be more truly comparative and more realistic, theorists have borrowed concepts from other intellectual disciplines and have used a variety of different techniques and approaches.

Inquiry in comparative politics has taken many avenues, started from various points, and been influenced by a variety of other disciplines. Fashion in political study has sometimes been as ephemeral as style in women's clothing. Political scientists have leaned on history for rules and examples but have learned to be wary of analogy, for history can be misleading as well as instructive. From law have come such essential concepts as rights, obligations, contracts, and procedure. Philosophy has influenced the examination of the ethics and values of societies and the clarification of terminology. From political sociology the study has borrowed analyses of social classes, the social structure, the roles played by political "actors," and the process of socialization. Economics has contributed the concepts of bargaining, input-output, information costs, and equilibrium analysis. Psychoanalysis has aided the study of personality in politics, individual and group behavior, and the correlation of personal traits with social activities. Anthropology has shown the significance of the total culture of a community, including its knowledge, beliefs, art, law, ethics, and customs. From biology students of politics have drawn on the organic analogy and the ideas of homeostasis and of functions in the making and maintenance of systems. The new science of cybernetics has stressed the importance of communications, feedback, and control mechanisms. A new subject of inquiry, "peace research," applies the techniques of social scientists and mathematics to the study of international conflict.

Data for comparative inquiry has been assembled from a wide variety of sources: from studies of elites, mass opinion polls, voting statistics, content analysis, aggregate data such as economic, demographic, or census material, history, and other social sciences yielding information about political behavior.[5]

The techniques of comparative politics have included case studies, model building and game theory. *Case studies* dealing with unique situations have been used to identify the various factors, persons, and problems involved in political activity in order to come to fruitful generalization. *Models* or typologies have been created for categorizing and analyzing complex data; these characterize a period of time or a system by emphasizing its dominant features. By using mathematics and by simulating a situation, *game theory* tries to provide an understanding of social interaction and to define the nature of rational behavior among people agreeing to some minimum set of rules; players, areas, and objectives are designated and various degrees of uncertainty are allowed for. Using a model stemming from game theory, William Riker has proposed a theory of political coalitions that, assuming rational behavior, demonstrates that coalitions will be created that are just large enough to insure a winning combination.[6]

The different approaches in comparative politics start from the recognition that society and the political system consist of individuals, while at the same time individuals cannot be understood apart from their society or system. Historically, political analysts have varied between *macroanalysis* which focuses on the whole society or political system as the unit of analysis, and *microanalysis* which is concerned with the individual parts to a greater degree. Plato and Jean-Jacques Rousseau saw the body politic as a whole in which individuals played their part, whereas René Descartes and Thomas Hobbes tended to view society as the sum of its individual parts. Contemporary political analysts differ in similar fashion. Some prefer the study of individuals and groups, people rather than institutions, and analyze political behavior or participation. Some prefer the Gestalt approach of studying sequences of wholes rather than their constituent parts. Some, following the example of Thucydides when he compared the "civic cultures" of Athens and Sparta, see an individual society as possessing a political culture, a coherent pattern of thought and action (including knowledge, beliefs, ethics, norms, attitudes, orientation, expectations, and symbols), and purposes that differentiate it from other types of society. Some prefer area studies, which assume that the cultural uniformity in the area allows cultural traits and patterns to be identified and compared. Some emphasize the similarity of political functions in all regimes; others frame generalizations that help distinguish political behavior in the older from that of the newer nations. Some compare the working of a particular institution as it operates in different countries or areas. Some compare one system through time; others compare systems with others of the same type.

A technique, a method, an approach, is merely a tool by which to reach political understanding. Because differences exist about what is significant for purposes of comparison and about what activities ought to be compared, it is not surprising that many approaches are used by or may be appropriate to the political scientist. Two of the major and influential contemporary approaches, systems analysis and structural-functionalism, are discussed in this chapter: others, including group, modernization, and development theories, are dealt with in later chapters.

The Political System

In recent years some writers have spent considerable energy and imagination in trying to determine the limits of politics and the nature of the political system. Most of these writers have been influenced by the sociologist Talcott Parsons, who has tried to frame a theory of society suggesting that the unit of study is the entire social system and the main purpose of the system is survival or self-maintenance. This system can then be divided into subsystems, one of which is the political system. According to Parsons, all systems perform four functions: 1) adaptation, 2) attainment of goals, 3) integration, and 4) maintenance of patterns.[7] A systems approach to politics would thus mean assessing what are, or must be, the functions of a viable political system, examining how members and institutions within the system interact, and postulating the means by which stability is maintained and change introduced.

In political science, *systems analysis* is most closely identified with David Easton, who conceives political life "as imbedded in and surrounded by other social systems to the influence of which it is constantly exposed."[8] The political system responds to environmental influences and obtains information feedback that enables the system as a whole to regulate its behavior and respond to stress. Easton is concerned with "the basic processes through which a political system . . . is able to persist as a system of behavior."[9] For Easton the political system absorbs inputs in the form of demands on authorities and supports from institutions and the political community, and produces outputs in the form of policies and decisions.[10] Arguing for a comprehensive theoretical scheme to guide research, he regards the political system as concerned with "the authoritative allocation of values for a society." By this Easton means that values, in the form of material goods or other rewards, are distributed on the basis of decisions that are regarded as legitimate and therefore acceptable.

Closely related to the systems analysis approach is that of *structural-functionalism*. This approach is also concerned with the definition of particular functions as well as with the roles played by political structures and processes in the maintenance and adaptability of political systems. The most prominent advocate of this approach is Gabriel Almond who holds that all political systems have a structure, that all political structures perform many functions, that the same functions are performed in all political systems, and that none are either completely "modern" or completely "primitive."[11]

For Almond the political system is a unique process characterized by four input functions—political socialization and recruitment, political communication, interest articulation, and interest aggregation—and by three output capabilities—rule making, rule application, and rule adjudication. By these terms Almond means the following:

Inputs

political socialization: the transmitting of the political values and norms of the society;

political recruitment: the obtaining of political leaders;

political communication: the sending of messages within the political system and between the system and the outside;

interest articulation: the voicing of political demands to the decision makers;

interest aggregation: the managing of those demands by bodies such as parties and interest groups.

Outputs

The three terms correspond closely to the familiar division of political powers, legislative, executive, and judicial, but they also allow for a wider interpretation than these powers normally suggest.

To counter the criticism that his concept was rather static, in a later version of his approach Almond suggests three different kinds of functions: capability functions, conversion functions, and system maintenance and adaptation.[12] Capability functions comprise regulative, extractive, distributive, and responsive activities; conversion functions consist of interest articulation, interest aggregation, political communication, and the three former "output functions"; system maintenance and adaptation includes political socialization and recruitment.

Other similar approaches to Almond's include those of David Apter and Karl Deutsch. David Apter combines a structural and behavioral approach; he maintains that political systems can be analyzed by studying the choices made about systems of values and conceptions of man as well as the context in which the choices occur.[13] Karl Deutsch regards the political system as a network of communication channels for the achievement of goals by the acquisition and use of information; the feedback of such information insures that an organization can change its state in response to information received.[14]

Yet though these views on the political system have often been quoted by students of politics, the definition of what is political (and is thus worthy of attention by students of politics) and the political activities with which it is concerned remains inexact and is not self-evident. A few examples may illustrate the point. Baseball may be simply a national sport with some slight statistical interest or it may be the object of governmental antitrust legislation. College students may be simply inhabitants of an academic institution or members of a revolutionary street mob. The Venus de Milo and the Mona Lisa may be esteemed objects of esthetic appreciation in the Louvre or symbols of "French" civilization and greatness. An Irish wake may be an occasion for private grief or an opportunity for political machination. The Olympic Games may be seen as an international athletic competition or as a demonstration of national chauvinism. Striped pants and morning coats are usually only of sartorial significance, but their use by envoys to the Commission of the European Economic Community led Charles de Gaulle to protest that their wearers were being endowed with undue diplomatic importance. Sexual relations are particularly private in nature, but the fear of world overpopulation and changing moral attitudes about homosexuality have led to political interest in those relations. Music lovers differ over the merit of Richard Wagner and Richard Strauss, but for Israel these composers are politically distasteful and their works remain unheard.

Structural-functional analysis has been useful in formulating a set of functions deemed essential to an organized political unit and in suggesting that these functions can be performed by different institutions at different times or in different places. But this approach says little about the significance of politics in social life or of whether politics can be distinguished from other social activities. In itself the theory provides no way to determine what is truly "functional" or "dysfunctional" (i.e., useful or unuseful) for maintaining a society. Thus Carl Friedrich has argued that even unadmired behavior such as political corruption and secrecy may be functional in allowing the adaptation of structures to changing communal values, interests, and beliefs.[15]

Underlying both systems theory and structural-functionalism are analogies between a biological organism or a mechanism and society. But these analogies are misleading because the members of a social system are more autonomous than the cells of an organism. Moreover the view of the system as a self-sufficient, internally consistent entity, in which equilibrium may be upset by the dysfunction of some element thus threatening the "health" of the whole system, converts a metaphor useful for analysis and making generalizations into a useless abstraction. This oversimplification by both systems analysis and structural-functionalism has led advocates to assume mistakenly that a particular function is essential and to accept unquestioningly that existing systems are healthy.

In addition to these faults shared with structural-functionalism, the systems approach runs into additional difficulties because it does not necessarily lead to causal explanations, works on a high level of abstraction remote from empirical findings, and is somewhat one-tracked in its conception of the way political systems operate. The view of David Easton that all the variables influencing political situations must be brought within a conceptual structure that can illustrate the dynamic relationship among those variables logically means the study of the whole of human activity — a forbiddingly difficult task.

The student of comparative politics can rarely be engaged, either singly or in collaboration, in such an ambitious endeavor. His or her dilemma is an acute one. To deal with large subject areas is a formidable task, but the more limited the area and topic of study, the fewer valid generalizations are likely to flow from them. Students therefore tend to equivocate between attempts at universality and concern for the unique qualities of a particular phenomenon or system. The larger the number of systems or phenomena studied, the more difficult becomes the search for generalizing concepts. It is usually more rewarding, as well as more manageable, to treat the subject matter of politics at a middle-range level.

The advice of Lord Acton to historians was "to study problems not periods."[16] For students of politics this still seems the most useful advice. In studying problems they must look for political information, understanding, and explanation. But the empirical problem, as Giovanni Sartori has argued, is that "we badly need information which is sufficiently precise to be meaningfully comparable," while the theoretical problem is that "we grievously lack a disciplined use of terms and procedures of comparison."[17] To meet this problem there appears to be a growing consensus in the field of comparative politics that a lower level of abstraction than universality is desirable and that the study of partial segments of systems and partial theories addressing themselves to particular aspects of political behavior and institutions are the most profitable line of inquiry.[18]

Politics: Art or Science?

Social scientists in recent years have called for the use of scientific method in the collection of empirical data about behavior and institutions and in the analysis of decision-making. But there is no exact parallel between the study of politics and of the natural sciences. Social and political phenomena are different in kind from physical phenomena. Causal relationships are more difficult to establish in political affairs. Great events may grow from small causes: for Leo Tolstoy in *War and Peace* the movement of a few birds was the immediate cause of the Battle of Borodino. Historians warn against attempts to make events seem automatic or inevitable rather than contingent or unpredictable: they differ on the essence and even the dating of major historical periods. The uniqueness of historical events, the difficulty or impossibility of experimentation with the raw material of politics, the intractable elements in behavior that are not quantifiable, the possible effect of the observer and the act of investigation on the behavior observed, are warnings to those who try to find more pattern in things than is actually there. An insuperable difficulty in political studies is that people react to what is said about them, thereby reinforcing or denying prophecies.

Decision making is often a disorderly process; analysts may try to impose patterns on situations where the relevant participants have flexible positions and act to deal with immediate difficulties. The power of governments to control events is limited, and the result of their action is often unintended. Political activity is influenced by the pressure of events, by the cumulative effect of past programs, and by current administrative needs rather than by coherent party programs. The "output," seen by Almond and Easton as the end product of political activity, is not in many cases easily summarized. It would be difficult to measure the "output" of the United States State Department in any useful sense. Politics, as one recent British prime minister said, is largely trying to empty the in-tray. Political problems are resolved temporarily rather than solved permanently; politics seeks approximation, not the absolute.

Before turning to the discussion of substantive issues in following chapters, it may be worthwhile to look at the variety of problems that beset the scientific analysis of comparative politics.

The Existence or Maintenance of Nonrational Behavior

Political behavior is not necessarily conducted on a rational basis or on scientific principles. This renders scientific study difficult if not impossible. The conduct of Senator Joseph McCarthy in his anticommunist hearings in the 1950s seem, in retrospect, inexplicable and irrational. Caesar's decisions to fight his battles were made on the basis of an inspection of the insides of chickens, while Prime Minister Mackenzie King of Canada communed with voices from the spirit world.[19] Politics provides frequent examples of irrational behavior and of a divorce between intended form and political reality. Max Weber observed that an organization may continue when it has no function to perform because an official may be living off it. The official fly swatter to the sultan of Morocco continued into an era of air conditioning. A grenadier guard was sent to be on duty outside 10 Downing Street 175 years after an attempt had been made on the life of the prime minister, Sir Robert Walpole. Institutions, as well, continue though they may perform no function. The British Board of Trade remains in nominal existence but never meets. The Swedish Minister of Education has the right to appoint university professors, but never exercises his power.

In postwar Indonesia volcanic eruptions have been the decisive factor in some political decisions; in Burma, astrology has been an instrument of political planning. Making concessions to the supposed magical number 9, the 1967 South Vietnamese constitution (written by a constituent assembly composed of 117 members) contained 117 words in its constitution which included 117 clauses. Religious dignitaries may be associated with political violence as are the Jan Sangh and other Hindus in India, Buddhists in Ceylon and Vietnam, and Muslims in Indonesia.

Alas for neat generalizations, laws are not always just or rational and people do not always choose to be good. Few today would accept René Descartes' notion that human nature is uniform and perfectible; they are more likely to be aware of what James Madison called "a degree of depravity in mankind" and Friedrich Engels "the wicked passions of man."[20] Moreover, motives of the political actors are an intangible with differing degrees of self-interest and regard for the public interest always mixed. Consequently, political action is inherently ambiguous. Even the former Russian leader Nikita Khrushchev acknowledged that his acquisition of the post of prime minister as well as that of leader of the Communist party represented "a certain weakness," the bug of ambition, as well as dedication.[21]

The view of theorists like Anthony Downs that political behavior is akin to economic behavior, and that, assuming the operation of rational self-interest, individuals try to obtain maximum political satisfaction and parties the maximum numbers of votes, disregards the fact that behavior in social organizations is more complex than in economic matters.[22] Political decisions are normally made to accomplish a specific purpose, but they may also often enhance the power of the individual or group making the decision. The wielding of influence takes diverse forms: the corridor may be more meaningful than the committee room, social relationships more than official statements and discussion. Fanaticism may compete with reason. Men, as John Henry Newman said, will die for a dogma who will not even stir for a conclusion.

The Value-Laden Observer

Differing values and beliefs of analysts affect their political perspective. Since Lenin, Marxists have seen "imperialism" as the highest and last stage of capitalism, in which capitalists demand markets for their investments and hence conflict arises out of competing economic interests. Non-Marxists may view the same phenomena as the outcome of autocracy or the result of the search for power rather than profit. For Soren Kierkegaard social leveling meant the destruction of the individual; for Harold Laski equality must be the informing spirit of social relations. Freud wondered pessimistically whether cultural development would succeed in overcoming the disturbance of social life resulting from the instinct for aggression and self-destruction. Gustave Le Bon saw crowd psychology—the behavior of people in crowds—as an example of abnormal psychology and of unconscious action and instinct; modern historians see the crowd in revolutionary situations as rationally defending its interests against its enemies and suggest that the high price of bread can be the determining factor in its behavior.[23] Criminals are normally regarded as unworthy members of society but some Far Eastern cultures have treated them as gods and Fyodor Dostoevsky looked on them as redeemers. The *lumpen proletariat* that Marx despised has become for Frantz Fanon the group that will inspire violent catharsis.

Political analysis, in other words, is infused with value. If the values of society are molded by existing facts and behavior, it is equally true that facts, and the search for relevant facts, are conditioned by the values of the analyst. A value-free social science is appropriate for computers, not for men. For the student of comparative politics a sense of irony may be as useful as a computer, and an understanding of *fortuna* as indispensable as knowledge of Fortran.

The Imprecision of Terminology

Political scientists are partly engaged in the same enterprise as Confucius and modern-day linguistic analysts: the rectification of names. The use of scientific method is partly aimed at clarifying terminology and making it more precise. But definition of political terms has always been difficult and meaning elusive. The habitual terms—power, influence, authority, control, left and right, radical or traditional, democracy or dictatorship—can be given an infinite number of meanings. Even seemingly clear terms have been put to peculiar uses; coins of the French Napoleonic era bore the inscription "Emperor of the French Republic."

Life is a swallow and theory a snail: our political terminology always lags behind changing reality. A "radical British foreign policy" was one thing in the prewar world in which the sun never set on the British Empire; it is quite another in a world that is one-third communist and in which British power has declined. The rhetoric appropriate to the ideological division of the world between East and West continues in a period when the nature of the systems in those countries is changing and when the major confrontation may well be between North and South, the developed and the underdeveloped countries.

The Problem of Change

Analysis tries to capture political systems in a state of equilibrium, and structural-functional analysis almost requires such a state, but the law of life is constant change and flux. The continual demands people make on the still scarce resources available and the conflicting pressures exerted as they pursue their different ends may mean that the period of temporary equilibrium is very short. It is change rather than equilibrium that is the normal state of affairs. Robert Michels' argument that "power is always conservative" does not deny the introduction of appropriate changes in organization and actions.[24]

The incredible rapidity of change is a novel feature of our age, and the political consequences are not easy to assimilate. In the period since World War II the real gross world product has quadrupled, adding three times as much to annual world productive power as in all previous history. This has been accompanied by a great increase in population, increased life expectancy, reduced infant mortality, and a change in territorial distribution. The current world population of 4 billion is likely to double in the next 30 years. In Latin America, where population has tripled between 1930 and 1970, food production must be increased by over 3 percent annually simply to keep pace with population growth. Although about 60 percent of the world's population is rural, the percentage living in towns is increasing: over 300 million have migrated from rural areas in the last 25 years. About three-quarters of the world's population now live in the developing countries.

Internationally the number of nation-states has increased by 65 since 1947. In 1914 about 84 percent of the world's land area was occupied or controlled by Europeans; at the end of World War II there were only three fully independent African states. Decolonization has been rapid, and few areas now remain under Western rule. In the United Nations the Afro-Asian bloc of 60 is now the largest single group. Economic, social, and technological developments and the problems of food, population, energy, inflation, and global disparities have to be set in an international rather than national context. The contemporary concern for oil and fish has already led to proposals for the extension of territorial waters from the traditional 3 miles to 12 and for an exclusive economic zone extending 200 miles from a nation's shoreline since this area includes four-fifths of the world's sea fisheries and nearly all its exploitable offshore oil. New weaponry and strategic arms have not led to political advantage but rather to nuclear stalemate.

In developed nations social and economic organization has become more complex and interdependent, the task of government more vital as well as more difficult, and the cost of public services very high. The American government at all levels employs over 14 million people, at a cost of $523 billion—about 37 percent of the gross national product compared with 12 percent in 1929. In Britain government expenditures account for 60 percent of the GNP. European economies in general have been dependent on 15 million migrants as blue-collar workers in the last 20 years.

In the developing nations, where economic activities range from the use of hydroelectric dams to subsistence farming, thought from magic

and witchcraft to scientific education, and ways of life from the traditional, unchanged for centuries, to modern Western behavior, movements of national revolution have in a brief time been changed into
organs of state power. The great difference in comparative study of
the older and the newer nations is that the former have a large number of fixed points around which changes can be made and can fit
into a generally acceptable and understood pattern. In the newer nations there are few fixed positions of this kind, and future change will
bear less relationship to their indigenous ways of life and behavior.

Political conflict in both developed and developing countries may
take the form of parliamentary debates or civil war, and societies may
be held together as much by the constraint necessary to mitigate such
conflict as by consensus. Political systems may be seen to some extent
as lying in a spectrum ranging from those regimes using violence as a
last resort to those prepared to use it immediately. Change often occurs through violence, coups, or conspiracy. Africa between 1963 and
1966 witnessed 17 coups; between 1963 and 1975 there were 18
coups in the former French colonies of Africa. In Argentina there
were 7 military coups between 1955 and 1976. Violent action recently
has included sectarian assassinations, kidnapping, hijacking, sabotage,
and a diversity of terrorist activities. Understandably, terrorist groups
do not exist in dictatorial systems, which are more apt than liberal societies to suppress them. Violence is nothing new in politics, nor is the
use of violence by political manipulators, as in the Roman Republic
when the "scum of Romulus" were instigated to act. Yet political
analysis has often tended to regard violence as exceptional rather than
as a constant factor and to see political stability as the norm in world
politics.

The most dramatic form of political change is by revolution. Internal conflicts may erupt into revolutions because of some incompatibility between existing social and economic conditions and the
nature and operation of the political system. Social tensions may also
result from conflict over authority, excessive state ambitions, and
weaknesses in the political structure. For Aristotle the main cause of
revolution was the resentment against existing inequality and the feeling of injustice in social arrangements. Crane Brinton, in his comparative study of four revolutions, suggested certain factors were present in all four cases: (1) a society that was advancing economically;
(2) increasing class or status antagonisms; (3) a ruling class that had lost
faith in itself; (4) a financial crisis; and (5) a disaffected body of intellectuals.[25] But revolutions have been more complex than is sug-

gested by Brinton's thesis. Chalmers Johnson has argued that revolutions may arise when an existing elite is unable to act and to control the social consequences resulting from some new process or factor such as rapid economic growth, imperial conquest, new ideas, or technological advances.[26] Revolutions become more probable if there is a revolutionary organization already in existence, if there is a leader who can inspire support, and if the regime has been defeated in war. To aid comparative analysis, Johnson has formulated a classification of revolution consisting of six types—jacquerie, millenarian, anarchistic, jacobin communist, conspiratorial coup d'état, and militarized mass insurrection—depending on the nature of the regime, the ruling body, the revolutionary movement, and its ideological convictions.

The Complexity of Political Systems and Behavior

Political life, like personal behavior, is rarely all of one piece. John Locke argued for political liberty and defended slavery. James Mill advocated birth control and fathered nine children. Thomas Jefferson wrote the Declaration of Independence but never freed his own slaves. All systems have some traditional and some modern elements, and the nature of the system is determined by the relative quantity it contains of the different elements. Democratic Britain has a House of Lords still largely based on heredity. England is a monarchy without royalists; France is a republic, some of whose citizens prefer a monarchy. Democratic Switzerland denied women the vote until 1971. In democratic United States not all citizens have effective civil rights. In many Latin American countries European mores and civilization have been superimposed on an Indian culture based on religious belief and ritual revolving around the land and agriculture. Labor union federations in Holland are still divided along religious lines. A highly developed Japanese economy and urban society coexist with small-scale industry, paternalism, and personal factionalism in politics; Kabuki plays and Kimono coexist with baseball and color television. Neither official Marxist-Leninist ideology nor periodic persecution has eradicated the importance of religion for many Russian citizens. Communist China on a number of occasions has produced the astonishing spectacle of government by graffiti and Peking wallposters.

All systems have complexities of this kind. The newer nations suffer to some degree from internal conflict between traditional and Western influences and between central authority and local groups and traditions. Dress, behavior, education are all subjects of dispute. India is beset by the debate over whether to use English as the official language or whether to use a native tongue, Nigeria by whether to use Muslim law or British common law, Egypt by whether to abide by Islamic divorce laws or amend them, Israel by whether to adhere to traditional Jewish dietary laws, Kenya by how to balance the authority of traditional local courts presided over by tribal elders with the system of courts following the British model.

The new African countries and Turkey are torn between traditional Islamic rules and modern secular trends, with the forces favoring an Islamic community and nationalism coexisting unhappily. In contemporary Morocco the traditional monarchy exists alongside a new multiparty system. Turkey since 1960 has introduced new constitutional and parliamentary institutions while maintaining traditional forms of social relations. Thirty years of communist control in Yugoslavia have not ended clan attachments in politics or traditional Balkan rivalries. Kwame Nkrumah, while in power in Ghana and planning the Volta hydroelectric dam, used a cane to protect himself from evil and had little bags attached to his chair to ward off evil spirits while at the same time keeping on his desk a copy of Machiavelli's *The Prince*. In Saudi Arabia some religious dignitaries insist that the world is flat, while the air force makes use of modern radar. In newly emancipated former colonies, politicians differ on whether to speak the language of their former masters, English or French, or their own native language as a symbol of national resurgence.

Simplistic or reductionist explanations of the dominant forces in political events—"Eastern bankers," the Establishment, Catholic doctrine, the Freemasons, race, economics, the communist conspiracy, Zionist expansion, colonialism, American imperialism—vary between the incomplete and the paranoic. Millenarian beliefs, often advocating a thousand-year reign of the saints, appeal to an original tradition of faith in the face of troubles and events arousing fears. Equally improper are attempts to explain political behavior in terms of a single psychological variable such as an inferiority complex or authoritarian personality, or to argue that a single factor—love, power, the need for achievement, custom, sympathy—is the dominant feature in political behavior. Each political theorist either has his or her own list of motives, preferences, or values that propel people or suggests a list of needs that should be satisfied, but no list does full justice to the complexity of human motives and actions.

Another related problem arises from the fact that although regimes imitate activity or institutions in other systems, dissimilar activities or consequences often result. The Weimar Republic, seeking to achieve a stable balance between the legislature and the executive, imitated the British method of parliamentary dissolution with disastrous results. Formally similar presidencies may be constitutional in the United States and autocratic in Latin America. In Britain adjournment motions are used to draw attention to an issue. In India they are treated as motions of censure, and only rarely can they be discussed in the legislature. The Soviet Union may have a formal legislative assembly, the Supreme Soviet, but many of the normal functions of legislative bodies are performed by other organs such as the Central Committee of the Communist party. The Australian Senate was created in imitation of the American model as the chamber of the states in a federal system, but it has not functioned in this way. Political reality often does not coincide with institutional form: elections in Nazi Germany, constitutional provisions for liberty in the Soviet Union and China, the formal election of a Mexican president bear little relationship to the reality.

The Figures in the Political Arena

Politics is largely limited to those who are taken into account in the making of decisions or to those who can make claims on government. Paul Goodman has argued that many of the frustrations of modern youth arise from the fact that their important problems are treated by their elders as nonexistent.[27] Politics is essentially concerned with what people do, not with what they failed to do. History is largely a record of the successful: as G. W. F. Hegel said "only those peoples who form a state come under our notice." Only in recent years has the term "the People" become synonymous with the whole adult population of a nation rather than the more limited parts meant by the term until the twentieth century. Even in the most developed countries the political rights of women are of very recent vintage.

It is a political axiom that the squeaky wheel gets the grease. If conflict propels people into politics, it is equally true that some groups, such as consumers, have been unduly neglected because they have no voice or powerful organ to express their needs or to unite them. Some have argued that the bias in a political process or culture may lead to "nondecisions," the ignoring or disregarding of issues or prevention of a challenge to the values or interests of decision makers.[28]

Political analysis is rendered more difficult by the uncertainty of the role capable of being played by individuals who are considered to be part of latent or "potential" groups.

Patterns and Analogies

For Aristotle, the person who existed outside of a political system was either a beast or a god. Modern politics assumes a society that is a permanent community, in which social relationships extend beyond the family, household, village, or tribe. From an anthropological or historical perspective humanity has passed successively through the savage stage, the most primitive cultural stage, and the barbarian stage associated with the beginning of agriculture and the use of bronze, into the civilized age, linked with the beginning of writing and the use of iron.

Certain patterns of activity seem inherent in economic modernization and in political development. All developed political systems are marked by a concentration of power, by centralization of authority, by a large number of activities performed by government.

The newer nations are all struggling to develop politically. Their goals include the greater formalization of political organizations and procedures, the greater differentiation of organization and specialization of function, the growing capacity of the system to take effective, coherent action and to adapt readily to new problems and conditions, and the development of rational bureaucracy.

But development in both older and newer nations is not necessarily in one direction and there is no inevitability about the process of historical development or political change. In a Europe where persuasion was replacing coercion, Joseph Stalin and Adolf Hitler became heads of regimes based on terror as a controlling instrument. In a world where secularism is rapidly replacing religious convictions, the Islamic League was formed in 1962 to unite the Muslims of the Middle East on a religious basis in adherence to Islamic law and education; there are now 42 Islamic countries whose representatives regularly meet for discussion. In Ulster the bitter dispute between the 1 million Protestants and the half-million Catholics seems unresolvable. The belief of democratic theorists that the expansion of the suffrage would lead to greater tolerance and political understanding has been belied by contemporary evidence that intolerant extremist movements are often more likely to be supported by the lower class than by the middle and upper classes. Reform of the franchise has not ended class antagonism nor thrown them into the shadows of oblivion as William Gladstone believed it would. As long as political will can be exercised, historical trends will not be synonymous with scientific laws.

Political analogies serve a valuable comparative purpose. It is useful to illustrate the medieval nature of some contemporary systems by showing the similar behavior of the Glaoui family in twentieth-century Morocco or the sheiks of Saudi Arabia with that of the barons in the English Wars of the Roses in the fifteenth century. It may help both understanding and practice to indicate the parallel between the changing relationship and reduction of conflict between Protestants and Catholics in the sixteenth and seventeenth centuries and the possibility of coexistence between East and West in the contemporary world. Light is thrown on the disputes among the science advisers of Winston Churchill in World War II or the group around Franklin Roosevelt when they are compared with earlier court politics.

But political analogies must also be treated carefully. Opposition to United States policy in Southeast Asia in the 1960s was not necessarily analogous to the appeasement policy of the Western powers toward Hitler in prewar Europe. Though interesting parallels may be drawn between the French and Russian revolutions, it is dubious that their pattern was enough alike for Leon Trotsky to see Stalin's conquest of power as the Thermidor of the Russian Revolution or for Alexander Kerensky to refuse to be the Russian Marat. For all students of politics the trap of historical inevitability is an ever-present danger. It is also misleading and sometimes dangerous to take metaphors too seriously, to equate Oswald Spengler's imagery of the spring or fall of a culture with the inevitability of decline of a political system, or to regard the United States as a "sick society" because of some undesirable features or incidents in the society.

Notes

[1] Fernand Braudel, *The Mediterranean and the Mediterranean World in the Age of Philip II* (New York: Harper & Row, 1972–1973).

[2] N. R. Hanson, *Patterns of Discovery* (New York: Cambridge University Press, 1965), p. 72.

[3] Michael Balfour, *States and Mind* (London: Cresset Press, 1953).

[4] R. A. Dahl, "The Behavioral Approach in Political Science: Epitaph for a Monument to a Successful Protest," *American Political Science Review* (December 1961), p. 767.

[5] Karl W. Deutsch, "Recent Trends in Research Methods in Political Science," in J. C. Charlesworth, ed., *A Design for Political Science, Annals* (1966), pp. 149–178.

[6] William Riker, *The Theory of Political Coalitions* (New Haven, Conn.: Yale University Press, 1962), p. 47.

[7] Talcott Parsons, *The Social System* (New York: Free Press, 1951).

[8] David Easton, *A Framework for Political Analysis* (Englewood Cliffs, N.J.: Prentice-Hall, 1965), p. 25.

[9] Ibid., p. x.

[10] David Easton, *The Political System* (New York: Knopf, 1953).

[11] G. A. Almond and J. Coleman, eds., *The Politics of the Developing Areas* (Princeton University Press, 1960).

[12] G. A. Almond and G. B. Powell, Jr., *Comparative Politics: A Developmental Approach* (Boston: Little, Brown, 1966).

[13] David Apter, *The Politics of Modernization* (University of Chicago Press, 1965).

[14] Karl Deutsch, *The Nerves of Government* (New York: Free Press, 1963).

[15] Carl Friedrich, "Political Pathology," *Political Quarterly* (January – March 1966), pp. 70–85.

[16] Lord Acton, *Essays on Freedom and Power* (Boston: Beacon Press, 1948), p. 25.

[17] Giovanni Sartori, "Concept Misformation in Comparative Politics," *American Political Science Review* 64 (1970), 1052.

[18] Joseph La Palombara, "Macrotheories and Microapplications in Comparative Politics," *Comparative Politics* 1 (1968), 52–78.

[19] Bruce Hutchinson, *The Incredible Canadian; A Candid Portrait of MacKenzie King* (New York: McKay, 1953), p. 4.

[20] James Madison, *The Federalist*, No. 55.

[21] Nikita Khrushchev, *Khrushchev Remembers: The Last Testament* (Boston: Little, Brown, 1974), p. 18.

[22] Anthony Downs, *An Economic Theory of Democracy* (New York: Harper & Row, 1957).

[23] Harold Laski, *A Grammar of Politics* (New Haven, Conn.: Yale University Press, 1929); G. Le Bon, *The Crowd* (New York: Macmillan, 1896); Sigmund Freud, *Civilization and its Discontents* (New York: Cape, 1930); Soren Kierkegaard, *The Present Age* (New York: Harper & Row, 1962).

[24] Robert Michels, *Political Parties* (New York: Dover, 1959), p. 366.

[25] Crane Brinton, *The Anatomy of Revolution* (New York: Random House/Vintage Books, 1965).

[26] Chalmers Johnson, *Revolutionary Change* (Boston: Little, Brown, 1966).

[27] Paul Goodman, *Growing Up Absurd* (New York: Random House, 1960).

[28] Peter Bachrach and Morton S. Baratz, *Power and Poverty* (New York: Oxford University Press, 1970).

Chapter Two

Society
and the State

"If men were angels," wrote James Madison, "no government would be necessary."[1] For many, *anarchism*—the view that society should be based on the voluntary cooperation of individuals and groups, with governmental authority eliminated—is a philosophically attractive solution to problems of social relationships, but there is no escaping the present necessity for the exercise of power and the establishment of rules by which human beings can be governed and controlled. The rules may be the result of a particular conception of the public good or a response by decision makers to the needs or wants of individuals and groups.

Every organized society has an ordered structure and a political process to make rules that implement decisions and allocate power. The *political process* consists of the interactions of nongovernmental participants, such as individuals and groups attempting to exert political influence, and governmental institutions that collectively constitute the "state." The state wields or claims to wield *legitimate power* and *coercion*—that power and force which is accepted as legal and valid by those over whom it is exerted.

Underlying the political process in a society is its *political culture*, which has been defined by Sidney Verba as "the system of empirical beliefs, expressive symbols, and values which define the situation in which political action takes place."[2] Members of society are induced to accept and understand the political culture by a process of socialization.

This chapter discusses some aspects of the interaction of society and state useful for comparative analysis of the political process. These issues are:

1. The role of groups in politics and the nature of public policy
2. The significance of political culture and of personality traits for understanding the political beliefs and values of a society
3. The interrelationship between groups and government
4. The basis for claiming that a ruler's power is legitimate
5. The ideologies and values on which institutions rest
6. The problem of the creation of stable political systems
7. The end or purpose of political activity

Groups in Politics

Political action is played on a social stage occupied by many different individuals, groups, and associations—economic, social, religious, cultural, intellectual, tribal, or kinship—pursuing diverse purposes and conflicting objectives. Recent sociological literature may have overemphasized the shift in modern Western culture from the Protestant ethic based on the individual conscience to the social ethic with its stress on the group as the source of all creativity and on the need for belonging. But all individuals belong to some social groups that may have a life of their own and may outlive individual members and that generally have a structure regulated by rules and procedures. The web and totality of social relationships make up *society*.[3]

All politics can be seen as interaction among individuals and groups having conflicting interests and ends. It is futile to base political or social systems on concepts such as brotherhood or love, however admirable these concepts may be in the abstract and however meaningful they may be in small group relationships. Religions founded by Buddha, Lao-Tzu, Jesus, and Muhammad, and secular ideologies such as democracy, socialism, communism, and pacifism have sought in vain to establish the international brotherhood of the human race.

Indeed, provided it does not take too violent a form, conflict, as Lewis Coser has shown in *The Functions of Social Conflict*, may even be a constructive as well as a destructive factor in the functioning of a society, acting as a warning signal or as a means for introducing change. Moreover, the greater the number of groups with multiple, overlapping membership, the more probable it is that conflict will be reduced unless the groups are ideologically identical, and thus reinforce conviction.

For the theorists of group politics, public policy is the equilibrium reached in the struggle among groups, and the function of political institutions is to mediate among them. The most influential of these theorists have been Arthur Bentley and David Truman. Bentley held that a *group* was "a mass activity" that was directed toward some definite course of conduct."[4] Truman defined an *interest group* as a number of individuals who share some common characteristics and who interact to make claims on others in a society.[5]

Groups take many different forms. For purposes of comparative analysis classification may be made on the basis of:

1. The degree of formal organization of the group
2. The number of members and its strength
3. The basis of the composition of the group—whether class, occupation, ethnicity, religion, attitude, or issue orientation
4. The range of its interests
5. The manner and the intensity with which it pursues its interests
6. The degree to which its activity is planned or spontaneous
7. The impact the group makes on political circles

The major motives for the study of groups in comparative politics have been the desire to illuminate an often neglected area of political activity and the hope of finding where and in whose hands real power in a society is located. Considerable empirical data on nongovernmental organizations and activities have been accumulated, but this study raises some methodological and philosophical problems.

Most studies have been concerned with a particular group or a small number of groups rather than with comparative analysis on a wider scale that would provide a framework for ordering the data. Philosophically, critics of the view that politics is essentially a bargaining process among conflicting pressure groups see the need for institutions to relate groups to the community as a whole. There exists, according to the critics, a common good or general interest that can be known and defined, that is concerned with the "common preservation and general will of men" in Jean Jacques Rousseau's term, and that may require the subordination of individual or group interests. In moments of crisis or emergency or during a struggle for national independence, a sense of the general interest or a spirit of self-sacrifice and dedication often arises, and governments have always exercised the right to act for the public welfare. Even the dictators of Rome acted on the maxim "see no harm befalls the Republic."

Equally, the creation of certain conditions clearly benefits everyone—clean air, national seashores, parks, pollution control, cultural activities, internal order—and the public interest in these and other matters is more than simply "the process of group accommodation," or the result of group pressures exerted through conflict, compromise, or aggregation. Much of the political action of the last century in the politically developed nations has been concerned with attempts to establish community interests in the face of entrenched privilege.

But genuine differences may exist on what constitutes "the community interest" and on its alleged primacy over "vested," "sectional," or "selfish" interests. Since all decisions involve choice, the public interest is never immediately apparent nor automatically translatable into empirical terms. In its starkest form the choice is between "guns and butter," as it was for the Nazis; in less extreme form it may be between controlling billboards on highways and allowing advertisers to choose a location they like, or between subsidizing railroads with deficits and building alternative means of transportation. In small, homogeneous groups it is conceivable that a common interest may motivate all members. In large organizations, such a common interest is not self-evident and political leadership must articulate it. The concept of a public interest has been claimed as a standard by which political acts can be judged, and which is applicable to the whole community. To this end a government may seek to base its actions on a "felicific calculus"—on the greatest happiness of the greatest number—or on the public welfare. But more frequently the concept is claimed by a group interested in some particular objective.

The argument for a group will or interest and for a common or general will or interest must, however, always be treated with caution. It is dangerous to personify groups, endow them with a will, mind, or personality, or think of them as expressions of a collective mind with human attributes. It is misleading to use a biological analogy for groups and society, and postulate a theory of organization in which political organizations may share with biological organisms the attributes of metabolism, growth, internal transformation, homeostatis, information, and entropy.

History has given many answers to the problem of the relations between the state and groups and individuals, and the relative demands of public concern and private need. At one extreme is the view of the state as the fulfillment of a moral principle or ethical imperative, or as the organ that implements the general will that may ultimately, in Rousseau's words, "force men to be free." At the other is the view that the play of individual and group interests, with the state neutral or limited, will result in an underlying harmony of interests and a natural social order, efficient and free. The first emphasizes collective action and interest and the need for individuals to be malleable for some higher cause. The second view—grounded in the Jewish religious concept that God speaks to individual conscience and in Athenian political democracy, articulated as well in the humanism of the Renaissance that made man the measure of all things and in the Reformation that insisted on the priesthood of all believers—stresses individual rights and freedom. The tension between "public" and "private" has been continuous throughout history but some of the more disturbing analyses of modern social behavior suggest that individuals have become entirely private, imprisoned in the subjectivity of their own experience, and alienated from society as a whole. In this way the attraction of strong power or totalitarian regimes for "mass man," living in an atomized society in which the role of associations and groups has been reduced has been explained. Opposing established values and patterns of behavior, some alienated individuals recently have urged a new life style and consciousness, and have appealed for authenticity and embraced a counterculture more receptive to sensuousness and psychedelic drugs.[6] Change would occur by personal conversion or in compliance with a preferred guru or shaman. This concentration on private behavior has contributed to a loss of confidence in political institutions as well as in traditional authority in other parts of the social system.

Political Culture and Personality

For an anthropologist the concept of culture provides a total picture of the life, actions, and beliefs of a community. Giovanni Battista Vico was the first important philosopher to emphasize that all aspects of a culture—politics, economic structure, morality, art, literature, religion—are interconnected. The interconnection may be unexpected: George Orwell thought that one good guide to the social atmosphere of a country was the parade step of its army.[7] For a political scientist the shared values of a community or group are embodied in its political culture, which is the reflection of its attitudes toward politics and which conditions the manner in which functions are exercised and the nature of the persons who perform those functions.

A Hindu culture in which people are divided into a number of mutually exclusive groups arranged in a hierarchy determined by birth almost inevitably leads to a politics in which caste is a crucial characteristic. A Buddhist culture that emphasizes the importance of the moral law over social order is likely to be more egalitarian in spirit than the Hindu system. An Egyptian culture in which the country is regarded as the domain of the gods and of Pharaoh results in a dictatorship or autocracy in which the ruler is obeyed unconditionally. A British culture based on internal security, legality, and traditions of civility fosters political stability, respect for the rights of individuals and groups, tolerance, and a certain deference toward authority. A Greek culture in which loyalty to family and local community is supreme is likely to accept patronage and nepotism in politics. A Japanese culture in which ancestor worship exists is likely to embody reverence for the imperial ruler. A Western culture that stresses individual benefits, pleasures, and satisfaction of demands is likely to take a different view of sacrifice for the state than an Oriental culture that looks upon shame or dishonor as worse than death.

In their book *The Civic Culture*, Gabriel Almond and Sidney Verba suggest three types of orientation to political action: (1) a parochial orientation, when the individual is not aware of nor has opinions about the system as a whole but only of the local community; (2) a subject orientation, when the individual is aware of the system but is essentially passive and accepts decisions; and (3) a participant orientation, when the individual is an active member of the polity. In a highly regarded civic culture respect for authority is combined with individual independence, and the acceptance of the legitimacy of the political system with the belief that an individual can and should influence the system. In broad terms Almond and Verba identify four different types of political system:

1. The Anglo-American, with values of freedom, welfare, and security, homogeneity in ends and means, and differentiation of political roles
2. Continental European, where strong subcultures exist and political roles are often embodied in the subcultures
3. The preindustrial, which exhibits tension because of the cultural mix and political instability because of an imperialist past imposed on a traditional political culture
4. The totalitarian, in which there is a monopoly of political power by one party, strong coercion, and no voluntary associations

All regimes have some process by which acceptable, agreed upon political values, norms, and behavior patterns are transmitted from generation to generation and by which individuals are adjusted to the culture. This *political socialization*, produced by multiple forces such as the family, school system, churches, mass media, popular literature and art, folk heroes, and popular mythology, affects the way in which individuals understand and participate in political activity, and which type of individuals are politically interested. In established societies the influence of family is likely to be the dominant factor in socialization. Studies show that 91 percent of American voters knew their father's political behavior, and over 70 percent shared their party preference with their parents.* In less established or in developing communities the process of socialization takes place through a variety of agencies, either unconsciously or more deliberately through bodies such as the communes in China, the kibbutzim in Israel, or the reconstruction hamlets in South Korea. In all systems no doubt television will be a major force in the future in fostering a common set of manners, language, and culture for a society.

Less rewarding for comparative analysis than the concept of political culture has been the attempt to relate individual psychological characteristics to political behavior. Galen in ancient Greece suggested there were four different kinds of temperament—choleric, sanguine, phlegmatic, and melancholic—but few early writers related these to political characteristics. Political classification today can hardly be based on varieties of human motivation when psychological theorists from Sigmund Freud and Alfred Adler to Carl Jung and their various disciples provide such widely differing explanations of that motivation.

There has been considerable research on different types of personality, especially on the *authoritarian personality,* who is supposedly aggressive in behavior but deferential toward superiors and who thinks in terms of power, virility, and toughness. But it is doubtful that there is any automatic correlation between a personality type and political opinions or leadership. The major influence on this research has been *The Authoritarian Personality,*[8] which tried in general to measure personality type, or the pattern of attitudes or values held by a person that constitutes a more or less central trend or enduring structure in a person. In particular, the work attempted to construct a scale to measure antidemocratic and anti-Semitic attitudes. Individuals could thus be classified in a spectrum from democratic to authoritarian, depending on those attitudes. But it is not clear why anti-Semitic attitudes

*Angus Campbell et al., *The Voter Decides,* (New York: Harper & Row, 1954), p. 99. A more recent study, however, notes that the transmission of party identification from parents to voters coming of age in the late 1960s and early 1970s in the United States is less strong. See N. Nie, S. Verba, and J. R. Petrocik, *The Changing American Voter* (Cambridge, Mass: Harvard University Press, 1976), pp. 70–72.

should be correlated with any particular political position, since anti-Semitism is not confined to right-wing authoritarian politics. Nor is it clear that a certain personality type is interested in politics. On the contrary, different times and different political offices require varying skills and personalities. Harold Lasswell's view that the basic character-istic of a political type is the accentuation of a thirst for power in rela-tion to other values does injustice to the other characteristics and val-ues he lists as important to the politically interested—enlightenment, wealth, well-being, skill, affection, righteousness, and deference. More-over, Lasswell's argument that the desire for power results from de-privation "which is not overwhelming" is not very useful for empirical reference.[9]

Government and Groups

The state is indispensable for conscious control over affairs, for plan-ning, creation of social peace, and unified external action, and for choosing among the multiple goals desired. The state wields its au-thority over all individuals and groups in its territory, and contains citizens whose membership is compulsory. All social groups can exert pressure and influence behavior to different degrees. This influence has been exerted in a variety of nonviolent forms such as economic boycotts, industrial strikes, passive resistance, creation of parallel au-thorities, and even nonaction as advocated by Lysistrata. But only the wielders of state power can exercise legal coercion and prescribe legit-imate punishment. Coercion by groups—military coups, riots, lynch-ings, strong-arm methods—is ipso facto illegal, though it may be suc-cessful in achieving its end or influencing the action of the state.

The state possesses *sovereignty* in the sense of being able to wield ul-timate legitimate coercive power or exercise the power of ultimate de-cision. The term "sovereignty," formulated in the sixteenth century during the emergence of the state system out of the struggle between the European empire and the papacy, is no longer a fashionable one, for it is often difficult to ascertain which particular institution or per-son possesses the legal sovereign power. Nevertheless in problems re-quiring ultimate decisions—whether the conflict between the states in the United States in 1861 or the dismissal of General MacArthur by President Truman in 1951 or defiance of federal orders by Governor Wallace in Alabama in 1964—the ultimate power is made clear in one way or another. But a number of problems arise out of the interaction of the state and groups.

Competition for Loyalty

The state competes with groups and associations for the loyalty of citizens and for control over their behavior. Groups may differ, as David Truman said, in the degree of their stability, shared attitudes, formal organization, and interaction of their members, but they have a certain ethos, rules, and norms to which their members conform and to which they may feel loyalty.[10] Groups may indeed be more meaningful to their members, and have more influence over their behavior, than the political institutions of the state. The closed or union shop, the professional association that has the power to determine admission to the profession, the church whose edicts are unquestioningly obeyed, the street corner gang, the ideological party are all examples of groups that may punish rule breakers, coerce through expulsion, or limit membership.

Democratic societies recognize that the existence of groups is an expression of a free society, that groups may act as a counterweight to the possibility of an overriding state power, and that they may be more central to the concern of individuals than are the actions of the state. In principle the state may act if the group is acting illegally or harmfully. But the degree of state control over the members of groups or over the rules by which private organizations operate is always uncertain. Can the state allow conscientious objection in wartime? Can individuals refuse to be vaccinated by public health authorities on religious grounds? Does an oath of loyalty to the Ku Klux Klan take precedence over the duties of citizens? Can the state enforce national policies of desegregation if social groups or clubs refuse to be desegregated? Can a state school fire a teacher on account of his unorthodox views? Does the special obedience owed by members of the Society of Jesus to the Pope prevent the Jesuits from opposing his views on birth control?

In the newer nations the state is challenged by the power of castes and factions. African politics still largely revolves around the tribe, which is an extension of the family, a fellowship for its members, and which may be organized into age groups and religious societies. In Nigeria after independence the tribal chiefs were made presidents of local councils, and tribal clashes resulted first in election disorders and eventually in the downfall of the regime. Caste, formerly a method for allocating rights and duties in a stratified community, has been of crucial significance in the Indian states in determining employment, licenses, and economic privileges. In Islam the sharia religious law covers many aspects of individual and social life and the distinction between church and state is amorphous.

The Effective Limits of the Sovereign

Sovereignty is not unlimited or unconditional. There are always things the sovereign body will not or cannot do even though it has legal power to act. Even totalitarian or authoritarian states do not interfere in the whole range of social affairs. Moreover, the sovereign power is limited in all systems by natural forces and the physical conditions of the environment.

Internally, the sovereign power may find that certain policies and programs are so significant and well established that they restrict its power of maneuver. Or it may find that social behavior remains unaffected by legal requirements as in Israel, where the 1950 law establishing a minimum age of 17 for marriage for girls has not been observed by Yemenites and Moslem Arabs. Power, as Richard Neustadt said, is the power to persuade.[11] In practice a legal instrumentality may not be able to get its will accepted: it is meaningless to impose parking fines or prohibition if compliance is not obtained. Even a master political tactician like Charles de Gaulle was obliged in April 1963, to recognize the folly of trying to enforce a decree ordering striking French miners back to work.

Externally, a state is bound by a series of international obligations that restrict its freedom of action and power of making ultimate decisions. In some postwar constitutions—those of Japan, West Germany, Italy, France of the Fourth Republic—provision was made for international law to be directly adopted as part of the law. The nine countries of the European Community are not supposed unilaterally to alter their tariff systems. But in addition, all countries to differing degrees have lost the power of real self-determination. The critical gibe "When the United States sneezes, the rest of the world catches pneumonia" may have been unkind, but it is a reminder that the behavior of the powerful countries may effectively limit the freedom of action of the less powerful. A depression in the United States may lead to worldwide unemployment. The "gnomes of Zurich," the Swiss banking interests, allegedly imposed conditions on the behavior of the British Labour government in return for financial aid.

Formal and Real Power

The possessors of legal power may not be the real wielders of power nor be able to exercise coercive power. Internationally, the nominal leaders of a state may be subject to foreign control or persuasion. Dominance of key economic activities by foreign companies, corruption and bribery by those companies, and the ecological impact of their activities may make national control difficult. Total production of goods and services by the foreign subsidiaries of large firms is larger than the gross national product of every country except the United States and equals about one-tenth of the GNP of the whole noncommunist world. About two-thirds of this total represents sales by American firms; the largest firm, General Motors, has total sales that are larger than the net national income of almost all countries. Only 50 of the 100 largest economic units in the world are nation-states; the others are multinational corporations. Not surprisingly these corporations will influence decision making in the countries in which they are located. The communist countries of Eastern Europe provide another example of foreign influence; they have not yet completely emerged from control by the Soviet Union, which in 1968 used the phrase "proletarian internationalism" to justify its military intervention in suppressing the Czech reformers. Similarly Syrian troops intervened in Lebanon in 1976, supposedly to end that country's civil war. And, it was MacArthur who was largely responsible for Clause 9 of the Japanese constitution that imposed a ban on armed forces; it helped Japan ignore the ban by calling its army "a national police reserve" or "self-defense forces."

The difference between form and political reality has been apparent throughout history. In the Ottoman Empire, the sultan ruled at the head of a small group, the Ruling Institution, but his power was effectively limited by religious, military, and civil officials. In fifteenth-century Florence, the Medici, though nominally private citizens, were the real rulers rather than the formal system of legal councils and committees. In the seventeenth century Jan de Witt, though holding only the office of councillor-pensionary, was the real political leader in Holland for two decades. The oligarchy that sponsored the 1889 Meiji Constitution in Japan destroyed the power of the Tokugawa Shogunate, and the Meiji emerged as the real power rather than simply as an advisory group to the Emperor. Joseph Stalin, as secretary general of the Communist party of the Soviet Union, had undisputed final power though he long held no formal office. A local political boss may be more powerful than the mayor he has chosen, and had elected. A White House aide to the United States president may be the second most influential person in the country. Enrico Mattei as head of ENI, the national hydrocarbon company, was a major, if not the chief, force in Italian politics in the 1950s, although he held no political office. In Sicily the presence of the Mafiosi has been defended on the grounds that they maintain order.

The "real rulers" may be undiscoverable. Marxists argue that the holders of legal power are always subservient to those possessing economic control. Equally, supporters of the extreme right tend to see a communist conspiracy in all decision making. The bases of power or influence are varied and will differ in different historical periods and systems. Official holders of power may depend on or compete with the educated, the favored social class, the wealthy, religious leaders, popular personalities, the scientists, those controlling the information process, those possessing patronage, those controlling blocs of political support, or court favorites including the licensed jester or royal mistress who sometimes may be the only one allowed to tell the truth to the ruler, and eunuchs whom rulers used to defend themselves against bureaucrats and other groups. Official positions or formal institutions do not invariably identify the powerful. The order of names listed at an important Kremlin or Peking banquet is likely to provide a more accurate picture of power relations in the Soviet Union or China than organizational charts.

The Political Elite

Political analysts, including Machiavelli and twentieth-century writers such as Robert Michels, Gaetano Mosca, Vilfredo Pareto, Georges Sorel, and C. Wright Mills, have argued that all organizations are necessarily oligarchic in character, because leadership is indispensable and logically must be exercised by a small group. The group controlling the policy of political bodies is often regarded as a *political elite*, a homogeneous group distinguishable from the rank and file, holding similar views on affairs and sometimes conscious of its corporate identity. Its members may be linked by a common background, privileges, and tradition. Journalistically, the elite has been pictured as an establishment as in Britain, where a number of civil and ecclesiastical dignitaries seem to constitute a clique of the well placed and influential.

It is a truism that some individuals will have a greater influence than others in the making of decisions or control over policy, but the influence of a limited number of people does not imply a specific ruling group. The elite may be open to the emergence of new groups or talent rather than remain closed and exclusive. The influence may result from unusual factors, as in the *moka* ceremonies in New Guinea in which one participant achieves a superior position by giving a bigger gift in an exchange.[12] Moreover, there is no clear dividing line between the elite and the rest. Power, control over the behavior of others, is a relational concept, and there is a continuum in which differing amounts of power and leadership are exercised by particular individuals, formally or informally, on specific subjects. The attempt to identify a political elite has arisen largely as a result of the universal acceptance of the principle of the sovereignty of the people and the virtual ending of government by aristocracy, so that it is no longer self-evident which specific individuals constitute the rulers.

The Sources of Legitimate Power

Throughout history there have been numerous attempts to answer the biblical question: "Who made thee a ruler and a judge over us?" in order to gain recognition of the exercise of power as legitimate and to obtain obedience. Some of the explanations are hardly appropriate today; none has been universally adopted.

Divine Will and Heredity

Though religious coronation services are still used to enthrone a monarch and Francisco Franco, the caudillo of Spain, was officially responsible only to God and to history, few today will argue that divine right constitutes an acceptable claim to exercise power or that law is the product of a code of divine reason; or hold, like Sir Thomas More, that the voice of Christendom may be opposed to that of Parliament, because it is the duty of people to obey God and his lieutenant on earth; or accept the view of former Chinese regimes that the monarch was the Son of Heaven. But some rulers still claim, as does the King of Morocco, to be descended from the Prophet, to be the leader of the faithful, or to be regarded by their subjects as endowed with the power of divine inspiration. The emperor of Japan is the chief priest of Shinto, the national religion, and prays at shrines where he reports to his imperial ancestors and to the Amaterasu-O-Mikami, the sun goddess and legendary founder of the imperial dynasty.

Equally, though monarchies based on hereditary succession still exist in many nations and an anachronistic curiosity like the British House of Lords survives into the present age, heredity in itself is not usually acceptable as a justification of power, though it is sometimes the basis of political succession. President Kim Il-sung of North Korea named his son as his political heir; in Taiwan Chiang Kai-shek was replaced by his son. In the United States, though less formally, some political families in Massachusetts, Louisiana, and California appear to have created dynasties.

Tradition

The view that tradition and habit justify power is based on the premises that the maintenance of order is itself essential, that authority is natural and rests on the desirability of all accepting the existing social hierarchy, that rational calculation does not go far toward achieving political understanding, that actions or institutions may be evaluated by reference to the maintenance of the whole political system, and that chaos will result if the natural order is broken. The head of the body politic is held responsible for the preservation of the system: "Untune that string and hark what chaos follows."

Historical examples of the appeal to tradition to justify authority abound. In 1776 American independence was opposed because, in John Dickinson's words, "The English Constitution seems to be the fruit of the expression of all anterior time." The French Royalists used to talk of the 40 kings who made France great. In Japan the office of shogun, with its political and military functions, was held by the Tokugawa family from the early seventeenth century to 1867. The Spanish Carlists, conservatives devoted to the traditional monarchy and a powerful church, still believe in a "state of the Catholic king" and call for a theocracy in Spain.

That tradition is still a potent factor in political behavior is shown not only by the existence of traditional monarchies, such as that of Japan in which the current emperor descends from a line of 123 others, but also by the perpetuation of what Walter Bagehot called the "spirit of deference" in Britain.[13] All nineteenth-century British prime ministers, except two, were aristocrats; all in the twentieth century from Winston Churchill to James Callaghan were educated at Oxford.

Though manhood suffrage was introduced in 1884 in Great Britain, the Conservative party, the party of tradition, has won 13 of the 24 elections since then.

Frequently tradition sanctions longevity. In the United States this is illustrated by the practice of seniority in the hierarchy of legislative bodies. In the hierarchy of the Catholic Church in 1966, 45 of the 98 members of the College of Cardinals, the body electing the Pope, were over 75 years old, as were 22 of the 28 cardinals holding a position in the Roman Curia, the central administrative body of the church; only since 1970 have cardinals over 80 not been permitted to vote in the College. Chiang Kai-shek died in 1975 at the age of 87 after having ruled Nationalist China for 48 years. It is now a familiar experience that the communist regimes exemplify this same phenomenon of longevity. The Chinese regime in 1975 was ruled by an 82-year-old party leader, a 77-year-old government leader, an 89-year-old chairman of the standing committee of its Congress, and a 76-year-old army chief, all of whom have been in power for many years. In the Soviet Union the average age of the 16 members of the Politburo in 1975 was 66, and that of the top 4 leaders was over 70. The Yugoslavian regime is still controlled by the 83-year-old Tito who has ruled for 30 years.

The Will of the Ruler

Justification of power has often been based on the will of the ruler, the wise man, or philosopher-king. The argument propounded by Creon in *Antigone* is the perennial defense of the ruler: "The man appointed to govern must be obeyed, whether his commands be great or small, just or unjust. Disobedience is the worst crime." In Europe the challenge of estates, the representative assemblies, to a single ruler was ended in the seventeenth century in France, Portugal, Spain, and Brandenburg, as it had already ended in England. James I of England could argue, "I will not be content that my power be disputed" and Louis XIV could say "L'état, c'est moi."

The concept has lasted into modern times and has even been of major significance in nondemocratic regimes. In Japan, according to the Japanese constitution of 1889, the emperor was the basis of all authority in the state, although real power during the reign of the Emperor Meiji was exercised by an oligarchy. The most disturbing use of the concept in modern times has been by Hitler acting as the *Führer* of Germany and Mussolini as *Il Duce* of Italy, with many potential imitators in other countries. The most dramatic and eloquent recent formulation of the idea has been by de Gaulle who claimed to embody the legitimacy of France after its defeat in 1940.

The Laws

Since Aristotle, a recurring argument has been that power is derived from the law, or the Laws, or some natural laws that lie at the basis of civilized relationships. In the attempt to control the power of the monarch, the superiority of the common law was advocated. Edward Coke argued that "the King hath no prerogative, but that which the law of the land allows him."[14] The argument was embodied in the 1790 constitution of Massachusetts, which proclaimed a government of laws and not of men.

The idea of natural law is notoriously vague — for some, meaningless — and natural laws are difficult to deduce from any "essential" human nature. But modern history, which has witnessed commands and edicts of a despotic nature culminating in Hitler's "statutory lawlessness," has amply shown that enduring principles of justice and of humanity based on civilized relationships must be held superior to merely legal actions. The Nuremberg trials of major Nazi war criminals in 1945–1946 decided that individual policy makers were bound by the fundamental rules of the world community. But it is perhaps premature to regard this as a binding precedent.

The Supremacy of Parliament

Elected representatives of the people in a parliamentary body have also claimed legitimacy. By the eighteenth century William Blackstone could argue that the British Parliament was the supreme power, and this is still technically and legally true in the sense that Parliament can pass or amend any law that it wishes while no body or organization can declare a parliamentary statute invalid or unconstitutional. In the France of the Third and Fourth republics the Chamber of Deputies or National Assembly clearly regarded itself as a collective group embodying political legitimacy.

The Sovereignty of the People:
Vox Populi, Vox Dei

Most frequently today it would be argued that power is derived from the will of the people or from "Our Sovereign Lord the People" in Charles James Fox's term. Primitive as well as mature societies have acted on this basis. When the people of Oyo in Yorubaland lost confidence in their king, they would send him a gift of parrot's eggs, and he would then commit suicide. Even nondemocratic systems, such as Portugal until 1974 or the Soviet Union, have claimed in their constitutions that power or sovereignty resides in the people. The constitution of Ghana, even under Kwame Nkrumah, emphasized the will of the people as the ultimate source of authority and reserved to the people the power to repeal or alter certain provisions of the constitution. Modern constitutional changes emphasize the recognition of this concept. The Japanese emperor who in the 1889 Meiji Constitution was "sacred and inviolable" became in 1947 merely "the symbol of the people in whom resides sovereign power."

John Locke, while arguing that the legislature was the major political agency in any system, also held that there remained in the people a supreme power to remove or alter the legislature if it acted contrary to the trust reposed in it. This implies a contract made between the government and the ruled by which the latter can rebel and reclaim their original power if the rulers break their bargain and act improperly. Democratic though the idea of the power of the people may be, it is inherently ambiguous; this ambiguity is illustrated in the Italian constitution which says that "sovereignty belongs to the people, who exercise it within the forms and limits of the Constitution." It is not coincidental that the 1793 French constitution, the first real attempt to organize a regime based on the sovereignty of the people, was never put into effect. Sometimes a new constitution has been submitted for approval to a referendum of the people, thus endowing the new regime or institutions with legitimacy. Yet the concept of popular sovereignty assumes, somewhat dubiously, that a community has an identifiable will and that the will can be expressed. Certainly some regimes, especially that of Switzerland, provide for referenda and plebiscites, and rulers as diverse as Napoleon III, Hitler, and de Gaulle have used these devices to claim popular support for their actions. Yet, in spite of the fact that public opinion polls can reflect the feeling of the people on a given subject, it is improbable that any regime can operate by recourse to such polls or by continual resort to referenda. Only the exceptional importance of the decision on membership in the European Community justified the unique referenda on the issue put to the people of Norway and Denmark in 1972 and Britain in 1975.

Political Institutions and Myth

Though other forms of political organization still exist—such as the Philippine agama, in which a variety of units chiefly defined by kinship exercise administrative functions, or African clans and tribes, which have held together by ties of kinship, landholding, and religious ritual[15] — the Western pattern of territorial organization with a state power has been the norm of political development.

Political institutions are the outcome of social relationships within a community, past history, geographical situation, economic development and cultural setting, though there is no simple correlation between given political and institutional forms and the presence of particular economic, social, or demographic factors. Political institutions in all regimes attempt to perform certain necessary activities. They all seek to maintain internal order, to insure the effective operation of public services, to resolve political conflicts by peaceful means if possible and conciliate the conflicting demands of groups, to control the territory of the nation and defend it against external aggression, and to assure the stability and maintenance of the system while introducing sufficient change to allow adaptation to new conditions.

All regimes contain ideologies, belief systems, political formula and myths that underlie thought and behavior and values that determine the ends that are sought and the means by which those ends are obtained.

The first problem of politics is to establish and maintain a viable community held together by some common values and purposes in a society composed of groups and individuals that are neither angels nor beasts. All political systems are based on these shared values and fundamental assumptions shown by their ethical and social norms, ceremonies, symbols, and behavior, which both explain and justify power, which control sentiment and thought, and which shape the manner in which individuals see the world. Even coins, which for the Romans were "gazettes of the empire," have been used to diffuse ideas and propagandize, reflecting military victories, internal political changes, and ideological views.

Every society, according to Ernst Cassirer, has developed a system of taboo.[16] Anthropologists explain that in primitive cultures myth expresses, enhances, and codifies belief, safeguards morality, and contains practical rules for human guidance. In all systems myth, from Babylonian times to the present, helps cement the community, and symbols are used to manipulate people or to show the common interests of the group, from the Medicine Arrows and the Holy Hat lodge of the Cheyenne political organization to the flags of modern states. Ever since Plato's "noble lie," political formulae or intellectual constructions have been devised largely to make existing rule acceptable.

Force is not the *ultima ratio* (the final argument) of political life, and every government, as Michels has said, tries to support its power by a general ethical principle.[17]

Where society is relatively static and immobile, traditional values and mores will be accepted, consciously or unconsciously, as the basis for action. Religion in particular has been used from the Romans on to keep a population under control. Where societies are changing rapidly or dramatically, traditional or religious values no longer suffice, and social or political myths may be consciously created to help sustain social relationships or to propel individuals to action. Rulers are endowed with extraordinary qualities: Richard I of England was lion-hearted, Charles of Burgundy was bold, Catherine of Russia was great, and George Washington never told a lie. In recent years Nkrumah styled himself the "Osagyefo," the redeemer, the savior, the chief of chiefs; President Sukarno of Indonesia proclaimed himself "first leader of the Revolution," the king of Morocco "Prince of the Believers," and de Gaulle the embodiment of the legitimacy of France. Haile Selassie was the king of kings and the elect of God, Palden Namgypal the "chogyal," or god-king, of Sikkim; the shah of Iran was the "Shadow of the Almighty, the "Vice Regent of God," the "Center of the Universe," Franco "the finger of God" to Spanish parish priests; Mao was the "Great Teacher" and the "Great Helmsman," Mobutu the "Great Guide" of Zaire, and Mujib the "Father of the Race" in Bangladesh.

In Western countries the underlying values have been complex concepts, such as freedom or equality. Sometimes the political myth may not correspond to political reality. In France the myth of the revolution, with its accompanying belief in the perfectibility of human beings and the unlimited power of the people, has fostered attitudes and behavior largely irrelevant to contemporary needs. In the United States the myth of a free enterprise system persists in an age of large corporations, when the 50 largest firms have almost 3 times as many workers as the 50 state governments, and their sales are 5 times greater than the taxes gathered by all the states. The "independence" of nation-states is belied by the powerful presence of subsidiary firms controlled by multinationals with coordinated global policies.[18] Rhetoric on individual initiative is belied by the divorce between ownership of stock in corporations and executive or managerial control over their policies and activities. The myth of the moral superiority of rural over urban life has encouraged the perpetuation of disproportionate political representation for rural areas in a largely urban population. The belief, now rapidly declining, in masculine superiority has made governments reluctant to extend political rights to women or to allow them equal civil rights.

Political systems have been purportedly based on, supported, or opposed by ideologies or belief systems, which may consist of an integrated world view that is explicitly formulated or a more limited and vague view of political issues. Ideologies or sets of beliefs about human nature, the political world, and the organization of society may justify the existing system, support its legitimacy, provide a moral and legal basis for power, reduce the likelihood of conflict, and provide a theory of change. Or they may be the intellectual basis for challenging the system and proposing a more preferred society. They may be a conscious contrivance of leaders to determine goals and programs or manipulate people and institutions, as with nationalism or communism, or they may be the unconscious assumptions of the people about the working of the system, as in democratic systems. In the former case the set of beliefs may be regarded as authoritative for its adherents whose lives may be transformed by the ideology.

Every ideology is a mixture of facts, values, and mythology that provide some understanding of history and the supreme significance of or necessary leadership by a particular individual, group, class, or nation—whether it be the proletariat, the peasantry, the white race, blacks, guerrillas, intellectuals, the military, Moscow, or Rome. Ideologies enable a group to have the assurance of possessing the truth, to be actively committed to implementing its beliefs, and to form organizations dedicated to that purpose. The beliefs may also enable people to act and to distinguish friends from opponents. Sometimes the beliefs are simplified to stress one factor as the key to right action.

Documents or books may be accorded a special significance, and particular leaders unusual allegiance. Language may be used emotively: words such as "vanguard," "heroism," "father," "mission," "sovereign people," "master race," "colonial," and "male chauvinism," arouse the committed to action. Some ideologies are based on hatred and fear, others on sympathy, compassion, or promise of a glorious future. Some have been regarded as substitutes for religion: part of the attractiveness of Marxism has always been its appeal to salvation through revolution. Others, by their impact on esthetic, philosophical, or even sexual matters, may have an important effect on a wide range of conduct.

In developing nations, in which functions are not well differentiated and where the political process is relatively simple, the identification of the key political actors may not be difficult. Tanganyika, in seeking to prevent corruption by officials, defined national leaders as "members of the national executive committee of the Tanganyika African National Union, ministers, members of Parliament, leaders of all unions affiliated to TANU, leaders as defined by any question of rank, councillors and civil servants of the middle and upper group." But in any developed or pluralistic system the notion of a political elite becomes more nebulous as more participants are involved in political affairs. Francois Goguel talks of the French political class as consisting of the 15,000–20,000 party leaders, government officials, and newspapermen. The identification by C. Wright Mills of the power elite as those political, economic, and military leaders who inevitably have power or influence because of the centralization of decision making is a neo-Marxist oversimplification of contemporary social trends. David Truman's extension of "the intervening structure of elites" to include those holding leading positions in bodies such as corporations, trade unions, churches, and political parties is a more realistic view of social and political pluralism.[19]

Nation Building and Political Stability

"Without a political foundation," wrote Hobbes, "moral rules are impracticable." The first essential requisite for a viable political system is that it be stable with a capable, effective ruling group that is able to overcome aggressive, self-destructive forces and internal civil dissensions and that can provide protection against external states. Stability may be characterized, as Harry Eckstein has argued, by durability, acceptance of legitimacy, and effectiveness of government actions.[20] The effectiveness of regimes is measured by the absence of violence, the acceptance of the constitutional system by the people who will have loyalty and confidence in it, and the persistence of the system in its essential form while adapting to new conditions. Political decay has been equated with a loss of political capability.[21]

Few regimes have possessed these characteristics. Only 12 countries—the United States, Britain and its older dominions, Scandinavia, the Benelux nations, and Switzerland—have had stable systems since the beginning of the twentieth century. Even in the most stable systems in recent years instability has appeared; perceiving central government as inefficient or remote and desiring to maintain a local language and culture, regional forces have produced ferment and a demand for their own assemblies or for independence. In Belgium a considerable amount of power has been devolved from the capital, Brussels. Denmark, which in 1970 allowed greater powers including taxation to be exercised by the larger county councils, is planning to grant home rule to Greenland in 1978. Since 1972 Italy's agriculture, public works and road transport, and medical services have come under regional jurisdiction.

Britain has witnessed the rise of the National party to the rank of second largest party in Scotland. With 30 percent of the Scottish votes, it has 11 of the 71 members of Parliament in Scotland which already has its own churches, legal and educational system, a minister of state in the Cabinet, and a special legislative committee in the House of Commons. In addition, the Welsh Plaid Cymru has emerged with 11 percent of the Welsh vote and 3 members of Parliament, and separatist groups, both Protestant and Catholic, have come to the fore in Northern Ireland. Britain is currently planning some turnover of administrative, executive, or legislative authority to these areas. Even in France, Europe's most centrally administered country, with its 37,000 communes each with an elected mayor, 3,208 cantons, 95 departments, and 22 regions, and with its prefects appointed and dismissed by the Ministry of the Interior and controlling the departments and regions, there has been a substantial demand for regional assemblies or devolution of power and a resurgence of minority sentiment in Corsica, Provence, Brittany, Alsace-Lorraine, Occitania, and among the Basques. This upsurge of ethnic identity, the increasing tendency for people to insist on their ethnic distinctiveness and to claim group rights, has been a paradoxical feature of our age, which has also witnessed attempts to go beyond the nation-state and create larger federations or organizations like the European Community.

Ideally, political communities arise from peoples with a common language and culture, geographic continuity and unity, a common historical experience, a viable economy, and a fear of common enemies. Where all or most of these factors exist, a sense of national identity can emerge, consensus can exist, and the rules of the political game be acceptable to all through the process of accommodation and compromise. In Sweden consensus is so deep that few issues are the subject of partisan dispute and parties woo the marginal or absentee voter. In Norway cleavages—the result of class, geographical, linguistic, social, and religious-secular differences—became aggravated only with the referendum in 1972 on the Common Market, which showed a split between the modernist and traditionalist parts of the country.

In countries with strong social divisions, such as the smaller European democracies, stability is achieved by accommodation among the different elites. They deliberately counteract cultural fragmentation by renouncing simple majority rule and adopting proportional representation systems, by exercising mutual vetoes and forming concurrent majorities, by allowing considerable autonomy to subcultural groups and organizations that represent special interests.[22] In other countries it has been more difficult to create a nation with an identity of its own and a unified polity. Canada, with its 4,000 mile extent, and varied geographical regions, religious, language, and ethnic groups, has had trouble establishing an identity in the face of British and American influence and with the growing demand in Quebec for independence. To meet this problem Pierre Trudeau, prime minister of Canada, has called for a new Canadian constitution reflecting a Canadian nationhood to replace the 1867 British statute that has been accepted as the fundamental law of Canada. Israeli nationality still needs definition since the country is a Jewish state with an Arab minority, the majority embodying both a religion and a national identity, while the minority is part of a larger Arab entity outside the borders of Israel. Frequently the process of nation building in both the older and newer nations has been undertaken coercively and brutally.

In Western politics there have been four historic major causes of dissension in a community: (1) the nature of the political system, (2) religion, (3) regional and ethnic loyalty, and (4) economics. In Britain compromises between the aristocratic tradition and new democratic forces, the early ending of religious differences, the union of aristocracy and plutocracy, and the general agreement on a welfare state have helped maintain political stability, except in Northern Ireland where the implacable antagonism between Protestants and Catholics led to the downfall of the regime. Similarly, consensus in the United States is based on a middle-class, nonaristocratic ethos, a free society, a mixed economy with both private industry and government economic control, religious toleration, and acceptance of the principles of the Constitution, though the idea of the country as a melting pot is coming into question as ethnic groups act increasingly as interest groups.[23] But in continental European countries, each of the four factors mentioned is still capable of producing instability, as in France and Italy, where differences exist on the desirability of the political regime, on the equity of centralized power, on religious privileges, and on the justness of the economic system. In countries divided on religious or linguistic lines, as in Belgium and Canada, the fragile unity of the regime is easily shattered. Recent Belgium elections have shown a growing geographical polarization of support of the two largest traditional parties, which represent the Flemish and Walloon voters. In as stable a country as Switzerland the electorate of the predominantly French-speaking Jura area of the canton of Berne voted to establish a separate canton in 1974. Ethnic groups as varied as Slovenes in East Austria, Austrians in Italy's Alto Adige, Basques and Catalons in Spain, Greeks and Turks in Cyprus, Serbs and Croats in Yugoslavia, and Ukrainians, Armenians, and other nationalities in the Soviet Union have challenged the central administration.

Political stability also depends on individuals and groups accepting decisions with which they disagree, tolerating different views, acknowledging the authority of political institutions, being prepared to compromise, and ultimately agreeing on common procedures or action. These conditions are rarely present. Some systems have collapsed when disagreements were too acute, as in prewar Austria where town and country, "red" Vienna and "black" provinces, socialists and Catholics were diametrically opposed; the converse is shown in postwar Austria with the mutual acceptance of legislation by the two major parties. In countries like Japan and Pakistan parliamentary proceedings have been disrupted by opposition disagreements. In many Latin American countries military leaders have refused to accept the results of elections or have overthrown regimes whose orientation or behavior they disliked. Other regimes attempt to maintain stability by necessary compromise. Thus, in Belgium government coalitions containing a number of parties inevitably include Dutch-speaking Flemings, French-speaking Walloons, and bilingual inhabitants of Brussels, and a cultural council has been created for each of the two peoples; in Cyprus military, legislative, and administrative appointments were divided between Turks and Greeks between 1971 and 1974; and in Canada English and French are both official languages for activities of the federal government. Rarely is the compromise as elaborate as in Lebanon, where from 1943 until 1976 governmental and legislative positions were balanced on religious and sectarian lines, the president being a Maronite Christian, the prime minister a Suli Moslem, the foreign minister a Greek Orthodox Christian, and the legislative seats were allocated among fourteen different Christian and Moslem sects.

Other systems have tried to create stability by coercion or discrimination. The Soviet Union has subjected the various nationalities and groups to a process of Russification, though Russians constitute only 53 percent of the people. South Africa has imposed a system of apart-

heid on the black majority that has prevented blacks from being present in white areas without a special pass, deprived them of political
rights, and created nine separate independent homelands for them.
In Rhodesia the white minority has refused to accept the principle of
majority rule.

In most of the newer nations the sense of national identity has yet
to develop, while consensus is lacking in many others. To develop
such an identity Gandhi popularized the use of white homespun cot-
ton cloth in India rather than imported clothing. Some states are
united by fragile bonds. The two areas of Pakistan, West Pakistan and
Bengal, were held together only by common religion and common hatred of India until the eastern province seceded after a civil war in
1971 and declared itself the independent state of Bangladesh. In the
non-Western countries divisive factors such as racial, tribal, religious,
and national minorities existing in conditions of economic underdevelopment have produced instability. Collections of tribes living
within arbitrary boundaries set by colonial powers, as in Nigeria, cannot easily constitute a stable state or a settled economy. Most African
states have been created as a result of European rivalry for territory
in Africa. In some cases tribes were divided while traditional enemies
were thrown together in the same country. The problem is illustrated
in Ghana where the Ashanti peoples in the center have wanted to secede, while the Ewe peoples living on both sides of the Ghana-Togo-
land border have wanted to unite. The fragmentation of tribes is illustrated by the Hausas, who live in Mali, Upper Volta, Niger, and
Nigeria, and the Woloffs, who live in Senegal and Gambia.

The newer nations find difficulty in controlling internal divisive
forces. Sometimes this difficulty has been blamed on the former colonial powers, which tried to divide the rule through tribal chieftains, as
in Nigeria where the British government recognized different administrations, or which left competing groups in existence, as in the
Congo. Centrifugal tribalism has been at odds with centripetal nationalism. In Buganda in Uganda the forces of nationalism were checked
by the Kabaka, and the Baganda for a time refused to send members
to the central legislature. In Africa most countries have populations
whose chief loyalties are to tribal chiefs or regional associations, as in
Somaliland or Cameroons with over 400 peoples. Frequently the tribal
differences have been acute divisive factors, as in Kenya or in Nigeria
between the Hausas, Yorubas, and Ibos, leading the Ibos to attempt to
secede as Biafra in 1967. In Sri Lanka the Tamils have asked for re-

gional autonomy amid acute divisions between Buddhists and Christians, and between castes.

In the newer nations attempts have been made to create unity and obtain national integration by a variety of methods: by deliberate action of rulers, by crushing dissension, by creating a one-party system, and by adopting a lingua franca. Ngarta Tombalbaye, while president of Chad between 1960 and 1975, introduced the tribal ceremony of *yondo*, by which all officials had to swear allegiance to him as tribal chief. In Zaire, with its 200 dialects and tribal groups, President Mobutu Sese Seko has tried to create a sophisticated tribal structure by making himself paramount chief among the chiefs of eight regions and by encouraging "black authenticity" which requires the removal of European names, including the name of the country itself (the "Congo"), as well as foreign-owned business and clothing. A number of other African countries have tried to Africanize: Leopold Senghor of Senegal has used the idea of "negritude" which was formulated by Aime Césaire to stress the African personality and culture. In Burma, Indonesia, Egypt, as in Portugal, national unions or fronts have been created to foster unity; occasionally, as in Cambodia, where Prince Sihanouk apologized for the unanimous success of his Popular Socialist Community, the unity has been too great. States have crushed existing or potential dissenters: in Burma the military has fought against rebellious tribes like the Karins, communist guerillas, Moslem separatists, bandits, and Chinese smugglers, while nationalization measures have eliminated the influence of Chinese and Indian minorities. The Iraqis have tried to crush the Kurd minority, the Indonesians have dealt harshly with their Chinese minority, as Pakistan has with its Hindus. India—which has formidable minorities of 50 million Moslems, 8 million Christians, a quarter of a million Parsees and a quarter of a million Anglo-Indians, and which is faced with internal dissension from its 8 million Sikhs, from the Nagas and Mizos in the north, and the party for the Uplift of Dravidians in the south—has legislation allowing the government to ban any group or association advocating the "secession" of any area from India. The Malays adopted a policy of *bumiputraization* against the minority Chinese who have dominated business and the professions in Malaya.

Many of the newer states have adopted one-party systems, arguing that disunity would necessarily lead to sedition. Similar appeals to national unity have been argued by Sekou Touré and his Guinea Democratic party, the Neo-Destour in Tunisia, the Convention People's party in Ghana, the Tanganyika African National Union, the Malawi party in Malawi, and the Progressive party in Senegal.

To remove a major cause of contention caused by the large number of languages in a nation, English or French has been adopted as the language of most African states. When in Ethiopia, Amharic, the language of the politically dominant Amhara group, was imposed as the official language, and local languages were eliminated from schools, the move was resented by both the Moslems and the Monophysite Christians in the province of Eritrea. In India where 1,652 languages or dialects are spoken, English remains as an official language together with Hindi. Sometimes, however, a regime makes linguistic concessions to minority groups, as in Peru where the language of the Incas, Quechua, has been made an official language, and in Paraguay where Guaraní, an Indian dialect, is officially recognized. In Asian states disagreement on language still exists.

Political Succession

The problem of political stability is closely related to that of political succession. Stable systems are by definition those in which a change in political leadership does not disrupt activity or endanger the regime because the change takes place through some known institutional device and is accepted peacefully by all including those politically opposed to the leadership. The death or resignation of the incumbent does not produce chaos. The British monarch is succeeded by the eldest child. In the United States the president is succeeded on death or resignation by the vice-president, who may also follow him by his own electoral victory. In American history 13 out of 38 presidents have served as vice-presidents; since World War II half of the successful vice-presidential candidates have later become president, and 5 of 13 in this century have succeeded to the office. Occasionally in world history succession has resulted from accidental events; Saul went to look for his father's asses and became king of Israel. Sometimes the process has been fortuitous, as in the lottery system of Greece. At times the holder of power abdicates, but it is more common for incumbents to believe themselves indispensable than to follow the examples of Sulla, Cincinnatus, Diocletian, or Charles V, and retire from office.

But the number of regimes in which change of leadership occurs in a proper constitutional fashion or as a result of competitive, free elections or according to the immemorial principle of gerontocracy, or by legal arrangement is relatively few. More frequently change has been the result of violence, coups, or a bitter struggle for power. Since their independence after World War II, 23 African states have had a government overthrown at least once. Benin has had 5 military coups in 16 years. In Bangladesh there were 2 coups within three months in 1975. In the 36 years between 1930 and 1965, Latin America witnessed 106 illegal or unscheduled changes of heads of state. Ecuador had 11 unconstitutional changes in this period, and Mexico was the only country in which change always occurred by constitutional means. This type of power struggle is the familiar experience in dictatorships or in strong monarchies, such as Yemen, Ethiopia, and Saudi Arabia, where the regime may be disturbed by plots to overthrow the ruler. Equally, instability results when, as in Syria, political leadership is disputed between civil and military factions. In the new nations leadership during and immediately after the liberation from the colonial power has often been in the hands of a charismatic figure. But in the postliberation period, with its internal conflicts, leadership has emerged from the army or from the single existing political party that has made use of the myths and symbols of the new nation.

In regimes with limited constitutional monarchs, political leadership may change while a common loyalty is felt to the monarch who remains in office. But peaceful continuity may also be harmoniously achieved under a military dictatorship, as in Nicaragua or Thailand, or through the perpetuation of a dominant political party, as in India or Bolivia, or where the process of succession is known to all the political participants and where the successor is coopted after consensus has been reached among the different factions, as in Mexico. The problem of succession has perplexed the communist countries whose leaders have attempted to stay in power without adequate preparation for the future. The only constitutional device in these countries is that in Yugoslavia where the Federal Council for the Defense of the Constitutional Order was created in 1974 to settle the succession after Tito's death.

Purpose and Politics

Is there a purpose underlying political activity and can one compare political systems by their purposes? Some systems exist for simple purposes: for Zulus warfare seemed the chief purpose of their lives; for the state of Pakistan, the chief initial purpose was the creation of an independent Moslem state. For idealist philosophers, including Plato, the ultimate end of action is beyond the political realm. For Augustine and early Christian thought political institutions were valuable as a preparation for the true end of human beings in the City of God. For some politics is the implementation of aesthetic qualities such as beauty or order or the correct subordination of the part to the whole, a view that tends to reinforce conservatism if not tyranny.

Others have seen politics as a less ambitious endeavor. For Thomas Hobbes the maintenance of civil peace was almost a self-sufficient end. David Hume denied there was any ideal to be enforced or any City of God to be reached. Politics was therefore only one of "many social activities, by no means the highest, concerned with the ordinary business of life." For some observers an unidealistic pragmatism is sufficient. For example, Michael Oakeshott sees politics as a "boundless or bottomless sea" and Karl Popper as "piecemeal engineering"; in a similar vein, it may be seen as adjustment to social harmony or equilibrium or as the meeting of inescapable demands.[24] For Jeremy Bentham politics became the intervention of government to insure the greatest happiness of the greatest number, and political actions had to be based on utilitarian considerations.

More frequently politics has been associated with faith than with utility. Throughout history religion has been used to support the existing order or to preserve values held desirable. In a pre-Christian period Augustus tried to restore the ancient Roman rituals to prevent the decline of Roman morality. In post-Napoleonic Europe some rulers thought that religion could be used to recreate order and stability after 20 years of war. In Libya the ruler Colonel Muammar Qaddafi has formulated a puritanical version of Islam prohibiting foreign languages and alcohol as well as emphasizing Islamic culture.

Politics has also been seen as teleological, as history moving to some desirable goal: the Christian view of salvation, the Hegelian spirit of consciousness working toward freedom, the fulfillment of racial destiny such as the German *Herrenvolk* or the Japanese Yamoto race, the inevitable victory of communism or American destiny. Other analysts view all systems as undergoing an inherent logic of political development, from an initial concern with unification, stability, and self-defense to increased economic expansion and industrialism, greater satisfaction of wants, and more efficient and coherent use of political power. But this analysis blurs the distinction between evolution, which is any kind of orderly change, and progress, which implies change in a desirable direction.

For Aristotle, political activity only became meaningful when it was an expression of ethical purpose. Few today would see politics as Manichaean or agree with the Shah of Iran when he described a referendum in 1962 as a battle between Yazdan and Ahriman, the Zorastrian gods of good and evil. But notwithstanding the unhappy attempts to establish "a reign of virtue," which have resulted in tyranny rather than justice, many suggest that politics implements ethical concepts. An Israeli statute, imposing fines on workers and employers for working on the Jewish sabbath or religious festivals, attempts such implementation of an ethical and religious principle.

If political systems have ethical purposes, should they seek to create good men and women or the good society; should they try to alter human personality or concentrate on social reform? For J. S. Mill, the purpose of political institutions was largely to foster the intellectual and moral development of citizens.[25] Therefore, the only purpose for which power could be rightfully exercised over individuals against their will was to prevent harm to others. Similarly, systems have been judged admirable if they produced the Christian gentleman, or citizens with mental health or mature personalities.

However, most regimes exemplify the view that in every community there is a shared public morality which must be preserved if society is to survive and that the moral code is as significant as the political structure. Most developed states will have as their guiding principles the upholding of human dignity, which includes the recognition of civil and political rights and the establishment of desirable social, economic, educational, and cultural conditions, as in Ireland where the "Directive Principles of Social Policy" in the constitution include provision of an adequate means of livelihood for all citizens and the distribution of material resources on the basis of the common good.

Purpose is a neglected concept in contemporary political studies. This is not surprising in an age where modern techniques of salesmanship and hidden persuaders influence and may even determine the political message. Political style is sometimes more admired than performance. Moreover, pessimism has seemed to replace purpose in contemporary Western culture, where major schools of philosophy view life as meaningless and argue that there are no permanent values attaching to things or standards, where a significant part of modern culture has been, in Lionel Trilling's word, "adversary" to and contemptuous of the established, bourgeois values, materialism, and technology,[26] where there has been a sharp decline in religious beliefs, and where social psychologists have asserted the view of the alienation of the individual. One major problem is that, while particular actions can be purposeful, it is difficult to say the same about a whole society or state. Kant suggested that the essence of wisdom was the human capacity to harmonize all one's purposes in life. It is appropriate but even more difficult for political regimes to harmonize the heterogeneous purposes of their citizens. Not only is there no exact method by which the superiority of purposes can be established in any absolute way, but rarely do political goals enter into any purposeful design, for they are multiple, varied, and interrelated rather than simple and isolated. Nevertheless, analysts of comparative politics should be as much concerned with the different purposes behind political regimes as with the different sources claimed for the exercise of legitimate power, the political myths and formulas that help explain and defend that exercise, and the relationship between government and groups.

Notes

[1] James Madison, *The Federalist*, No. 51.
[2] Sidney Verba, "Comparative Political Culture," in Lucian Pye and Sidney Verba, eds., *Political Culture and Political Development* (Princeton University Press, 1965), p. 513.
[3] Robert MacIver, *The Web of Government* (New York: Macmillan, 1947).
[4] Arthur Bentley, *The Process of Government* (University of Chicago Press, 1908), pp. 203, 214.
[5] David Truman, *The Governmental Process* (New York: Knopf, 1951), pp. 23–24.
[6] Charles A. Reich, *The Greening of America* (New York: Random House, 1970).
[7] George Orwell, "Such, Such Were the Joys," in *Collected Essays*, vol. 4 (New York: Harcourt Brace Jovanovich, 1968).
[8] T. W. Adorno et al., *The Authoritarian Personality* (New York: Harper & Row, 1950), pp. 228, 971.
[9] Harold Lasswell, *Power and Personality* (New York: Viking Press, 1963), pp. 27–28, 40.
[10] David Truman, *The Governmental Process* (New York: Knopf, 1951).
[11] Richard Neustadt, *Presidential Power* (New York: Wiley, 1960).
[12] Andrew Strathorn, *The Rope of Moka* (New York: Cambridge University Press, 1971).
[13] Walter Bagehot, *The English Constitution* (Ithaca, N.Y.: Cornell University Press, 1966).
[14] The Question of Royal Proclamations 1610 in Carl Stephenson and F. G. Marcham, *Sources of English Constitutional History* (New York: Harper & Row, 1937) p. 441.
[15] Basil Davidson, *The Africans* (New York: Longman, 1969).
[16] Ernst Cassirer, *The Myth of the State* (New Haven, Conn.: Yale University Press, 1946).
[17] Robert Michels, *Political Parties* (New York: Dover, 1959), p. 15.
[18] Raymond Vernon, *The Economic and Political Consequences of Multinational Enterprise* (Cambridge, Mass.: Harvard University Press, 1972); and his *Big Business and the State* (Cambridge, Mass.: Harvard University Press, 1972).
[19] David Truman, *op. cit.*; C. Wright Mills, *The Power Elite* (New York: Oxford University Press, 1956).

[20] Harry Eckstein, *Division and Cohesion in Democracy* (Princeton University Press, 1966).

[21] S. P. Huntington, *Political Order in Changing Societies* (New Haven, Conn.: Yale University Press, 1968).

[22] Hans Daadler, "The Consociational Democracy Theme," *World Politics* (July 1974), pp. 604–621; and Arend Lijphart, *The Politics of Accommodation* (Berkeley: University of California Press, 1968).

[23] Nathan Glazer and Daniel P. Moynihan, *Beyond the Melting Pot*, 2nd ed. (Cambridge, Mass.: M.I.T. Press, 1970).

[24] Michael Oakeshott, "Political Education," in *Rationalism in Politics* (New York: Basic Books, 1962); and Karl Popper, *The Open Society and Its Enemies*, 4th ed. (Boston: Routledge and Kegan Paul, 1962).

[25] John Stuart Mill, *On Liberty*, chap. 3.

[26] Lionel Trilling, *Beyond Culture* (New York: Viking Press, 1965); and his *Mind in the Modern World* (New York: Viking Press, 1973).

Chapter Three

The Classification of Political Systems

Of the classifying of systems there is no end. Since every regime is at once unique and in flux, all classification is at best partial and temporary. Regimes exist in a continuum, somewhere between total reliance on either persuasion or coercion, differing in the amount of power exercised and the way it is distributed; they do not fit neatly in rigid categories. Nevertheless classification serves to illuminate the major politically meaningful similarities and dissimilarities between regimes.

The Classical Division

Aristotle was the father of comparative political analysis and classification. His classification of regimes was based on the number of people who participated in governing, on the ethical quality of their rule depending on whether it was in their personal or the general interest, and on their socioeconomic status. Those regimes that served the interests of the ruling group only were perversions of the true constitutional forms.

Aristotle clearly preferred the aristocratic form because the mean, philosophic and otherwise, was desirable. Other classic theorists, particularly Cicero and Polybius, thought that simple forms of government would degenerate so that monarchy would become tyrannical and aristocracy become oligarchic. Stability depended on the existence of a "mixed state," made up of all the social classes participating or being represented to some degree.

Historically the Aristotelian theory has been useful in indicating the numbers and nature of the governing group in a regime and whose

Table 1.   The Aristotelian Division

Number of rulers	Rule in the general interest	Self-interest rule	Social group
One	Monarchy	Tyranny	King
Few	Aristocracy	Oligarchy	The Wealthy
Many	Polity or Democracy	Ochlocracy	The Poor

interests were likely to be taken into account. Comparison might thus be made between monarchies such as France under Louis XIV or Prussia under Frederick the Great, aristocracies like fifteenth-century Florence, nineteenth-century England, or Brazil from 1889 to 1930, and democracies such as twentieth-century Sweden or the United States.

Modern elitists suggest that this classical division is limited in its usefulness. Since all political systems and organizations are oligarchic, the majority of people are in fact ruled by small minorities in all regimes. In Yeats' poem, an elite continues even if its members change:

> Hurrah for revolution and more cannon-shot!
> A beggar on horseback lashes a beggar on foot.
> Hurrah for revolution and cannon come again
> The beggars have changed places, but the lash goes on.*

An elite is as observable in the Soviet Union, with its dachas and personal privileges, and in Sri Lanka, where two families, the Senanayake and Bandaranaike, have alternated in the prime ministership, as it is in the Western world.

The extension of the suffrage has not so far made any appreciable difference in the composition of the political elite in democracies. In Britain the close connection between the ruling group and the well born and the wealthy has been maintained into the present century; the working class has had little access to key positions and not until 1906 did a man of working-class origin become a Cabinet minister; the leadership of the Labour party has been largely middle class while that of the Conservative party has remained almost completely upper-middle class. In the area of foreign policy it is even truer than in domestic affairs that a small group dominates the decision-making process.

*"The Great Day" reprinted by permission of The Macmillan Company from *Collected Poems* by William Butler Yeats. Copyright 1940 by Georgie Yeats. Also reprinted by permission of Mr. W. B. Yeats, The Macmillan Co. of Canada, and Macmillan & Co. Ltd for the Commonwealth.

Monarchies and Republics

Another important division was suggested by Montesquieu, who distinguished regimes as *despotisms*—those in which the sovereign was unrestrained—*monarchy*—regimes in which the ruler was subject to restraints of custom, local privileges, or his own law—and *republics*, which could be either democratic or aristocratic and which were more likely to be endowed with charity and patriotism than were monarchies. But this analysis is more appropriate for eighteenth-century than for contemporary conditions.

Machiavelli divided regimes into republics and monarchies, partly to distinguish free from unfree regimes. But this distinction is almost as unimportant as that of the Greeks who divided peoples into two categories only: Greeks and barbarians. In all monarchies the monarch serves as the formal head of state, whereas in republics this position may be exercised by different persons. But monarchies vary widely from the constitutional type found in Britain, the Netherlands, and Scandinavia, to the benevolent, as in Monaco, the traditional in Thailand and Buganda, and the autocratic in Saudi Arabia. They may even be nonexistent as in Francisco Franco's Spain, which was formally a monarchy but which had no king. Similarly, republics vary equally widely from the democratic to the despotic, and their number inevitably increases. The postwar period has witnessed the elimination of monarchies in a considerable number of countries including most of the newer members of the Commonwealth, which, since India set a precedent, have opted to become republics on attaining their independence. It is unlikely that a new regime will found a monarchy since it would be difficult in the contemporary world for a monarchical regime, to establish its claim to legitimacy, though a monarchy was founded in the Central African Republic in 1976.

A Marxist Classification

The determining characteristic of regimes for a Marxist is the nature of the economic system. History is propelled by the struggles between classes that are related to each other in the different processes of production, the essential conflict being always between those who own the means of production and those who do not. Social relationships arise from the processes of production, and the existence of classes is bound up with particular historical phases of the development of production.

The Marxist philosophy of history differentiates five broad successive types of social relationship: (1) *primitive communism* with its general equality, (2) *slavery* with its slave-owning and slave classes, (3) *feudalism* with its lords of the manor and its serfs, (4) *capitalism* with its capitalist and proletarian classes, and (5) *communism* with its abolition of economic classes. Because Marx was largely uninterested in the first three stages and because he regarded it as utopian to speculate in detail on the nature of the future communist society, he was essentially concerned with analysis of capitalism and the capitalist state in which all organs of power are organs of bourgeois dictatorship.

There is an obvious connection between social relationships, the economic system, and political institutions. A country like Ecuador, where 0.4 percent of the landowners own 45 percent of the arable land, is run by an oligarchy that controls business, the army, and the avenues to political power. A shift in the economic structure will usually lead to a shift in political power. As one example, in Brazil the economic growth of the south, which reduced the significance of the rubber and sugar plantations in the economy of the country, led to the traditional landowning oligarchy, controlling a largely illiterate population, being displaced by demogogic politicians allied with industrial and agrarian workers.

But an economic interpretation of political systems can only provide limited understanding. The widespread appeal of Marxist theory is due less to the incisiveness of its historical and philosophical analysis than to its logical rigor, the vigor with which the analysis is argued, the assurance of certainty and of ultimate victory that it provides, the deceptive ease with which supposed laws are deduced from political and economic phenomena, and the attractive ultimate communist society from which injustice and oppression have been eliminated. There is no automatic correlation between an economic basis and political institutions or actions.

The imperialism practiced by the European powers in the nineteenth and twentieth centuries is comprehensible less in economic terms than in prestige, national power, and security. And it caused its own destruction, not through economic disaster but by the intellectual ideas of equality and self-determination accompanying it. Marxist theory has not taken account of the complexity and heterogeneity of modern regimes; nothing in Marxism effectively explains contemporary extremist systems, the diversity of political forms that capitalist countries has taken, the rise of fascist and Nazi regimes, or the differences in political operation of communist regimes. Moreover, these regimes have come into existence not through the internal con-

tradictions of the capitalist system, as Karl Marx predicted, but by
revolutionary coups, guerrilla war, or the impact of an occupying
communist power. In addition, communist regimes can no longer be
regarded as a monolithic bloc. The acute disagreements and inter-
mittent hostility between the Soviet and Chinese regimes reflect both
ideological and tactical differences on communism and tension between two great powers. In his unorthodox Marxist theories Mao Tse-
tung emphasized the need for peasant insurrections, the role of army
units in the workers' revolution, the assertion of human will to overcome obstacles, the importance of guerrilla action, the creation of
people's communes throughout the country, and the desirability of fo-
menting revolution in the developing countries of the world. These
unorthodox theories, plus the determination of China to defend itself
against the power of the Soviet Union, to resist Moscow's domination
over the Chinese party, and to regain Chinese territory annexed by
czarist Russia, has lead to an armed clash between the two countries in
1969 and to continuing friction.

Above all, in spite of differences in nomenclature of systems, all
modern industrial systems use planning to a considerable degree, and
often, as J. K. Galbraith has argued, this has replaced consumer demand or "the market" as the determining force in the economy.[1] The
state plays a major role in planning, regulating demand, fixing prices
and wages, and assisting industry, which depends to a large degree on
the state as both supplier and buyer. The state has been called on to
intervene, stabilizing the economy and expanding employment, when
private enterprise has failed. The lines that theoretically delineate
communist and noncommunist systems on the basis of the ownership
of property seem less strong in actual current practice.

Constitutional Democracies

Although the history of the world has essentially been one of dictatorships of some kind, and freedom the characteristic of the exceptional
regime, almost all contemporary systems describe themselves as democratic. The Democratic Republic of North Vietnam and the German
Democratic Republic are both communist states; President Achmed
Sukarno of Indonesia thought of his regime as "guided democracy";
General Ayub Khan of Pakistan attempted to create "basic democracies" from the village level up; Sekou Touré is the head of Guinea
and leader of the only party, the Democratic party; "economic democ-

racy" is being created in Iran by the shah and the one party permitted.

The use of the category "constitutional democracy" enables those regimes with an essentially similar ethos to be classified in one group. These regimes are all marked by similar characteristics: strong regard for private rights, peaceful change, the existence of a wide variety of voluntary unofficial associations, the presence of effective restraints on the holders of power so that they act in responsible fashion, a pluralistic society in which no one group or element is dominant, tolerance of and freedom to dissent, free elections and the existence of a legal political opposition that will have some impact on decisions, political neutrality of the army and the civil service, civilian control over the military, traditions of civility, impartial justice for all, and the existence of the rule of law.

The rule of law is a crucial factor, insuring legal impartiality, the absence or reduction to a minimum of arbitrary behavior, no punishment except for an individual found guilty of a crime, everyone being subject to the law, the calculability of legal behavior, the protection of individual rights, an emphasis on procedural safeguards, an absence of retrospective legislation, a respect for law, an independent judiciary, and a free legal profession. Thus whose who make and enforce law must themselves be subject to law, all government acts must be legal and subject to control by appropriate authorities, and effective remedies must be available against the state.

These remedies have been exercised in the Anglo-Saxon countries and their former colonies by the ordinary courts and the common law system, which have enforced proper procedure, principles of natural justice or due process of law, and a strict interpretation of the reasonableness of administrative acts. In Continental European countries the same result has been obtained by the German *Rechtstaat*—an elaborate legal system controlling official behavior—and by administrative courts, such as the French *Conseil d'État,* which decide on the validity of administrative acts. Yet the problem remains that political ministers and administrative officials are given discretionary powers that may be difficult to control, while the need for strong government action may produce an atmosphere in which adherence to procedure is reduced.

Constitutional democracies exist, with few exceptions, in the older and more developed political systems and in societies with a modernizing middle class. Democracy in its traditional Western form has not spread to the newer nations of the world. According to a 1975 report only 19.8 percent of the population of the world live in relatively full freedom. Even in contemporary Western Europe, regimes such as the French and Spanish have come into existence by nonlegal action or pressure. The assumed connection between a constitutional system and an educated population is sadly dispelled by the reality that about one-quarter of the Nazi SS leaders possessed a Ph.D., that the extremely anti-Semitic Austrian Volkspartei was nicknamed the professor's party, and that the Austrian anti-Semitic parliamentary deputies were well educated.

It is a familiar experience that economic development, especially industrialization, tends to disrupt traditional social relationships and behavior, and that economic planning may require the acquiescence or submission of the population. A plausible conclusion is that regimes in the first stages of industrialization can rarely afford the luxury of political democracy or constitutional restraint on power. There are differing views on the relationship between democracy and socioeconomic factors. Some writers, including Seymour Lipset and Phillips Cutright, argue that democracy is related to a particular level of development that includes industrialization, accumulation of wealth, high education levels, urbanization, and extensive communication and transportation networks. Others, such as Deane Neubauer, hold there is no such regular relationships when factors such as the percentage of adults eligible to vote, the equality of representation of voters in the legislature, the distribution and availability of political information, and the competition of parties and their alternation in office are considered.[2]

Constitutionalism, the allocation of a higher sanction to the basic laws than to the immediate wishes of a ruler, marks an important stage to a democratic regime. The problem for the tyrant, as Aristotle knew, is to find people who will tell him the truth. Constitutional regimes rarely suffer from this particular disadvantage, even if they sometimes operate more subtly to allow policy makers to evade or be protected from public scrutiny. Much of the analysis of succeeding chapters will be devoted to the practice of constitutional regimes.

Nonconstitutional Regimes

Nonconstitutional democracies embrace a variety of different types, though all are dictatorial in differing degrees and lack an organized political opposition or a free press. They may exist because the country has no tradition of constitutional behavior or cannot agree on fundamentals. Dictatorship may result from the inability of the executive to rule, from the existence of a multiplicity of parties preventing the formation of a stable and coherent government—as in Italy with 12 parties in 1922, Germany with 15 in 1928, and Spain with 18 in 1933—from the attempt to implement an ideology, or from the concern about economic instability or failure.

Authoritarian Regimes

Outright tyrannies are rare in the contemporary world. Originating in Asia, where the despotic power of a ruler was able to check the aristocracy, tyrannical regimes are no longer as relevant to contemporary life as in the days of Oriental despotism. The Iraqi practice of selecting individual opponents for assassination is not now customary. Perhaps the rule since 1971 of General Idi Amin in Uganda, where people from the Acholi and Langi tribes have been massacred, at least 25,000 people eliminated, and 30,000 Asians holding British passports expelled, best exemplifies modern tyranny.

In *authoritarian regimes* political activity is controlled, all the media are subject to censorship, liberty is restricted, there is no legally recognized opposition, and parliamentary institutions are absent or meaningless. The system is not tyrannical, however. The society is traditionally oriented, power is exercised by small groups such as military leaders, bureaucrats, or religious figures, economic activities can still be pursued with considerable independence, there is a certain degree of cultural freedom, and voluntary internal and external travel is possible. Examples of such regimes are Argentina under Juan Perón, Spain under Francisco Franco, and Portugal under Antonio Salazar.

In Argentina, Peronism, marked by devotion to a charismatic leader who embodied social resentment, tolerance of the power of organized labor, and an ideology of "justicialism," was an ambiguous alternative to capitalism and socialism. In Spain under Franco, who was generalissimo and caudillo for 36 years until his death in 1975, political opponents were executed, imprisoned or deported, or obliged to pay considerable fines and gatherings of over 20 people had to be authorized; the vote was taken away from women as well as most men and the system was largely supported by traditional conservative groups such as monarchists and the clergy and by the Falangist party. In the Estado Novo of Portugal there was only one legal party, the press was controlled, elections were manipulated, dissenting officials were likely to be dismissed, spying by bureaucrats on their subordinates was common, strikes were illegal, and the secret and political police were powerful.

A large number of modern regimes embody similar characteristics. In the Brazilian system established in 1964, an authoritarian president can sign emergency decrees and has exclusive competence to make laws on finance, while civilians can be tried by military courts and those citizens who "abuse their individual right" may lose their political rights. In most Latin American countries political parties have been barred or suspended, the press censored, and opponents imprisoned arbitrarily. Over the two years, between 1974 and 1976, India appeared to be changing from a democratic to an authoritarian system in which the fundamental freedoms of speech, assembly, association, and travel have been suspended, due process and equality before the law put in abeyance, press censorship imposed, the power of the courts to review decisions on rights or censorship limited, political opponents imprisoned, without trial, and the constitution amended to stress the duties and obligations of citizens rather than their rights. This process was reversed with the defeat of the Congress party and Prime Minister Indira Gandhi at the 1977 election.

The constant dilemma for authoritarian systems is that rebellion or revolution may become the only way to register dissatisfaction with the regime.

Military Dictatorships

A fundamental principle of Western democratic systems is civilian supremacy over the military authorities, though this supremacy has been established in authoritarian systems such as Ethiopia as well as in democratic systems like Britain or the United States in which the military forces loyally uphold the regime and its policies. But throughout history, from Artaxerxes on, the military has interested itself in politics and in ruling. Military groups—the Sacred Band in Thebes, the Praetorian Guard in Rome, the Samurai in Japan, the Junkers in Prussia, the Janissaries in the Ottoman Empire, the army in France from the time of Napoleon—have often influenced political decisions. In past Asian regimes or the sultanates of the Middle East there was little distinction between civil and military authority; the monarch was both absolute ruler and the person who could command the support of the army. But the military itself rarely exercised power.

The military has often acted as a pressure group attempting to influence political decisions or has intervened on behalf of civilians, usually of a conservative disposition, as in Argentina since the fall of

Perón in 1955, with a brief intermission between 1973 and 1976. Sometimes civilian groups themselves urge the intervention of the military or depend on the approval of the military, as in Turkey in 1908 and 1960, and in Iraq and Syria. In some Latin American constitutions the military is given the task of "guaranteeing the constitutional powers." In that region today, 13 out of the 19 countries are under some form of military rule.

Sometimes, as in Colombia, the army leadership, regarding itself as the most honest, most efficient, and most advanced organization in a nation, may turn out the politicians or civilian rulers it believes to be corrupt, misguided, or inefficient. It may act where political instability results from irreconcilable political divisions or continual political crises, or when the nation has been humiliated by defeat in war. The military leaders form a small, highly disciplined and organized group, cohesive and hierarchical, often living apart from civilians and living by a different code of discipline and order, well educated, possessing technical knowledge as well as weapons, seeing itself either as a upper- or middle-class managerial group that guards the nation's honor or as the only group concerned with the national interest, essential for the preservation of law and order, and in the newer nations, acting as agents of modernization. The military council that deposed Haile Selassie in Ethiopia in 1974 sees its role as the creation of "Ethiopian socialism," to be established by people's communes in a one-party state.

Usually the military has withdrawn from political control after establishing internal stability. But its members may remain in power if there is no organized political group capable of maintaining stability. Brazil's army has produced 4 successive chiefs of state in the last 11 years, and the president has used his powers to suspend the legislature, make decrees, dismiss officials, and suspend political rights.

"Military moustache and tunic," in Marx's phrase, "are periodically acclaimed as the tutelary deities of society."[3] Historically a military dictatorship has bolstered the existing regime with its privileges and inequities. But if in countries like Chile, Brazil, and Uruguay the military has headed rather repressive regimes, it has in other countries such as Peru attempted to introduce social reform and economic programs. More recently, and especially in countries in the early stages of political development where the army views itself as the best modernizing group, the dictatorship has been aimed at changing the existing regime. This has occurred in Egypt under Gamel Abdul Nasser, Pakistan under Ayub Khan, Syria under Adib Shishakli, Iraq under Abdul Kassim, Thailand under Sarit Thanarat, Burma under Ne Win, Sudan under Ibrahim Abboud, and Lebanon under Fuad Chehab. By

1975, 18 of the 35 independent black states in sub-Saharan Africa had military rulers. This type of regime, based on the taking of power by the armed forces, is, however, different from a caudillo type regime of the Latin American past, where an individual used his own military following to maintain his power, acted on the principle of *personalismo,* and exercised both military and political power at the local level.

But the army is not a perpetual ruling mechanism, and power must inevitably be exercised in conjunction with civilians or transferred to them. Indeed the generals and colonels who originally staged the coup may begin disputing power and thus reintroduce political chaos, or they may establish themselves as a new class with special privileges.

Some regimes may be termed *Bonapartist:* they are dominated by a magnetic leader who is supported by the mass or a considerable part of the population, they lack doctrine but possess an ambiguous program of social reform, and they are nationalistic or militaristic in spirit. But even those regimes are logically obliged to transform themselves into another kind of political system as the need for continuous political organization becomes apparent and the administrative inadequacies and lack of governmental skills of the military become obvious. Often, as in the case of the two Napoleons, the regimes become autocracies.

Rarely has a military dictatorship itself prepared the way for a democratic regime or organized political parties, though as in Mexico, Turkey, and Portugal after 1974 it has sometimes been able or tried to establish a stable regime. The most recent attempt of military rulers to create a political party has been in Burma, where the military regime in 1962 formed the Burma Socialist Program party (Lanzin) to recruit, train, and indoctrinate a new political elite on the basis of an ideological program, *The Burmese Way to Socialism.* Until modern-day Portugal, Turkey under Ataturk was probably the only example of a regime in which a successful attempt was made to create a political democracy. After the military coup in 1960, the Turkish junta again tried to provide some democratic legitimacy for the new regime. And in Pakistan the system of "basic democracies" was introduced within a year of the declaration of martial law, though it was not implemented in reality. In Africa only in Sierra Leone has a military ruler been replaced by a civilian government up to the present.

Guided Democracies

In the newer countries dictatorship or authoritarian rule has been defended as necessary to achieve national integration, to unite potentially divisive groups such as tribes, and to bring together representatives of groups such as farmers, labor, youth, and the army. This has been true in Ghana under Kwame Nkrumah, Egypt under Gamel Abdul Nasser, or Guinea under Sekou Touré. Sukarno called his regime a "guided democracy" but he had powers to appoint and dismiss members of the assembly and to suspend parliament, and was responsible only to the People's Congress, which did not meet. Nevertheless his power was limited by two groups, the Indonesian Communist party and the army. Touré has called the Guinean regime a *communaucratie,* a combination of traditional African ideas of community and Marxist ideals, which contains some resemblances to a communist type of regime, though there is also greater participation by a variety of groups in political life. In Madagascar the *Red Book of the Malagasy Socialist Revolution* was written by the president to form the basis of the regime. The constitution of Zaire is based on Mobutuism—the thought, teachings, and actions of President Mobutu who is "head of the great Zaire family and father of the nation." In Tanzania Julius Nyerere is attempting to build a rural socialist society, village communities of brotherhood, and cooperative ventures across the country, and to create a social and national ethic for its members. In Pakistan General Khan had attempted to create a system of basic democracies by a four-layer system of representative government, from village representatives through county councils and district councils up to divisional councils, consisting of officials and appointed representatives, with the villagers voting only for the village council; his successor Ali Bhutto barred the main opposition party and charged its leaders with sedition. In Bangladesh Sheikh Mujibar Rahman planned in 1975 to crush "anti-social and anti-national activities."

Reality has not often corresponded to the theory of guided democracy. Rulers have justified dictatorial policies on the basis of long-term benefit and urged sacrifices for the sake of modernity or a socialist future. But the fall from power of Sukarno, Nkrumah, and Mujib and the death of Nasser have revealed that their regimes were more corrupt and inefficient than democratic. The megalomania of some of these rulers and others has led to a willful neglect of the welfare of citizens.

Reforming Dictatorships

Some regimes may be personal or party dictatorships supported by a large part of the population and aimed at general social or economic improvement. The regime may be ideologically based, as was

the regime of Fidel Castro in Cuba with its general Marxist orientation until it became formally communist in 1975, or the Nasser regime in Egypt with its vaguely socialist policy of land redistribution,
beginning of industrialization, nationalization of large companies, and
nationalism that recognized the importance of Islam. Or the regime
may be more pragmatic, like the Latin American systems that were
both nationalist and socially reformist and that had strong party leadership and support by mass movements such as the military or intellectuals; Peron in Argentina, Getulio Vargas in Brazil, the National
Revolutionaries in Bolivia, APRA in Peru, and the Acción Democratica in Venezuela were of this sort.

Reforming dictatorships aptly illustrate the contemporary difficulty
in drawing the distinction between regimes of the left and of the right,
a distinction analysts have tried to make since the French Revolution gave currency to these terms. Like other nondemocratic bodies
these have attended to the welfare of workers, these dictatorships are
pledged to economic and social reform and frequently receive strong
popular support.

Western views of the left have been a synthesis of Marxist and radical ideas, containing programs for social reform, proposing the end or
limitation of traditional privileges, and the widening of political participation. Various attitudes have been seen as the main characteristics
of the left: stress on rationalism, belief in liberty and equality, especially equality of opportunity, sympathy for the exploited, opposition
to racism, pacifism, hostility to organized religion, fear of strong
power, and support from the working class. The dilemma is that regimes of the left do not exemplify all these characteristics, while other
types of regime possess some of them. David Caute, in his *The Left in
Europe Since 1789,* argues that the key factor is that a regime of the
left be based on popular sovereignty; but the recent history of ple-
biscitary dictatorships calls for the qualification of this view.

The rise of communist systems since the 1917 Russian Revolution
has produced an attitude of ambivalence among the leftists. Not all
would agree with Jacob Talmon's view of these systems as types of totalitarian democracies or as representative of political messianism,
which postulates a preordained, harmonious, and perfect scheme of
things based on the idea of the essential goodness and perfectibility of
human nature, and which attempts to achieve progress and social harmony.[4] But the strong political controls imposed in communist systems, and the often callous disregard for human values, suggest political behavior regarded as more typical of the right than of the left.

The modern right is essentially a response to and reaction against the principles and attitudes stemming from the French Revolution. Philosophically based on the ideas of recognizing human limitation and denying equality, rightist thinking implies support for traditional values and institutions, including both religion and ecclesiastical authority, which in turn bolster it, and the implementation of desirable concepts such as order, discipline, hierarchy, aristocracy, and courage. Normally it emphasizes nationalism and the desirability of national unity rather than class consciousness, political party, or sectional interests. The purported aim of the right is not to liquidate democracy, but to rescue the state from the abuses of democracy and to restore morality to public life. In the modern era the right has always reached agreement on hostility to communism.

The existence on one side of politically leftist regimes that flout many of the basic principles of the left, and on the other of dictatorial regimes or systems dominated by nonleftists engaged in economic modernization, social reform, and the amelioration of the condition of life, raises the question of whether the left-right distinction is any longer a valuable way of distinguishing between regimes.

Totalitarian Regimes

The existence of some similar important features in the communist regime of the Soviet Union, the fascist regime of Italy, and the Nazi system of Germany has led some analysts such as Hannah Arendt, Carl Friedrich, and Z. K. Brzezinski to suggest a new category of "totalitarianism."[5] This concept implies the existence of a new twentieth-century type of regime based on a dominant leader supported by a mass party acting on an aggressive ideology that explains and influences political actions.

A totalitarian regime differs from an authoritarian system in that the former attempts to totally control and regulate behavior in detail, and subordinates all organizations to the state. In absolute monarchies, tradition and law limited the power of the monarch, who, in any case, did not interest himself in the whole social order. Even Louis XIV of France, the personification of absolutism, was not absolutely powerful in practice. But in Leon Trotsky's aphorism, if Louis XIV could say, "L'etat, c'est moi," Joseph Stalin could say with equal appropriateness, "La société, c'est moi." The basic concept of totalitarianism is that the state attempts to absorb all of society, to control lives and minds, and to mobilize the population, youth as well as adults, in all areas of life. In Nazi Germany membership in one or another of the youth organizations was compulsory; by 1938 the total membership was 8.7 million. Power is concentrated in the hands of an individual or group, and the regime eliminates all opposition parties, controls communications and the mass media, exercises control over the economy and over highly centralized planning, uses religion for its purpose though it is fundamentally irreligious, and makes deliberate use of terror as a controlling factor through the secret police, concentration or labor camps, and the completely amoral use of force. The existence of a single official ideology and a single party leads to a concentration of political, economic, and religious power in the same group, intolerance of dissension or democracy even within the one party, and the refusal to allow any standard of morality other than that of the party.

Some theorists have argued that totalitarian regimes are supported not simply because of economic benefits or promises, but also because they seem to offer a method of solving the problem of personal alienation and the division between individual and society. They are welcomed in an era when people are bewildered by the complexity of modern life and when the significance of previous unifying social ties such as the family, locality, or religion has been reduced.[6]

The three regimes regarded as prime examples of the totalitarian model—Nazi Germany, fascist Italy, and the Soviet Union under Stalin if not after his death—did not embody all of the characteristics of the model to the same degree. Moreover, there was in reality less coherence and unity in decision making in these systems than is suggested in the model.[7] But the three regimes were similar in their ruthlessness and extreme dictatorial behavior, and none of them was overthrown by the people living under them in peacetime. Yet the differences of ideology, in purpose, in spirit, in the kind of support obtained in the three regimes suggest that they do not fall completely into one category.

There was no inherent inevitability about Russian totalitarianism, and it was perhaps the effect of civil war and foreign intervention more than doctrine that led originally to opposition parties being forbidden and dissident groups within the Communist party itself being dissolved in 1921. Much of the cruelty and inhumanity displayed in the Soviet Union up to 1952—including the murder of 20 million people, among them the top political leadership, and the extreme use of security police—are more attributable to the personality or paranoia of the dictator Stalin than they are the result of objective needs or communist policies. As Robert C. Tucker has suggested, the personalties of the dictators have had an important impact on the operation of the three systems, and in the case of the Stalin and Hitler regimes, the dictators, driven by pathological hatred and fear of enemy conspiratorial forces, were responsible for the terror to a considerable extent.[8] Tucker explains Stalin's behavior by his desire to become Lenin's "alter ego and closest companion-in-arms" and by his view of the "enemy" within the party as potential betrayer of it and the revolution.[9] Stalin's control over the Communist party was complete. Of the 139 people chosen in 1934 to constitute the central committee of the party, 98 were later arrested and killed by Stalin. The cult of personality was so extreme that he imprisoned for 7 years Madame Kalinin, the wife of the president of the Soviet Union. Party congresses were called at his will; after an interval of 13 years a congress was convened in 1952 at which the members of the Politburo, supposedly the top decision-making body, were informed of the agenda and their assignments.

Italian fascism was the response to the political and economic difficulties experienced by the country after World War I; it emphasized the glorious past of the country menaced by barbarism, the national genius, the need for a unity that transcended individuals and their rights, the necessity for action, the assertion of state authority, and the resurgence of Italy as a world power. Its leader, Benito Mussolini, an admirer of Lenin with a revolutionary socialist background, presided over a movement that appealed for social harmony and order, advocated a corporate society, and included within it contradictory elements, religious and atheist, Catholic and anticlerical, monarchical and republican, socialist and conservative. In practice Mussolini, glorified as *Il Duce,* was a skillful opportunist who maintained his supremacy by maneuvering among the different groups within the party as well as those outside rather than by implementing any corporativist principles: he symbolized external aggression, colonial expansion, and militancy, and dealt with political dissenters by using physical violence, imprisonment, and even castor oil. For Mussolini the appearance of action was more important than the reality. The party was gradually subordinated to the state under Mussolini who destroyed the vision of some party members of an "integral syndicalism" that was to include employers and employed in a cooperative relationship. The term "totalitarianism" was coined in Italy in 1925, but Mussolini did not eliminate any of the existing establishment—monarchy, religion, civil service, or the military.[10]

The nature, the essence, the objectives of Nazism remain puzzling today. Plausible explanations of its motivating characteristics,— counterrevolution, nationalism, German expansion, antirationalism, antiutilitarianism, antidemocratic feeling, rural revolt against urban domination, or petit bourgeois reaction against big business—all seem inadequate. The most convincing argument seems to be that of George Mosse, who, in *The Crisis of German Ideology*, sees the major factor in Nazism as its ideology of race that urged the creation of a *Volk* from which the impure such as the Jews would be excluded. This ideology led to control over personal behavior as well as over intellectual products, over dress and makeup as well as over books and plays. Other groups and organizations supported or acquiesced in the Nazi activity. Political parties were outlawed, the trade unions broken; the churches, with rare exceptions, remained silent, and the educational system was a compliant tool. Within the Nazi party and the SS, the elite group exercised total power under the orders and ultimate control of Adolf Hitler, the charismatic leader. The Nazi regime, which was supposed to last for 1,000 years, was characterized by the excessive brutality and violence and agressive nationalism; in a chain of concentration camps throughout the country over 6 million Central European Jews were murdered.

The one regime that survived World War II, the Soviet Union, has changed in a number of ways, suggesting that any common totalitarian aspects may be transitory. Assumptions about the monolithic nature of communism, both inside the countries that have adopted it and within the communist camp of countries, need qualification. In the Soviet Union since the death of Stalin collective leadership has alternated with rule by a dominant leader, the interests of social groups are expressed and taken into account, the extremism of the police state has been reduced, there is less use of terror and coercion, and some critical opinion has been tolerated. But the official ideology remains paramount and controls have been reimposed on dissenters. A growing bureaucracy controls planning. The maintenance of labor camps with a population of 1.25 million, the extension of the death penalty to "economic crimes," the reluctance to allow emigration, the detention of dissenters in mental institutions as well as their punishment by nonjudicial means such as dismissal from a job, expulsion from a union, and harassment over residence, all indicate that dictatorship still pervades the whole of life. To prevent the spread of unofficial documents or dissident opinion, documents are still copied by hand rather than by photocopying machines.

The current nature of the Eastern European communist systems is also not an apt reflection of the totalitarian model. In Poland the power of the church and the voice of intellectuals has been a restraining influence on communist political power. Successive changes in Yugoslavia—decentralization in industrial organization and a more self-regulatory economy, an unwillingness to press for the collectivization of the peasantry, a partial return to a free market in agricultural commodities, the reduced role played by the Communist party and the divorce of the party from government and administration, a more liberal constitution, and even the resignation of the government of the republic of Slovenia in 1966—illustrate that communist regimes are not inherently totalitarian. In other Eastern European countries economic management has differing degrees of autonomy, and a small private business sector exists. The monolithic communist unity was ended by the Yugoslavian refusal to accept Russian domination and its expulsion from the Cominform, which was founded in 1947 to coordinate the activities of communist parties, in 1948; by the denunciation of Stalin by Nikita Khrushchev in 1956, which weakened the Russian control over other Communist parties; by the advocacy of polycentrism by the Italian Communist Palmiro Togliatti in the 1950s; by the Sino-Soviet schism in the 1960s; by the independence of Rumania in foreign affairs since 1963; and by the extreme Maoist groups in a number of countries.

Perhaps the closest current approximation to the totalitarian model is China. The government totally controls all political activity through the structure of revolutionary committees, mobilizes labor for common purposes and has attempted to instill a revolutionary will into the peasantry, indoctrinates people beginning in the nursery to create a new consciousness, has tried to change human nature by removing all bourgeois behavior or motives and to end family control and the traditional authority of the father, and makes advancement contingent upon ideological conformity. The system was dominated until his death in 1976 by the leader Mao Tse-tung, who manipulated the party and other organizations at will, tried to limit bureaucracy, combatted revisionism, and pressed for uninterrupted revolution. In the evolving power struggle in China, Mao Tse-tung during the Cultural Revolution of the 1960s seemed to abandon his belief in the party as the chief instrument of revolution and to put more emphasis on the army and the Red Guards for implementing policy, thus dividing power among the party, army, and administrators, especially in the creation of communes along the lines of the Paris Commune. As in the Soviet Union the party organs have met at the will of the leadership; after an interval of a decade the Chinese National People's Congress, an instrument of the party, finally met in 1975.

The paradox exists that the more matters in which a totalitarian regime interests itself, the less the controlling group can know of actual conditions, with the result that the political leaders may in fact have considerably less freedom in making decisions than at first seems the case. Experts and specialists necessarily exert substantial influence in those areas in which they possess knowledge, such as education, military strategy, or industrial management.

Western and Non-Western Regimes

The vast increase in the number of new nations in the postwar period has led analysts to consider them as a different political category from the older nations, which are characterized by a highly differentiated system of governmental organization, a rational, scientific, and secular basis of decision making, coherent political parties, bureaucratic administration, regulatory behavior based on the rule of law, personal and social rights, a high degree of literacy, economic affluence, and technological innovation.

By contrast the newer nations, economically undeveloped with a very low standard of living and a low rate of capital formation, are characterized by political fluidity and instability, abrupt changes, lack of consensus on the ends and procedures of politics, frequently charismatic leadership, a highly nationalist or ideological orientation, a lack of any clear differentiation in the roles of political and other leaders, a lack of any real opposition groups, few organized autonomous or nongovernmental interest groups, a relatively young political leadership, and a lack of unified communication. Politics may revolve around a pattern of personal associations and cliques, each of which may support the regime in return for certain powers and privileges, and which easily shift allegiance; in Pakistan the khan of Mamdot took his group of followers in and out of three parties in nine years. There is an absence of any considerable number of highly trained administrative personnel; often administration is inefficient or wasteful in countries marked by limited education or literacy and with little previous experience in self-government. Civil services are often much larger than is necessary because existing governments habitually put friends on the civil service payroll.

In internal affairs these countries generally pursue policies requiring state economic control and different forms of socialist ideology, while maintaining a neutralist attitude in international affairs. There is an enormous discrepancy in the conditions of life in the older and newer nations. In the Western countries the average life expectancy is about 70; in the Afro-Asian nations it is about 30. The widest gap is between the average per capita income in the United States of $5,041 and the Afro-Asian average of about $150. The industrial democracies account for 65 percent of the world's production and 70 percent of its commerce. The non-Western countries are not only less industrialized but are also deficient in technical skills, power, transport, production of capital goods, a balanced economy, and adequate development of natural resources. The abysmal poverty of most of the world's population coupled with the fact that it is predominantly non-white (whites constituting only about 30 percent of the world's population) has inevitably led to tension with the wealthier and white part of the world. The problems of these poorer nations are aggravated by an estimated 800 million illiterates.

Useful though a contrast of this kind is analytically, one major problem is that it would put developed nations, such as the United States and the Soviet Union, in the same group because they are both highly industrialized, prosperous, materialistic societies in which politicians are an identifiable group and managers control industry. Moreover a dichotomy between Western and non-Western systems omits many regimes of Latin America, which do not clearly fall into either group and which are differentiated by a variety of political institutions, social conditions, philosophic beliefs, and types of leadership and parties, and countries such as Brazil, Japan, and Taiwan, which are prosperous societies with politically varied systems. To focus on Japan, which has experienced the fastest economic expansion in history since the 1940s, that country is now the second industrial deomocracy in the world, though it is neither Western in cultural origin nor white in race.

Stages of Political Development

Philosophers, sociologists, and anthropologists have suggested a variety of ways in which societies may be differentiated. Emile Durkheim spoke of mechanical and organic solidarities, Ferdinand Tönnies of *Gemeinschaft* (community) and *Gesellschaft* (society), Leopold von Wiese of sacred and secular societies, Robert Redfield of folk society and urban civilization. The most influential of such theories has been Max Weber's tripartite typology of traditional, charismatic, and bureaucratic societies.[11]

Traditional societies are characterized by conformity and are ruled on the basis of tradition and divine law by a monarch or aristocracy whose power is made legitimate by status or heredity. In the contemporary world a diminishing number of countries fall into this category.

The concept of *charisma,* implying a gift of grace, was appropriated from religion to indicate political leadership based on personal magnetism and devotion and often exercised by a military leader or religious prophet. The *charismatic figure,* partly by manipulating symbols and myths, gains the loyalty of citizens who place particular faith in him or her. The developed nations have in recent years been led by outstanding figures of this kind, such as Dwight Eisenhower, Winston Churchill, and Charles de Gaulle. In the newer nations leaders such as Norodom Sihanouk, Sungman Rhee, Habib Bourguiba, Gamel Abdul Nasser, Jawaharlal Nehru, and Achmed Sukarno have attempted to create internal cohesion. Some writers have suggested that charismatic leaders are invaluable as agents of political transition in most of the newer states. But all too often the political equilibrium these agents have sought to establish has been in the familiar pattern of dictatorship. And in both developed and undeveloped countries, it is difficult to see what "charismatic" means in practice except a strong, attractive personality who can command political support.

Weber's *bureaucratic system* is essentially a constitutional regime in which legal rules are established and followed, with the holders of offices adhering to those rules irrespective of their own personalities or desires and with power exercised according to known procedures. Characteristic of such a system is that it is objective, depersonalized, and reliant on specialized expertise and routine.

Weber himself did not specify the relationship between the three types of system, nor suggest that societies were likely to follow particular patterns, nor argue a unilinear theory of social change though his implication was that less-developed societies are "traditional," while more modern societies are "bureaucratic." Other writers have argued, however, that systems have gone through certain similar stages of development. Anthropolgists have traced a four-fold development of regimes from (1) hunting groups bound by blood or marriage, to (2) large tribes organized in kinship groups, to (3) chiefdoms with some form of governmental organization, and finally (4) large united policies. Aristotle traced associations from the household to the village and finally to the polis, the political association. Giovanni Vico viewed history as alternating between periods of progress and retrogression. G. W. F. Hegel saw regimes illustrating stages of the spirit of consciousness working toward freedom; Claude-Henri Saint-Simon saw an alternation of organic and critical periods; Herbert Spencer spoke of the change from homogeneity to heterogeneity. Auguste Comte saw regimes progressing from a theological through a metaphysical to a positive phase of history.

Interest in the problem of political development has been stimulated by the attempt of the newer nations to create viable political systems and to modernize economic and social conditions. There is easy agreement on the essence of economic modernization, but like the proverbial elephant, politically developed countries are easier to identify than to define.

Economic and social modernization and political development are clearly connected. Weber saw the development of formal legal rationality and secularism, accompanied by efficiency and a calculus of ends and means, as related to the rise of modern capitalism. Weber and R. H. Tawney both discussed the interconnection between the rise of Protestantism in Europe and the emergence of capitalism, though a causal relationship has been challenged.[12] Religion can rarely be an independent variable; though Buddhism is traditionally anti-materialist and therefore seems logically incompatible with economic development, Japan has succeeded though Mahayana Buddhism is important there, and Theravada Buddhist countries have varied in their economic behavior.

Emile Durkheim regarded the change from mechanical to organic solidarity and from repressive to restitutive legal sanctions as the result of the division of labor. Henry Maine explained the rise of contract in terms of the declining role of kinship as an exclusive base of social organization.[13]

There is a close relationship between political underdevelopment and factors such as limited industrial capacity, backward agriculture, a gulf between urban and rural areas, an illiterate or uneducated population, and an impoverished people. But there are no exact comparable indices of economic modernization and political democracy. Modern science and techniques have been introduced by widely varying social systems. A particularly startling example is Germany, where economic modernization and industrialization did not lead to liberal democracy. German society remained quasi-feudal rather than producing a self-confident bourgeoisie with its own political aspirations.[14] The existing society remained because of the early emergence of large economic units, the state assistance to industry, state ownership of many enterprises, a generous state social welfare system, and the official stress on national ends.

Modernization implies economic growth, the increase of gross national product and of per capita income, economic planning, greater industrialization, the accumulation of capital, increasing urbanization and a reduction in the proportion of those engaged in agriculture, scientific advance, improved transport, and a higher rate of literacy. It signifies a move from a subsistence to an industrialized economy and a social change from an extended to a nuclear family. The "takeoff" point for economic growth often occurs when agriculture claims less than 45 percent of the working population. From an economic point of view the implicit assumption is that economic and technological growth and increased consumption is inherently desirable, an argument that today is not accepted automatically either by economists or ecologists.[15]

Walt Rostow has argued that all important economic systems, with the partial exception of the Anglo-Saxon countries, have depended on government intervention for sustaining growth, transferring of agricultural surplus to new sectors of the economy, increasing savings and fostering industrial manufacture, and accumulating capital.[16] This is essential both for rendering labor more productive and for sustaining the division of labor on which, Adam Smith argued, the wealth of nations largely rests. A major contemporary problem is whether self-sustaining economic growth is possible in the underdeveloped countries without some form of temporary dictatorial regime that has to amass capital by brutal means, as was done in the enclosure movement by British landlords in the eighteenth century, manufacturers in the United States and Germany in the nineteenth century, by the Meiji rulers in Japan, and by Soviet commissars under Stalin.

The concept of political development is more ambiguous than that of economic change and implies changes in many areas of thought and behavior. Samuel Huntington argues that development and political order exist when institutional and organizational growth are compatible with the rate of social mobilization, the rise of new social forces and groups, and the expansion of political participation.[17] The term "social mobilization" means the breaking away of people from their social, economic, and psychological commitments and their induction into new patterns of group membership, organization, and commitment.

All states exist in a continuum between primitive economies and technically sophisticated ones, between subject and participant political cultures, between societies that are closed and those open to merit, between cultures based on kinship and those with nuclear family units, between religious and secular societies. Development can be regarded as the move from one member of the pair to the other.[18]

In recent years a number of typologies have been proposed to help classify the large number of developing systems. One of the most interesting has been that proposed by David Apter in *The Politics of Modernization*, in which he suggests the existence of three types of developing regimes: (1) modernizing autocracies, (2) mobilization systems, and (3) reconciliation systems. In the first type innovation is introduced by traditional authorities or institutions, as in Ethiopia or Morocco. In the second type the mobilization of the people is attempted, usually by a single party, to deal with economic and cultural deficiencies and to achieve certain specific goals; Guinea and Tunis are examples. In reconciliation systems such as India and Nigeria a variety of groups, institutions, and government bodies compete in the developmental process. But Apter's tripartite division cannot take sufficient account of the wide political and social differences that exist in over 100 developing nations.[19]

Gabriel Almond and G. Bingham Powell also suggest three types of political systems in the development process—traditional, transitional and modern—with the system changing in response to internal and external pressures.[20] Systems can thus be compared by the degree of specialization of structures, differentiation of political roles, and specificity of functions.

Various characteristics have been suggested to indicate developed polities. These have included: (1) a rationalizaton of authority, ability to maintain law and order efficiently, management of tensions, creation of a national legal order, and willingness to seek specific secular and political ends; (2) a differentiation of governmental structure so that different organs and personnel perform legislative, administrative, judicial, and military functions, and organizations and procedures are institutionalized; (3) a more complex political organization so that government can handle information effectively; (4) the decline of traditional elites and of claims to legitimacy based on outmoded factors; (5) the widening of political participation to a considerable part of the population who then become involved in activities of the state, help choose the rulers, and have their interests taken into account; (6) an increase in the speed and extent of change as the result of the proliferation of knowledge; (7) efficiency in the making of policy; (8) political as well as social and geographical integration to achieve a coherent, unified, stable regime which can assimilate new social forces and be accepted by all; (9) the presence of the chief characteristics of an open, constitutional democracy; (10) a regime adaptable enough to perform new functions or meet new needs; and (11) a regime in which, as Lucian Pye has suggested, personal identity, trust, and psychic well-being can be fostered.[21]

In a somewhat different formulation a country is said to be "developed" if it has successfully dealt with crises in (1) identity, or problems arising from territory, social cleavages, subnational groups, and the consequences of rapid social change; (2) legitimacy, or problems arising from the nature and bases of authority; (3) participation, or problems arising from changes of social stratification and demands made by individuals and groups; (4) penetration, or problems concerning the extent of governmental power to execute policy; and (5) distribution, or problems over the increase or distribution of goods.[22]

An underlying problem in such classificatory schemes, is that economic modernization may occur in a political situation where development is not taking place but rather is retarded by dictatorship, internal strife, corruption, and the decline of effective political institutions.

Moreover, there is no unilinear way to change or inevitable process of political development, nor is there any particular modernizing elite group. In Japan change was fostered by the aristocratic oligarchy, in Western Europe by commercial traders and capitalists, in Latin America by strong executive leaders, and in revolutionary countries by leaders of political parties. Barrington Moore has suggested three different paths taken by societies on the road to modernity: (1) a bourgeois revolution resulting in Western democracy, (2) a conservative reaction leading to fascism, and (3) a peasant revolution leading to communism. The first road is followed only if certain preconditions exist such as a balance between a strong monarch and an independent landed aristocracy, the development of commercial agriculture, a weakening of the landed aristocracy, a break with the past, and the prevention of an alliance between the bourgeoisie and the aristocracy against the peasants and workers.[23] Another analysis offers seven different patterns of modernization depending on when the transfer of political power took place, whether it was due to internal or external change, whether it took place within a single territorial state, whether it succeeded colonial rule, and whether it had a base in already developed institutions.[24]

The most highly developed states in the Western world are those that Daniel Bell has termed "post-industrial societies."[25] In industrial societies corporations are the chief economic and social institution, the machine has a major impact on the character of work performed, and there is conflict between capital and labor. In postindustrial societies, whose people are affluent and have a relatively high standard of living, the corporation has a less central place, work relations are more people oriented, the importance of industrial norms is less apparent, and a lesser proportion of the labor force works in industry than in services;* it is also true of such societies that scientific and technical elites are prominent, universities, research institutes, and knowledge in general have a prominent role, merit rather than property is the principle of social stratification, group competition replaces class warfare, and the social structure has a more rational and efficient basis. The economic function is subordinated to the political order because the government is responsible for planning; experts and the bureaucracy play a large role in such planning, and the state intervenes in the economy for a broad variety of reasons, a trend that challenges some aspects of democracy and constitutes a danger to individual rights.

Colonial and Noncolonial Powers

From the perspective of the newer nations, a meaningful classification might be to differentiate the independent nations from the former or remaining colonial rulers such as Britain, France, Portugal, Holland, and the United States. The new nations have argued that the colonial powers made fortunes out of the slave trade, instituted the color bar, plundered resources, disrupted native institutions, were largely uninterested in the social welfare of the inhabitants, and ruled in authoritarian fashion, often using emergency regulations, detention without trial, and various forms of restriction. Above all these nations have complained that the paternalism of the colonial powers, though they established order and a basic administration, left them unprepared to

---

*Of the 11.2 million jobs created in the United States between 1968 and 1976, 8 million were white-collar, 72 percent of which were filled by women, 2.5 million were service, and 1.5 million were blue-collar jobs.

rule themselves. Not until 1957 did Belgium allow local elections in the Congo it administered. The British—who maintained a tradition of a semiautocratic governor, an executive council of senior officials, and a nominated legislative council with local governments based largely on hereditary leadership created to deal with the diversity of existing native societies—were often accused of maintaining control over the colonial possessions through indirect rule. Yet, as Nkrumah wrote, "If colonialism deserves to be blamed for many evils in Africa ... surely it was not preceded by an African Golden Age or paradise."[26] A heritage of colonialism need not lead to a cycle of self-perpetuating poverty. Some ex-colonies, in Latin America, West Africa, and Malaya, have made considerable economic progress. Others that were not subject to colonial control, such as Liberia and Ethiopia, have remained among the poorest African countries.

Some of the newer countries have deliberately encouraged an attitude of raucous anticolonialism in part to help consolidate internal national sentiment; symbolically, Sierre Leone created the Order of the Mosquito because the insect had kept the white man out of Africa. Their fear of continued Western control and of the preservation of some special privileges or interests by stronger nations has led them to be wary of suspected "neocolonialism," taking the form of economic imperialism, dollar diplomacy, and intellectual control, which might undermine their sovereign power. Despite these suspicions, total aid from the West has actually risen sharply from $15.7 billion in 1970 to $27.6 billion in 1975. The Yaoundé Convention of 1963 between the Common Market and 16 African states allowed the latter to expand their trade, and the Lomé Convention of 1975 links the Common Market with 300 million people in 46 African, Caribbean, and Pacific countries, which have free access for all their industrial and 96 percent of their agricultural products. Yet independence has not inevitably meant unity among the new nations, as shown by the experience in African countries where two blocs were temporarily formed: the Casablanca group of Ghana, Guinea, Mali, Morocco, the United Arab Republic, and Algeria, and the Monrovia group of more moderate systems. Africans still differ in their goals; some remain attached to tribal loyalty, some are nationalist, some believe in a wider loyalty.

Regional African organizations have been sacrificed on the altar of national integration and sovereignty. The two ambitious federations proposed by Britain in East Africa and in Central Africa, the Union Africaine et Malgache (The African, Malagasy, and Mauritian Common Organization) proposed by De Gaulle, the West African Federation suggested by Nkrumah, and the East African Federation by Nyerere have all failed to materialize. The organizations that have been established—the Economic Community of West African States and the Union Douanière et Économique de l'Afrique Centrale (The Central African Economic and Customs Union) in Equatorial Africa—as yet are of little importance. On a broader front, however, a number of regional blocs—the 47-member Organization of African Unity, the 24-member Organization of American States, the 20-member Arab League, and the Afro-Asian members of the Commonwealth—now composed of 36 members with 850 million people—have strengthened the former colonies.

The Bandung Conference of 1955, attended by 29 African and Asian countries, tried to portray the homogeneity of the Afro-Asian bloc. It led to a Third World group of non-Western countries that do not have communist governments and that were accordingly to be nonaligned in disputes between Western democracies and communist countries. All these countries reject any form of colonialism or concept of white supremacy, manifest a desire for political and economic independence and political consolidation, and emphasize nation building through a spirit of nationalism to overcome traditionalism and localism. But the Third World has been as marked by internal dissension on economic and political matters and boundary disputes as have the two other world blocs. Containing 70 percent of the world's population and accounting for 30 percent of global income, the Third World includes oil-rich Saudi Arabia and impoverished Bangladesh. Some Third World countries, such as Iran, Algeria, India, Brazil, and Nigeria, are important politically; some, such as Singapore, Hong Kong, Israel, Mexico, Thailand, and Taiwan are stable states. The Third World does not vote unanimously as a bloc at the United Nations, nor does it possess a common attitude to politics or to the other two groups. In West Africa a schism has developed between those countries such as Senegal, which believe in black consciousness or negritude, and others such as Nigeria, which hold that African culture should embrace the world of Islam. Nevertheless, the common stand taken by the Third World at the important United Nations Conference on Trade and Development at Geneva in 1964 and at subsequent meetings showed the solidarity of the economically underdeveloped countries in demanding concessions and preferential treatment from the rich man's club of developed countries, and in wanting to share in the making of decisions by the economic institutions of the world as well as in controlling the production of their own natural resources.

In recent years the Group of 77, which now contains 112 members, has been planning strategy for the Third World at a time when the reduction of foreign aid, the rapid increase in population in the underdeveloped world, monetary difficulties, and Western inflation have left most of the members unable to advance economically. The quadrupling of oil prices and the imposition of a selective embargo on the West by the Organization of Petroleum Exporting Countries (OPEC) in 1973 led the Third World to think of their natural resources as bargaining weapons with the developed West. Though there is no unanimity on the issues, the Third World in general has argued for stabilization of commodity prices at high levels, a system of indexing that links the price of commodities with world inflation, a moratorium on debts, technological assistance, more aid to the poorest countries and greater access to Western markets.

Classifications of typologies of political regimes throw light on various aspects of the political behavior or institutions present in societies. But no one classification can capture in any permanent manner the kaleidoscopic characteristics of a large number of different systems. New divisions of systems are always occuring. An increasingly acrimonious one exists between the world's 100 coastal countries and those that are landlocked or have inadequate coasts; the latter want guaranteed access to the sea and a share in offshore resources and fisheries. The group of 52 landlocked countries, anxious to obtain transit rights over the land of coastal nations, includes such diverse countries as Switzerland and Uganda. The most useful typology is the one that, for the observer, illuminates either the largest number of features in the regime—economic, social, and cultural, as well as political—or the particular features of politics in which the observer is interested—the claim to legitimacy or authority of the political rulers, the values and political culture of the regime, the relative power of the various institutions, groups, and personnel, the degree of freedom of citizens, the restraints on government, the stability, strength, and efficiency of the system, or the major internal and external policies.

Notes

[1] J. K. Galbraith, *The New Industrial State* (Boston: Houghton Mifflin, 1967).
[2] S. M. Lipset, *Political Man* (Garden City, N.Y.: Doubleday, 1960); Phillips Cutright, "National Political Development," in N. Polsby et al., eds., *Politics and Social Life* (Boston: Houghton Mifflin, 1962); and Deane Neubauer, "Some Conditions of Democracy," *American Political Science Review* (December 1967), pp. 1002–1009.
[3] Karl Marx, *The Eighteenth Brumaire of Louis Bonaparte.*

[4] Jacob Talmon, *The Origins of Totalitarian Democracy* (New York: Praeger, 1960).

[5] Hannah Arendt, *The Origins of Totalitarianism* (New York: New American Library/Meridian Books, 1958); Carl Friedrich and Zbigniew Brzezinski, *Totalitarian Dictatorship and Autocracy* (New York: Praeger, 1961); and Carl Friedrich, M. Curtis, and B. Barber, *Totalitarianism in Perspective: Three Views* (New York: Praeger, 1969).

[6] Erich Fromm, *Escape from Freedom* (New York: Avon Books, 1965); and Peter Drucker, *The End of Economic Man* (Briarcliff Manor, N.Y.: Stein & Day, 1939).

[7] E. N. Peterson, *The Limits of Hitler's Power* (Princeton University Press, 1969); Merle Fainsod, *Smolensk Under Soviet Rule* (Cambridge, Mass.: Harvard University Press, 1958); and A. L. Unger, *The Totalitarian Party: Party and People in Nazi Germany and Soviet Russia* (New York: Cambridge University Press, 1974).

[8] Robert C. Tucker, "The Dictator and Totalitarianism," *World Politics* (July 1965), pp. 555–583.

[9] Robert C. Tucker, *Stalin as Revolutionary, 1879–1929* (New York: Norton, 1974).

[10] Denis Mack Smith, *Mussolini's Roman Empire* (New York: Viking Press, 1976).

[11] Max Weber, *From Max Weber*, H. H. Gerth and C. Wright Mills, eds. (New York: Oxford University Press, 1946).

[12] Max Weber, *The Protestant Ethic and the Spirit of Capitalism* (London, Allen and Unwin, 1930); and R. H. Tawney, *Religion and the Rise of Capitalism* (New York: Harcourt Brace, 1926).

[13] Emile Durkheim, *The Division of Labor* (Glencoe: Free Press, 1949); Henry Maine, *Ancient Law* (London: Murray, 1906).

[14] Ralf Dahrendorf, *Society and Democracy in Germany* (Garden City, N.Y.: Doubleday, 1969).

[15] D. H. Matthews, ed., *The Limits to Growth* (New York: Universe Books, 1972).

[16] W. W. Rostow, *The Stages of Economic Growth* (New York: Cambridge University Press, 1960).

[17] S. P. Huntington, *Political Order in Changing Societies* (New Haven, Conn.: Yale University Press, 1968).

[18] Dean C. Tipps, "Modernization Theory and the Study of National Societies," *Comparative Studies in Society and History* (March 1973), pp. 199–226.

[19] David Apter, *The Politics of Modernization* (Chicago: University of Chicago Press, 1965).

[20] G. A. Almond and G. B. Powell, Jr., *Comparative Politics: A Developmental Approach* (Boston: Little, Brown, 1966).

[21] Lucian Pye, *Politics, Personality and Nation Building: Burma's Search for Identity* (New Haven, Conn.: Yale University Press, 1962).

[22] Leonard Binder et al., *Crises and Sequences in Political Development* (Princeton University Press, 1971).

[23] Barrington Moore, *Social Origins of Dictatorship and Democracy* (Boston: Beacon Press, 1966).

[24] Cyril Black, *The Dynamics of Modernization: A Study in Comparative History* (New York: Harper & Row, 1966).

[25] Daniel Bell, *The Coming of Post-Industrial Society* (New York: Basic Books, 1973).

[26] Kwame Nkrumah, "African Socialism Revisited," in W. Cartey and M. Kilson, eds., *The African Reader* (New York: Random House, 1970), p. 203.

Chapter Four

The Fundamental Rules of Regimes: Constitutions, Conventions, and Law

Ordered society exists on the basis of accepted rules. These rules have been largely derived in five ways: (1) from a constitution, (2) from statutes, (3) from judicial decisions and the accumulation of judge-made law, (4) from administrative regulations and actions, and (5) from conventions or customs accepted by all as constituting the rules of the political regime.

Constitutions

The most vital and important political rules are normally elaborated in constitutions, exemplifying Talleyrand's remark that if a thing goes without saying, it goes still better for being said. Constitutions are usually regarded as of a higher validity than other rules, thus bestowing legitimacy on those who claim to wield power according to constitutional rules. Constitutions reflect different aspects of the life and behavior of a community. Essentially they are the outcome of the socio-economic conditions of a community, even if they are not the exact image of social forces. They state certain basic principles to which the regime is dedicated. The Irish constitution includes "the directive principles of social policy" while the Indian constitution includes "the directive principles of state policy." Constitutions often claim to express the purpose and ethical values of a community and to reflect its political culture. The 1917 Mexican and the 1936 Soviet constitutions are purportedly implementations of a socialist system; the 1937 Eire constitution begins by invocations to the "Most Holy." The 1964 constitution of Iraq declares itself Arab and Islamic as well as independent and sovereign. Pressure by Hindus forced the inclusion in the Indian constitution of a sentence urging banning of the slaughter of cows in the section on the organization of agriculture and animal husbandry. The Chinese constitution was revised in 1975 to designate the system as "a socialist state of the dictatorship of the proletariat" instead of "a people's democratic state."

Often the constitutions may bear little relationship to existing reality, as in Latin America where almost 200 constitutions have been used during the last century and where they serve as periodical publications. As Lloyd Mechan has shown, the expressions of idealism and overoptimism, insistence on legality, and approval of revolution that are to be found in the Latin American documents show that they are only regarded as of temporary value in a continent where coups have been the constant element in producing change.[1]

Constitutions, as Plato said, do not "come out of sticks and stones, but result from the preponderance of certain characters which draw the rest of the community in their wake."[2] They therefore tend to reflect the needs, preoccupations, and interests of the politically influential groups in the society. They may also be the result of certain current problems or conditions. Political instability in France led in 1958 to a constitution devised largely to meet the views on governmental affairs of one person, Charles de Gaulle. The 1961 Rhodesian constitution was related to educational development since the rate of political transition to majority rule was connected with graduation from secondary schools, and therefore indirectly to the perpetuation of white rule. Constitutions must be acceptable to the people: "Every constitution" said Walter Bagehot, "must first gain authority and then use authority."[3]

Written and Unwritten Constitutions

Almost all countries have written documents that are regarded as the basic constitution. These documents vary considerably in length, from the brief American document to a lengthy document such as that of India which includes 97 items for federal control, 66 for the state list, and 47 for the concurrent list of powers; or that of Kenya, which in allocating functions between the central authority and regional governments discusses the subjects of animal disease control, barbers and hairdressers, and disorderly houses. Only in rare instances, such as those of Great Britain and those countries influenced by its political behavior like Israel, or of Spain under Franco, where organic laws were introduced from time to time—is there no single written docuement regarded as the constitution. Even in Israel a number of basic laws establishing the fundamental principles of the governmental system have been passed with the aim of eventually codifying them into a formal constitution.

But the distinction between regimes with a "written" and those with an "unwritten" constitution—formerly a means of comparing Britain and other systems—is not today of great political importance. Regimes possessing constitutions may be of any nature, democratic or dictatorial, liberal or conservative, communist, capitalist, or with a mixed economy. What is significant is that political actions adhere to an agreed pattern of behavior or the generally understood principles of the political system. In Britain these principles are partly the result of historic statutes and declarations going back to Magna Carta in 1215 and including the Petition of Right (1628), the Bill of Rights (1689), the Habeas Corpus Act (1679), the Act of Settlement (1701), and the various franchise statutes, which do not differ from other statutes in form but only in their constitutional importance. But the principles are also the outcome of the cumulative development of *common law,* the law resulting from judicial interpretations of the behavior of persons and the working of institutions, and of those rules and practices known as *conventions* or *customs* which enable the system to operate more effectively. In addition, political nature imitates art for certain celebrated books, such as Walter Bagehot's *The English Constitution,* A.V. Dicey's *Introduction to the Study of the Law of the Constitution* and Erskine May's *Parliamentary Practice,* are regarded as so authoritative that their analyses of constitutional correctness become commonly accepted as valid and thus influence future behavior. As a young man Prince Charles, heir to the British throne, read Bagehot in order to understand how a constitutional monarch is expected to behave.

In countries with a written constitution, legislation or action regarded as contrary to that document can often be declared unconstitutional by a high court or some other formal body. In Britain unconstitutional action would be that which does not adhere to the principles of agreed working of the system. Generally agreement is easy to reach, but legitimate differences of opinion may arise about the constitutionality of particular actions such as the limitation of debate in the legislature by the government.

The Reasons for Written Constitutions

There are five major reasons for the existence of written constitutions:

1. They are the sign of successful internal revolution against the former rulers as in the Soviet Union; or revolt against external rulers as in the United States.

2. They signify the existence of a regime after the downfall of the previous regime in war or internal collapse. Examples are France of the Third and Fourth Republics or postwar Italy and Germany.

3. They illustrate concessions made by ruling groups to rising groups in the community, as in France in 1814 or in postwar Morocco, where democratic institutions were established while the authority of the monarchy was reinforced.

4. They mark the creation of a new regime formed by a union of hitherto separate units, as in federal or confederate regimes.

5. They are the sign of independence granted by a former colonial power or military victor as in the British Commonwealth countries whose constitutions are formally statutes of the British Parliament. In this case there may remain some ambiguity about the complete independence of the new regime. In both South Africa and Ghana particular methods of procedure laid down in the constitution represented a limitation on the power of the regimes when they wished to introduce changes by methods not allowed in the original constitution. Both countries claimed that the granting of independence made them sovereign states and gave them the power to alter their own constitutions in the way they thought most desirable. The High Court in South Africa for a time delayed the amendment of the "entrenched clauses" of the constitution by a simple majority of the legislature rather than by the two-thirds majority legally needed. In Ghana the legislature in 1958 passed a statute allowing constitutional amendments to be made by simple majority rather than by the two-thirds of the total assembly required by the 1957 constitution.

The constitution of Canada, in effect the British North America Act of 1867, also leaves Canada's independent status somewhat ambiguous. For some time it could be amended only by the British Parliament. In 1949 Canada was ceded the power of amending its own constitution, except those sections affecting the authority of the central and provincial governments, the use of French and English languages, and educational rights, which are still technically reserved for amendment by Britain. Some Canadians are now proposing a new constitution that would put all power of amendment in Canada's hands.

Sometimes constitutions are devised by existing rulers to give legality to their actions. Normally they are drafted by a regular parliament or by a constituent assembly chosen especially for that purpose but which may also turn itself into a legislature, as in India and Pakistan. They may also be drafted by a selected group—university professors in Turkey or civil servants in France in 1958—and then submitted to the people for approval. It is rare for the electorate to reject the proposed document, as did the French in 1946, and almost equally rare for the electorate to accept it by as small a proportion of the vote, as in France later in the same year, when only 36 percent voted for the constitution.

Difficulties arise when constitutions do not come into existence in approved legal fashion but as a result of unilateral or illegal action. In the American colonies and in many other cases military success endowed the new constitution and the regime with a halo of legitimacy.

> Treason doth never prosper; what's the reason?
> For if it prosper, none dare call it treason.
>
> *John Harrington*

But in a similar situation the Rhodesian constitution, introduced in 1965 by the government after a unilateral declaration of independence from Great Britain, was declared illegal by the Rhodesian High Court, though the court also held in apparent self-contradiction that the government of the country must be recognized as the de facto administration.

Constitutional Restrictions

Regimes have imposed constitutional restrictions on themselves either at their own behest or through outside pressure.

Sometimes a constitution may restrict the powers of its own system. A number of countries have provided for international authorities to exercise some national functions. Denmark in 1953 and Norway in 1962 amended their constitutions to allow the delegation of expressly defined national authority to supranational organizations.

Restrictions placed in a constitution also resulted from the Allied occupation of Austria and Japan after World War II. In Austria the Allies agreed to independence only after Austria declared its neutrality and agreed to incorporate this declaration in its constitution. Moreover the neutrality was reinforced in the State Treaty, signed with the four former occupying powers, which forbids actions leading to unity with Germany. The Japanese constitution, largely through the influence of General MacArthur, contains the provision in Article 9 that "the Japanese people forever renounce war as a sovereign right of the nation and the threat or use of force as a means of settling international disputes"; and also as a result of American influence, that constitution is essentially democratic in nature.

Fundamental Law

A constitution is not just the formal embodiment of the sovereignty of a community, the symbol of unity, and the focal point of loyalty. It is also the reflection of the basic consensus underlying the regime or of the basic beliefs held by the politically significant groups. Constitutions are therefore considered to be the expression of fundamental law, or the "superior paramount law" in Chief Justice John Marshall's phrase, that controls all statutes and political action.[4]

In the eighteenth century Edward Halifax wrote that a true fundamental, if undermined, will bring down the whole house. But it is not always apparent what is to be considered fundamental in political, economic, or ethical matters, especially on subjects such as property and personal relations. The argument of Sir Edward Coke that the English common law will control acts of Parliament and sometimes judge them to be utterly void[5] has often been quoted. From his view has been drawn the conclusion that the common law was fundamental, and that statutes were affirmations of the common law. Yet Coke himself was inconsistent on whether the royal prerogative was subject to common law. His argument was never a valid analysis of English constitutional practice, for it was largely the force of Parliament, rather than common law, that allowed the "undisputed powers of the King" that James I spoke of to be disputed and controlled. Nevertheless, the fundamental nature of a constitution, at least nominally, is recognized whether it rests on common law or on those principles of reason and justice and rules of civilized relationships that underlie all law.

The superior status of the constitution is illustrated not simply by the emotional regard felt for it or the empirical belief in its practical utility, but also by the normal difficulty in amending it. James Bryce argued that a major distinguishing characteristic of constitutions was between those that were flexible—capable of being amended by the same procedure and rules as was needed to amend ordinary legislation—and those that were rigid—needing a different, and logically more difficult, method of change.[6] Very few regimes come in the first group, and constitutional amendment is consequently considerably more rare than amendment of ordinary legislation.

Constitutions are amended in a number of ways or combination of ways: by the legislature, by the electorate, or by a special convention. Where the legislature is used, a qualified or absolute majority is normally needed. This is true in West Germany or in the U.S.S.R., where a two-thirds majority of both chambers is required. Sometimes, as in Norway and Sweden, the dissolution of the legislature and the holding of an election based on the issue is also required. Amendments may be submitted to the people by mandatory requirement as in Eire, Australia, or Switzerland, or under certain conditions. In France an amendment goes to the electorate if it has not been passed by a three-fifths majority in joint session of the assemblies. In Italy it is submitted if it does not receive a two-thirds majority of each house at the second legislative reading. Amendment procedure in federal systems normally requires an electoral majority in both the whole country and in a majority of the regions that make up the country. This is true in Australia, the United States, and Switzerland. Federal regimes also usually include a provision that no state be deprived of its territory or its relative representation without its own consent. A number of regimes, recalling political experience during World War II, also forbid constitutional amendment while the territory of the country is under foreign control.

Constitutions and Governmental Functions

Constitutions provide the method for allocating functions and determining the organization of political institutions, and also the method for imposing restraints on those exercising power.

The existence and exercise of governmental powers has been analyzed in a variety of ways. Some writers, following the analysis of F. J. Goodnow and Woodrow Wilson, have suggested that there are only two essential functions, policy making and administration.[7] Others have argued that there are three essential activities of government: determination, execution, and supervision of the policy adopted or of the decisions reached. Harold Lasswell proposed seven categories through which the decision-making process could be analyzed: (1) intelligence, (2) recommendation, (3) prescription, (4) invocation, (5) application, (6) appraisal, and (7) termination of policy.[8] Theoreticians of the structural functional school or of systems analysis provide an even more elaborate analysis. Gabriel Almond and G. B. Powell speak of three categories of functions of the political system: (1) capabilities, (2) conversion, and (3) system-maintenance and adaptation functions that allow the system to change. These functions are then classified still further. The classification of conversion functions that lead to policy making includes the articulation of interests, the aggregation of those interests, rule making, the application of rules, adjudication, and collection of information. The capability functions that will determine the limits within which action can occur include the extraction of human and material resources, regulation, distribution, symbolic, and responsive functions. But intractable political behavior rarely allows itself to be fitted into rigid categories of this kind.[9]

The method used most frequently in dealing with developed, ordered societies, and still the most useful because it is both universally understood and free from occult jargon, is to see politics as concerned with three essential functions: (1) the *legislative function*, involving deliberation on public affairs and the enactment of general rules or norms of conduct; (2) the *executive function*, involving the application of general rules to specific cases; and (3) the *judicial function*, dealing with the resolution of disputes between individuals or between individuals and government bodies. But these functions are not invariably performed by any one given institution.

Constitutions elaborate the way in which functions are to be exercised and the institutions that are legally responsible for that exercise. (These functions and institutions are compared in Chapters 8–10.) But the framers of constitutions, worried that the wielders of power may become corrupt or tyrannical, have generally also sought to establish methods through which power could be controlled. This control has been attempted in varying ways: by a mixed state, by checks and balances, by a division of power normally through a federal system, and by a separation of powers.

The basic idea of a *mixed state* is that all political elements in a system share legislative power and each is given a particular function, as in ancient Rome where Imperium, Senate, and popular assemblies shared in the legislative process. For James Harrington in the seventeenth century the need for restraint indicated the desirability of a balance between the various social orders in which the Senate proposed the laws, the people consented to them, and the magistracy executed them. In addition to the joint legislative power possessed by the king, House of Lords, and House of Commons, each element was also assigned particular functions such as foreign relations, the power of adjudication, and the right to propose taxes.

Systems possessing governmental *checks and balances* seek to prevent concentration of power or undue influence of any one element or institution by devices like impeachment, judicial review, executive power of pardon, sharing of budgetary responsibilities, or participation by the legislature in certain aspects of foreign policy such as declaration of war.

Because both the division of power in federations and the separation of powers are such important constitutional controls, we will look at each of these in detail next.

Division of Power: Federal Systems

Since the United States Constitution created a federal system that has been widely imitated, a useful division can be drawn between this kind of system and a *unitary state*. The latter is one in which the central set of political institutions exercises legitimate authority, as in England or France. Local authorities obtain their powers from the central authority which can amend those powers if it desires.

A *federal system* is one in which the functions of government are shared between a central authority and regional authorities, both sets being autonomous in certain areas and deriving their respective powers from the constitution or interpretations of it, not from each other. A federal system stands somewhere between a unitary regime and a *confederation*, in which the power of the individual units is safeguarded to a greater degree. Though there are differing degrees of central power in federal systems, as there are differing degrees of decentralization in unitary states, they are all marked by this coordinate sharing of power and of decision making between the central and regional authorities. Certain limits are thus imposed on the power of each set of institutions. Federalism is a more complex system than a unitary regime, usually more difficult to operate and more fragile.

In older countries, such as the United States, Canada, and Switzerland, federalism was created to preserve strong existing diversities while maintaining sufficient unity to insure that limits were put on the power of the center; sometimes, as William Riker has suggested in *Federalism: Origin, Operation, Significance*, it has been a result of a political bargain between those wishing to extend the area of territorial control and those prepared to surrender part of their independence. Similarly, in newer nations like India and Nigeria the device of federalism has been used to hold together societies in which tribalism is strong and divisive, and nationalist sentiment and allegiance is weak; but the results have rarely been happy.

In federal systems the crucial characteristic is the relationship between the central and regional governments and the relative powers exercised by both. The allocation of powers varies from the simple distribution in the United States constitution to the highly detailed allocation in the Indian constitution. In all cases the function of foreign affairs and defense belong to the central authority although sometimes a regional government may concern itself with these subjects, as when West Bengal, a province of India, directly negotiated with the World Bank to obtain a large loan, or when Quebec in 1967 established its own foreign ministry.

An interesting variant of this type of allocation of functions is the West German system where Länder, or regional units, existed before the central institutions were created in 1949. Each of the 10 Länder has its own legislative and executive. The Länder now provide the 41 representatives who, together with 4 from West Berlin, comprise the membership of the Bundesrat, the second chamber in West Germany. Most legislative functions are given to the federal institutions, and most administrative functions are exercised by the Länder, which are limited in the areas in which they can legislate. The federal government can implement most of its rules and laws only with the cooperation of the Lander. Some central ministries are little more than planning and policy-making bodies with the actual administrative functions being performed by the Länder.

In federal regimes the territorial integrity of the units, as well as their functions, is normally safeguarded since the central authority cannot form new states or alter the boundaries of any state without the consent of the state involved. Occasionally, however, a system may allow the central authority to annul the rights of a state in an emergency situation, as India did when the Communist party controlled the province of Kerala.

Similarly, secession of a unit without the consent of the central authority is technically difficult and likely to lead to political chaos and the destruction of the regime. In the United States the problem was solved by war. In Canada and Australia threats to secede by Quebec and western Australia have remained bargaining weapons. In Nigeria differences between its four regions resulted in the downfall of the regime, and civil war. Paradoxically it is the federal regime of the Soviet Union, the regime least likely to allow political independence of its constituent parts, that allows legal secession of a unit.

The major difficulties in federal regimes are uncertainty about final power—the concept of sovereignty is ambiguous in them—and possible inequities in the way units are treated. The central government can never be sure that its power will prevail: in the United States the South did not automatically carry out desegregation laws; in India the southern provinces have resisted the imposition of the Hindi language; in Canada the provincial legislatures have tended to provide the major opposition to the will of the federal government.

The larger states in federal regimes always claim to be treated unfairly. Political concessions will often be made to smaller states, such as equality in an upper legislative chamber, membership in executive bodies, or disproportionately larger representation in the legislature. In Australia the two largest states, New South Wales and Victoria, complain that they receive considerably less in services than the amount collected from their residents in the annual distribution of tax revenue. In Yugoslavia the developed republics such as Croatia and Slovenia complain that they help subsidize the development of more backward areas such as Montenegro and Macedonia.

Federalism has been subjected to many criticisms. Many since Harold Laski have argued that it is obsolescent,[10] that it is essentially negative in its effect and is not suitable for positive action, that it cannot act rapidly, that it is too reliant on compromises, that it is financially expensive due to duplication of work and waste of time in compromises and negotiation, that it is difficult to determine responsibility of the different units, and that conflicts of loyalties may confuse individual rights and obligations. Certainly it is true that federal regimes logically limit the power of the center, but it is not therefore necessarily true that the states will be greater protectors of individual interests than the central government. The states may be as subject to political pressure as the center, and may resist reform desirable for the welfare of the whole, as in eighteenth- and nineteenth century Spain, where the central government was often the source of administrative, educational, and religious reforms while municipal and regional independence became a cloak for reactionary interests. Also, the existence of a number of nondemocratic federal systems suggests that federalism does not inevitably safeguard political liberty or provide for an opposition to be expressed through the units.

In all countries the power of central authorities has been increasing.

In federal regimes the center now is often able to make the states follow policies it desires and has power to act in areas such as labor, education, crime, taxation, health, housing, and recreation, where the individual units may not possess sufficient resources to take appropriate action. The central government may establish direct relations with local authorities, thus bypassing the states, and in some matters may deal directly with the public. But sometimes it allows other bodies to act, as in Australia where the Commonwealth Conciliation and Arbitration Commission deals with wages and the Tariff Board with tariffs. Federalism depends on cooperation among the different units, at both the executive and legislative levels.

Canada with its policy of "cooperative federalism" and the United States with its ideal of "creative federalism" are both seeking to create conditions in which the provinces will have greater flexibility and local governments will play larger roles within a framework established by the center. But the complexity remains enormous in a system like the American, which comprises a federal government with hundreds of agencies, 50 state governments, 80,000 local administrations, and 24,000 school boards, all involved in applying 170 federal aid programs financed from over 400 appropriations.

Though the distinction between federal and unitary systems is still a useful one, modern trends in the amount and nature of power exercised have blurred the distinction. While the central institutions in federal regimes have grown stronger, there have been attempts at greater decentralization in unitary states; Britain, France, and Italy have all experimented with regional bodies or groupings. Britain has responded to the recent enthusiasm for Scottish and Welsh nationalism by making proposals for the devolution of power that might lead to the disintegration of the United Kingdom.

As a model, federalism remains analytically useful, but in practice its operation may not be too distinct from unitary regimes.

Separation of Powers

The most celebrated method of political control is by the *separation of powers*, originated in the seventeenth and eighteenth centuries, in part to prevent absolute monarchs from ignoring the needs of important parts of the nation. This involves the establishment of three separate departments or institutions, a legislature, an executive branch of government, and a judiciary, each of which is almost exclusively respon sible for the exercise of one of the three functions of government, and has little to do with the other two functions. Separation of function is reinforced by separation of personnel, which is created by forbidding any person to be a member of more than one institution.

The model exemplifying the concept of the separation of powers is the American constitution, which incorporates all three features of the theory: tripartite division of governmental functions, the creation of three institutions corresponding to those functions, and the separation of personnel. The 1790 French constitution, which prevented judges from interfering with the work of administrative bodies, also claimed to embody the principle.

The theory is based on the premise that law is general and universal in its application. The legislative power issues general rules that are applicable equally, impartially, and impersonally to all individuals and groups, the executive makes specific decisions and rules relating to individuals, while the judiciary applies the general rule. Because the legislative power was assumed to be the supreme power and the executive had some share in this power, it was particularly important, especially to Montesquieu, that the judiciary be a separate, independent group and that people be tried in accordance with the settled rules and known procedures of the courts and not by reference to the legislative power.

This is the significance of the theory in Britain and France and those countries influenced by them such as the Commonwealth in the one case and Belgium, Italy, and Greece in the other. In Britain important features are the independence of the judiciary from the executive, the principle that everyone is subject to the law administered in the ordinary courts, and the assurance that public authorities act in accordance with law. Correct and known procedures of the courts, not legislative policy, determine the rights of accused persons.

But it is the absence, not the existence, of a separation of powers that is the crucial characteristic of Britain, for its parliamentary cabinet system is based on the fact that members of the government, with rare exceptions, are invariably chosen from among the membership of Parliament. The government, by its control over a strong and disciplined party in the Parliament and by its control over the procedure, timetable, and activity of the House of Commons, is able to control the legislature. This concentration of power has allowed the exercise of strong government. But that exercise has not become tyrannical nor has it been abused, largely because of the spirit of constitutionalism or adherence to the political norms of tolerance and moderation that pervade the system.

The French Declaration of the Rights of Man in 1789 held that a country does not have a constitution if it has not applied the principle of the separation of powers. But in France this has largely meant a separation of judicial and administrative functions, and an emphasis on a code of administrative law and a set of tribunals including the *Conseil d'État* that can determine the legal validity of executive action and behavior by officials and hear appeals against an executive department. The power of the French executive to make rules through decrees and ordinances is a continual denial of any rigid separation of the legislative and executive functions.

The classic case for the separation of powers in *Federalist Paper 47* argues that the preservation of liberty requires that the three branches of government — the legislature, executive, and judiciary — should be separate and distinct. John Locke had pointed out the danger that, whereas the legislature need not always be in session since its work was not continuous, the executive power was always needed and present and therefore members of the executive might exempt themselves from obedience to the laws.[11] The premise of the *Federalist* is that any person possessing power may be tempted to abuse it unless controlled, and that power can be checked only by power. The separation of powers attempts to create a balance among the competing units.

Yet a separation of powers need not lead to a weak executive or a stalemated governmental system. This is demonstrated by the prominent role of the American president in the political system in recent years. The role of the president in the conduct of foreign affairs and control over the decisions to enter into and end war, the activist nature of Democratic presidents in economic and social matters since the 1930s, and the growth of the presidential staff have led to his prominence. At its worst, under Richard Nixon, executive authority was abused by unusual secrecy and by illegal behavior such as wiretapping, burglary, and income tax harassment of opponents. Power was concentrated in the White House, in which the president and his staff were virtually isolated, with the result that Congress was often ignored and the cabinet relegated to minor significance. Since the resignation of Nixon in 1974 for fear of impeachment, Congress has reacted against the possibility of such presidential dominance and tried to reassert itself in policy making and to gain a position of at least equality in political decision making. To this end Congress in 1974 established budget committees with power to present a systematic congressional budget. It imposed controls on executive seizure of appropriated funds and, through the War Powers Act, limited presidential foreign policy-making powers. The increasing use of the *legislative veto* allows the Congress to pass a statute with certain provisions that can become effective only after further legislative approval.

Useful as the theory of separation of powers may be in limiting tendencies to excessive power, there is no political system in which the three governmental institutions are so completely separate that one does not exercise some of the other's powers. The medieval British Parliament was almost as much a court as a legislative body, though the legislative and adjudicatory functions could not easily be distinguished. In both Spain and France the judicial institutions exercised some political functions until the sixteenth century and later. The French Parlements obstructed the executive not so much to defend liberty as to preserve their own privileges.

In all modern systems, institutions exercise overlapping functions of some kind or provision is made for some degree of cooperation between the different organs and branches to perform the work of government. The executive officials as well as the legislature, together with informal organizations and nongovernmental personnel, may participate in the process of deliberating about and formulating legislation. Many rules and regulations, decree laws, and emergency powers are framed and put into effect by the executive and administrative agencies. Nomination and approval of appointments or the ratification of treaties may be shared by legislature and executive. The judiciary may exercise some executive functions, such as control over licensing, may be capable of enjoining illegal actions by the executive or declaring legislation unconstitutional, or be used for special nonjudicial missions. Judicial or quasi-judicial functions may be exercised by administrative tribunals, ministerial departments, or legislative committees.

Though other factors may be equally or more significant in the maintenance of a free society—the mores that foster free speech, press, or religion and the existence of a multiplicity of groups and associations—the value of a separation of power by dispersing functions among different political institutions is that it attempts to provide a limit to political power and a brake on action by constitutional devices. Power must be limited if liberty is to exist, for unchecked power is as dangerous as the unity of temporal and spiritual powers: the prophet armed has been equally harmful in Stalinist Russia as in medieval Islam. But the concept of separation of powers has been impossible to realize in any complete way. Moreover, an undue insistence on the concept may be harmful in creating friction in the government, dividing responsibility so that it becomes difficult to assess, and producing political stalemate or a lack of a cohesive policy. The hope of those who framed constitutions in the eighteenth and nineteenth centuries that they could establish equilibrium among the different branches of government has proved to be unduly optimistic. A world in which war, economic crises, physical disasters, and famines are common is one that needs power to be used as well as controlled and one that must view constitutions as documents providing for the exercise of power as well as acting as a restraint on power.

This need is clearly shown by certain characteristics of postwar constitutions. They are invariably based on political equality and universal suffrage. They provide for advisory bodies or chambers for economic affairs and planning. They all provide for the constitutional exercise of emergency powers in time of crisis. But above all they try to strengthen the executive power and keep it stable by reducing the opportunities for the assembly to defeat the government, as in Germany where the chancellor can be forced to resign only by "a positive vote of no confidence." This means that a new chancellor must be elected by a majority of the Parliament on the same vote that defeats the incumbent. In a number of regimes, motions of censure or of no confidence in the government have been made more difficult since they may need a minimum number of signatures of deputies to be introduced, a period of delay between their initiation and any consequent debate on them, and a special majority to be passed.

In most modern constitutions, such as those of Germany, Italy, India, and Japan, the effective power of the head of state has been reduced so that he or she has largely become a ceremonial figure. The real political leader is the head of the government whom the head of state may have the power to choose.

The need for exercise of stronger power is also shown by the reduced role given to parliaments and especially the weakening of second chambers, even where greater autonomy has been desired by regions or territorial areas in the larger whole. Moreover, although a number of modern constitutions have tried to create federal regimes or regional institutions to take account of and make concessions to racial, national, or tribal diversities, they have rarely been successful. Most, like those in Nigeria, the West Indies, Malaysia, Rhodesia,

Nyasaland, Tanganyika, Uganda, Kenya, and Brazil, have failed, while others, like those in Germany, Italy, and India, are not really meaningful from the federal or regional point of view.

Limits on Power

Constitutions provide limits on the exercise of power for a number of reasons: to impose restraints on rulers, to protect individuals, groups, and minorities, to safeguard human rights, and to preserve the regime. The *Federalist Papers* stated clearly that constitutions need to provide checks on the ambitions of the powerful and the passions of the populace, and that the exercise of authority had to be kept within the bounds of God and the law.[12]

All systems, including dictatorial regimes such as Ghana under Kwane Nkrumah or the Soviet Union under Joseph Stalin, purport to protect individual rights. Constitutions formerly concerned themselves with civil or political rights; in the twentieth century they have also included economic and social rights, dealing with land, labor, employment, education, religious freedom, and new protections such as control of noise. Yet regimes have often not implemented the rights inherent in their constitutions or, like the former Nigerian constitution, have stated that many rights were subject to limitations that were reasonably justifiable in a democratic society. In heterogeneous or divided societies minority rights or privileges may be protected, as are minority lands in Malaya, minority languages in India, a minority educational system in Canada; in some countries minorities are allotted a number of government positions.

Since the first requirement of a regime is that it remain in existence, constitutions may attempt to preserve the system. The West German constitution forbids extremist parties and undemocratic attacks on the regime; the Italian constitution forbids the Fascist party. The French and Italian systems forbid the changing of the republican form of government. In 26 countries Communist parties have been outlawed, but this has not always been done by the constitution itself.

Conventions and Rules of the Game

The real constitution of a state, said Jean Jacques Rousseau, "is not graven on tablets of marble or brass, but on the hearts of the citizens."[13] Consequently a people may be kept "in the ways in which it was meant to go" by morality, custom, and public opinion.

Important though a constitution is in providing a basic political foundation for a regime, even more significant may be the spirit in which it functions and the rules of the political game that influence its operation. No political system can work without accepted rules of the game—customs, or conventions that are not legal agreements but understood ways of political behavior that amplify the legal provisions. They are the necessary flesh added to the bare skeleton of the constitution, enabling orderly government to exist, creating harmony among the political institutions and parties, permitting institutions to function more efficiently, often obtaining political responsiveness to electoral feeling and recognition of the underlying power of the electorate, and safeguarding minority rights.

Conventions, thus, are always concerned with the real substance of power rather than its shadow, with the "efficient" elements of a system rather than the "dignified" that may be of little real significance. Conventions insure, for example, that the British monarch appoints as the prime minister the leader of the party controlling a majority in the House of Commons rather than his or her own personal choice, that the electoral college in the United States elects the person who has already been implicitly chosen by the people, that the president of Germany will act essentially as a ceremonial figure, that the rights of the opposition will be respected in democratic countries, that all six states in Australia will be represented in the cabinet, that several of the fourteen major religious groups in Lebanon will be represented in the government, that the Sinhala and Tamil languages will both be used in Ceylonese politics, that all Canadian cabinets will contain both English and French-speaking members, and that a Swiss government will always contain members from the two largest cantons, Zurich and Berne, and will never have more than five of its seven members from German-speaking cantons. Even in the Soviet Union, conventions seem to exist as in some of the Supreme Soviets of the individual republics where the elected body shows consistent arithmetical relations among its different elements, men and women, party and nonparty members, natives and immigrants.

These conventions and rules of the game are acceptable because they reduce the possiblities of friction and enable the system to operate. If they are broken, no illegality will have been committed and no legal punishment ensue, but the result may be political chaos or difficulties.

In fact, the rules of the game may be adhered to more than are the constitutional requirements with which they may be in conflict. In the French Fourth Republic the delegation of legislative functions was forbidden, but it nevertheless became a necessary part of the political system. The provisions in the United States constitution for periodical reapportionment have remained largely inoperative. President Sukarno violated the Indonesian constitution by appointing members of Parliament and by making laws in the form of decrees instead of submitting them to the legislature for approval.

The Judicial Function

Constitutions are part of the primary rules that guide political action and behavior. But in every community there must be some method of deciding what exactly is to be considered a primary rule, how it is to be interpreted, and whether it has been contravened. The application of rules always needs interpretation, and this is the core of the judicial function in politics.

The *judicial function* is the determination of the meaning of laws and rules, the imposition of penalties for violating those rules, the deciding on the relative rights and obligations of individuals and the community, the determination of the area of freedom to be allowed persons within the political system, and the arbitration of disputes between individuals and officials.

This function can be performed by a single individual, a tribal leader, a religious dignitary, or a king, or it can be done in the king's name. It may be performed by a political body such as the Athenian Areopagus, the Roman Senatus or the British House of Lords, which is still the highest legal body in Britain though its judicial function is exercised by a special group of nine law lords. But justice is normally dispensed by judges, individually or collectively, in regular courts of law organized hierarchically and acting on the basis of procedure, known prescribed rules, impartiality, and fairness. However, in nondemocratic countries the judicial function may be exercised by executive officials. Special courts of public order may be established, as in Francisco Franco's Spain, to try political cases, or the military may be responsible for deciding the complicity of those accused of terrorist acts.

A crucial characteristic of all free societies is an independent judiciary, autonomous and subject only to the law. Some regimes, such as the Italian and the West German, protect this independence in their constitutions; others do it by statutes like the British Act of Settlement of 1701, which provides that judges cannot be removed during good behavior and thus ends the fear of dismissal at will. Impeachment processes by which delinquent judges can be ousted exist in most regimes.

Hopefully, impartiality and incorruptibility are also characteristics of the judicial process. As early as the twelfth century Henry II of England established a system of impartial justice for all, with writs and a jury system that was used to accuse criminals and settle property disputes. Judicial impartiality implies not only the impartiality of judges, but also the existence of elaborate procedural safeguards to insure a fair trial. Underlying the operation of the law in all its aspects are the principles of "due process of law" or "natural justice."

Selection of Judges

Judges are selected in a variety of ways, though in almost all systems they come from the upper strata of society.

In prerevolutionary France judicial offices were bought, sold, and inherited by the wealthy. This practice did not inevitably lead to abuse since individuals as gifted as Michel de Montaigne and the Baron de Montesquieu became judges. Legal purchase of judicial offices is rare today, but rumor has it that some municipal judgeships in the United States are available for contributions to party funds.

Some judges are elected by the people, as in a number of states in the United States, some cantons in Switzerland, and in some instances in the lower courts of France. Candidates are usually sponsored by a political party, but many are unopposed or receive endorsement by bar associations.

Appointments by the executive is the procedure for obtaining judgeships in the higher courts of the United States, Britain, a number of Commonwealth countries, and some Latin American countries. Judges chosen in this way, though they may have been members of a political party, will rarely have been partisan figures who receive judgeships as a political reward. In Britain and countries that imitate that country, judges are chosen from distinguished members of the bar, as distinct from Continental European countries where the judge is a public servant and the bench constitutes a career of its own to which individuals are appointed by competitive examination.

In a number of systems judges are selected by parliament. In Switzerland the Federal Tribunal is chosen for a six-year term by the two chambers in joint session, though the incumbents are usually reelected if they so desire. By convention the choice of judges will include individuals from all major parties, religions, and languages.

In West Germany the Federal Constitutional Court is chosen by the two chambers, half by the Bundestag and half by the Bundesrat, although judges in the lower courts are appointed by the minister of justice and a committee of the legislature. In the Soviet Union, too, judges of the senior courts are chosen by the parliament and are subject to recall by it. In other regimes, such as the American, the legislative approval of the nominations of the executive is required.

There are a variety of other procedures, some of which are illustrated in France, Italy, and Israel. In the French Fifth Republic judges are appointed by the High Council of the Judiciary, composed of the president of the republic, the minister of justice, and nine others appointed by the president. In Italy the Constitutional Court is chosen for a twelve-year term partly by judges named by the magistracy of the three highest courts, partly by the two-house legislature, and partly by the president. In Israel judges are chosen by the president on the advice of a committee of nine from a list of candidates proposed by the minister of justice, the president of the Supreme Court, or three members of the advisory committee.

Law and Judging

Both the concept of "law" and the nature of judicial activity are subject to controversy. *Law* has been viewed as a body of binding obligations, as the commands of the sovereign power, as a set of rules that define correct behavior or uphold the moral fabric of society, or as prophecies of what the courts will in fact do.

Acute differences exist on the relation between law and morality and on whether the law should punish immorality as such. One school, following John Stuart Mill, argues that there is an area of morality with which the law cannot interfere if no harm is done to others. Its opponents argue it is the task of law to suppress immorality because there is a shared morality that must be preserved and enforced if society is to survive.[14]

Judges do not enact laws; they interpret statutory provisions and regulations when deciding on individual cases. But there is no agreement on the method by which they reach decisions. The *slot machine theory* is that judges, who are conceived to be subject to legal rules, precedents, and principles, apply these precedents to the particular case in automatic fashion, as if they were part of what Oliver Wendell Holmes called "The brooding omnipresence in the sky." The *legal rationalist view* states that law is the method through which the will of the people can be made known, and judges are those experts exercising judicial power who logically deduce decisions that are in accord with the public interest. Law fulfills social ends, and because these are in continual flux, judges must continually examine ways in which to adapt law to meet those ends. A related view is that judges make choices among alternative public policies, deciding on the basis of a balance of different interests or on what they conceive to be the welfare of society or according to the principles of natural law. Underlying their activity may be some fundamental concept, such as a moral or religious view, regard for the rights of property, or belief in the desirability of free speech.

To the *orthodox view*, which emphasizes the significance of legal rules and precedents in its explanation of the judicial process, is opposed the *realist view*, which regards them as rationalizations for the judges who really decide on the basis of their personal disposition, social background, personality, philosophy of life, intuition, and hunches. It is true that the judge is rarely able to decide on purely personal lines, for, as Karl Llewellyn has argued, "the common law is a high wall surrounding the judge".[15] But the realist point of view emphasizes the importance of nonlegal factors in the decision of cases and makes apparent the unpredictability of judicial activity. The judge, as Walter Murphy has suggested, may weigh a large number of variables other than the law itself, such as the prestige and professional reputation of the court, the condition of public opinion, and the attitudes of politicians and interest groups toward the case in question.[16]

Control Over Power

The judiciary was once regarded as an organ subordinate to the executive and the legislature, and the king was seen as the source of justice. In most systems the independence of the judiciary is now established and an indispensable judicial function is to insure that wielders of power are kept within the bounds of their authority. Recourse to a form of judicial review or reference to higher moral laws may allow the courts to review the constitutionality of legislation or to decide jurisdictional conflicts among other power holders.

Equally, the judiciary attempts to prevent the abuse of power by the executive or the use of power for an improper purpose. The judiciary insures that executive and administrative actions are correct in form, limited to their proper jurisdiction, and that power will be exercised in a fair and equitable manner, whether the case involves dismissal from office, cancellation of a license, demolition of buildings, or appropriation of land. In Britain the judiciary declares if an action is ultra vires. The 1947 Crown Proceedings Act allows the Crown itself to be sued for actions performed by officials. In France the *Conseil d'État* is empowered to check administrative actions that are improper or that have abused discretionary powers or injured individuals. Similarly in the United States the judiciary, especially since the 1946 Administrative Procedures Act, has power to review the behavior of executive agencies.

In *Federalist Paper 48* James Madison argued that all power is of an encroaching nature. To limit the possibility of excessive power, a high court in some systems is given the power of *judicial review,* by which it is able to decide the meaning or intention of the constitution or declare whether statutes and acts are in accord with that constitution. To allow the legislature to interpret the constitution would be, as Chief Justice Marshall argued, to permit a legislative intrusion into a judicial monopoly. Asserted by Marshall in *Marbury* v. *Madison* (1803), judicial review implies that the United States Supreme Court is the final authority on the meaning of the Constitution and is the chief guardian of it. It means the right to declare actions of other branches and agencies in the federal government and official actions in state governments unconstitutional. Since 1789 over 100 federal laws and some 800 state laws have been declared unconstitutional. American-style judicial review has been imitated in a number of other countries, including Australia, Canada, and Japan. The courts, by their interpretation of the constitution, statutes, and actions, have permitted the system to develop to meet changing needs. They have allowed the executive to exercise necessary and sufficient power to insure internal and external stability and security, have tried to balance the powers and relations among the organs of government or among the different governments in a federal system, and have clarified the rights of individuals and groups. They have changed race relations, altered political districts, and laid down principles on personal and social matters such as abortion and capital punishment.

Sometimes, as in Ireland, West Germany, or Pakistan, the power of judicial review is explicitly given to a superior court. This is not the case in the American system, which, as discussed above, acquired the power through judicial interpretation of the constitution. It is noticeable that a number of European regimes, affected by the prewar experience of dictatorial and totalitarian regimes, created some stronger form of judicial control in their new constitutions. West Germany or Italy is able to assess constitutionality of federal and regional legislation, as well as decide conflicts between the center and the regions, arbitrate among the different organs of government, try impeachments against officials, and declare that the existence of certain organizations, such as extremist political parties, is contrary to the political system and is destructive of individual rights. Even in the French system, which, strictly speaking, does not implement the idea of judicial review, the judiciary has considerable discretion in interpreting abstract concepts such as "order," "good morals," or "security of the state" when applying the law in particular cases. In its interpretation the *Conseil d'État* acts on the fundamental premise that the public interest is superior to private interests.

Limits of Judicial Activity

In some political matters the judiciary is unable or unwilling to act. Courts may be excluded from jurisdiction in certain subjects, as in Switzerland where federal laws cannot be challenged in the courts, or in France where *actes de gouvernement* remain outside the province of the courts.

But judges themselves do not always willingly enter the arena of political controversy, or "the political thicket" in Felix Frankfurter's phrase.[17] They may become embroiled in controversy, as in the United States in 1936, or may find that their decisions cannot be enforced. In 1966 the Rhodesian High Court could argue in a cautious and ambiguous manner as the United States Supreme Court did in *Texas v. White* in 1869. In the latter case the court held that the Confederate Constitution had not been the lawful constitution of the country and that the Confederate government had not been the lawful government of Texas. Nevertheless it was obliged to acknowledge that the statutes passed and the administrative measures of that government had to be obeyed.

The judiciary has been the main instrument for making judicial decisions. Regimes have tried to preserve the autonomy and independence of judges by forbidding extraordinary tribunals, by preventing legislatures from making juridicial decisions through bills of attainder, by preventing the crown from dispensing justice unilaterally, and by not permitting parliamentary investigating committees to exceed their powers.

Judge-made law provides for flexibility as well as continuity, but it suffers from certain disadvantages. In some countries the excessive length of judicial proceedings and the steady increase in the backlog of cases have virtually produced, as in Italy, a paralysis of the judicial system: a lawsuit may take 12 years to get to court, and "justice delayed is justice denied." But also on certain subjects the judiciary is not in a satisfactory position to determine all the complex repercussions of a decision or action. Changing conditions may make laws obsolete and produce injury before the courts can act. On the Palais de Justice in Paris is the inscription: "Hora Fugit—Ius Stat" ("Time flies but justice remains"). Nor does judicial lawmaking allow for planned programs of change or for the establishment of political priorities.

The leaders of the French Revolution mistrusted judges for their conservative leanings, and consequently judges were forbidden to interfere in governmental and administrative functions. An administrative jurisdiction, independent of the ordinary judicial apparatus, was therefore created to judge disputes in which the administration was involved and to control the activities of the civil service.

The 1957 Committee on Administrative Tribunals and Inquiries in Britain (the Franks Committee) was dubious that it could draw a distinction between "judicial" and "administrative" law. For that body, the characteristics of openness, fairness, and impartiality should pervade all adjudication. The true question is whether the policy of the legislation is so settled that it can be embodied in a series of detailed regulations on which a tribunal could decide, or whether it remains flexible and so needs implementation by the civil service.

In recent years, with the vast increase in governmental functions and responsibilities, an increasingly familiar pattern in regimes has been that decisions, judgments, and uses of discretion are now made by administrative bodies composed of political ministers and civil servants. Dicey in his *Introduction to the Study of the Law of the Constitution* and writers supporting the position argue that administrative tribunals are denials of the principle of the common law and of the rule of law. But these tribunals, created for their flexibility, cheapness, informal and simple procedure, ability to act quickly, and possibility of using experts, are now an indispensable part of the governmental apparatus.

In France there is a clear division between the judicial courts that hear ordinary civil and criminal cases and administrative courts that are concerned with actions by officials in the performance of their state functions and that act according to a code of administrative law. In cases of doubt the *Tribunal des Conflits* decides which set of courts should adjudicate on a particular matter. A number of Continental European regimes also provide for a system of administrative courts through which the claims of citizens against public authorities can be heard. In the basically common law system of Britain, administrative tribunals have been developing their own case law and redressing grievances that result from the conduct of public authorities. Administrative tribunals may annul decisions, issue an order of mandamus requiring a person or agency to perform its duty, annul a general administrative act, or award damages against the administration. The proposal of the Franks Committee that a standing Council on Tribunals be established was accepted by the government, and since 1959 the council has published annual reports on the work of the administrative tribunals. But the small number of officials and the inadequate facilities of the council prevent it from exerting any strong control over the behavior of the tribunals.

Notes

[1] Lloyd Mechan, "Latin American Constitutions: Nominal and Real," *Journal of Politics* (1959), pp. 258–275.

[2] Plato, *Republic*, 544d.

[3] Walter Bagehot, *The English Constitution* (Ithaca, Cornell University Press, 1966), p. 61.

[4] In Marbury v. Madison (1 Cranch 137) 1803.

[5] In Dr. Bonham's Case, 8 Reports 118 (1610).

[6] James Bryce, "Flexible and Rigid Constitutions," in *Studies in History and Jurisprudence,* vol. 1 (New York: Oxford University Press/Clarendon Press, 1901), pp. 145–254.

[7] F. J. Goodnow, *Politics and Administration* (New York: Macmillan, 1900); and Woodrow Wilson, "The Study of Administration," *Political Science Quarterly* (June 1887), pp. 197–222.

[8] Harold Lasswell, *The Future of Political Science* (Englewood Cliffs, N.J.: Prentice-Hall, 1963), pp. 15–16.

[9] G. A. Almond and G. B. Powell, *Comparative Politics: a developmental approach (Boston: Little, Brown, 1966).*

[10] H. J. Laski, "The Obsolescence of Federalism," *The New Republic* (May 3, 1939), pp. 367–369.

[11] John Locke, *Second Treatise on Civil Government,* chap. 13.

[12] *Federalist Papers,* No. 51.
[13] Jean Jacques Rousseau, *The Social Contract,* Book 2, chap. 12.
[14] Patrick Devlin, *The Enforcement of Morals* (New York: Oxford University Press, 1965); and H. L. A. Hart, *Law, Liberty and Morality* (Stanford University Press, 1963).
[15] Karl Llewellyn, *The Bramble Bush* (New York: Columbia University Press, 1963).
[16] Walter Murphy, *Elements of Judicial Strategy* (University of Chicago Press, 1964).
[17] In Colegrove v. Green, 328 U.S. 549 (1946).

Chapter Five

Representation and Voting

All modern regimes claim to be to some degree the product of the will of the people or the implementation of that will. Since it is clearly impossible, in spite of the arguments of Aristotle and Rousseau to the contrary, for a people to meet and exercise the functions of government as a collective body in any contemporary system, this claim is implemented most easily by some form of representation through which persons or groups are given the right to act for others who are able to choose them.

The original main purpose of modern representative systems, as Karl Mannheim has argued, was to balance the power of the absolutist bureaucracy.[1] But representative government serves or may serve a number of other useful purposes. It helps integrate the social forces or groups of the community, allowing competitive ideas to exist, to be taken into account, and to form part of agreements reached. It insures both a change of political officials and a constructive use of opposition. It enables the rulers to be made accountable in a general way for their actions and makes them responsible to those who have chosen them. The electoral process enables the citizen body to choose individuals to formulate and execute rules, who can act for those represented, and who can be held accountable and made responsible for their actions.

Even nondemocratic countries hold elections. In the Soviet Union no real electoral choice exists because officially there are no antagonistic classes, though in other communist regimes, such as those of Poland and Yugoslavia, there are more candidates than legislative seats, even if all candidates come from a single party. In Hungary a voter may theoretically choose among the 349 single-member constituencies into which the country is divided, but in the 1967 election only in 9

111

constituencies was more than 1 candidate nominated. In the 1971 election, in which 98.7 percent of the electorate voted, there were alternative candidates in 48 constituencies. Elections thus supposedly demonstrate the solidarity of the people with existing political leadership and are intended to promote consensus. But to be meaningful an election must present voters with alternative candidates, parties, or issues from which to choose, and elections must be fairly and honestly organized. A system such as the Malayan, where nominations have been kept secret until the last moment, is hardly meaningful.

Meaningful representation is the reflection of a free society and exists only in the presence of certain conditions. Elections must be periodic, and they must offer a real, uncoerced choice to the voters who can give their general approval to an individual representative or to a government. Elections must allow for peaceful change of government, and electoral violence must be limited or nonexistent. There must be general agreement on governmental rules and expectation that the opposition will abide by them, while at the same time minorities should be permitted to oppose the policies approved by the majority. Free articulation is central to a true representative system. Optimistically, the electorate should be sufficiently politically educated to appreciate, if not enter into, the political dialogue. But balance is also essential, both in the compromise between majority and minority and between social groups.

The concepts of government based on the consent of the governed and the right of citizens to choose representatives fairly and openly are relatively new in history, though in politically developed countries these are now considered among the most significant human rights. Representation, "the vital invention of modern times" as Lord Acton called it, developed over a long period for a variety of reasons and under a diversity of influences.

Few today would accept the view that representation can be traced back to the ancient sacrifice of individuals in the belief that they represented the sins of the society, or to the Greek view of the representative sufferer in tragedy. Similar skepticism applies to the old view that representation came out of the Teutonic forests and the Germanic approval of the chief through the clashing of spears, or from the provincial assemblies of the Romans in Spain and Gaul, or from the love of freedom of the Anglo-Saxons.[2] Some historians stress the influence of the religious orders, especially of the Dominican friars who chose a representative to speak for them; elections, secret vote, and seniority system were used in the medieval period for ecclesiastical purposes. The principle of majority rule as binding all because the majority represents all slowly developed out of the behavior of corporate bodies.

Representative assemblies arose out of political convenience and bargaining. At first primarily useful for the monarch in an age when agriculture was significant, the representative principle became a mass weapon once literacy became common. The king as the representative of the whole nation, the man who could weld the warring factions together, the embodiment of Thomas Hobbes' "unity of the representer,"[3] was able to obtain advice and consultation and gain some knowledge of the beliefs of citizens through the early assemblies such as the Spanish Cortes composed of representatives of all social groups—ecclesiastical, military, and popular. The advice was not necessarily taken, but the assemblies were also able to present lists of judicial or political grievances to the king or to petition the Crown on the various operations of government. The memory of a historic struggle is embodied in the First Amendment of the United States constitution, which forbids Congress to abridge the right "to petition the government for a redress of grievances."

Assemblies became a way of obtaining assent to taxation and attending to the king's shortage of money, at first through representation of estates and later by personal representation on the basis of the Roman principle: *Quod omnes tangit, ab omnibus approbetur* ("What touches everyone should be approved by everyone"). Only later were the petitions presented by assemblies converted by royal approval into law in some countries. For John Locke the determination of taxation was more important than the determination of legislation; it is noticeable that the introduction of money bills in the assembly is still in the hands of the government in Britain, France, and Germany. However, in France the financial needs of the monarchs did not at first strengthen representative institutions. The Estates General were not summoned for considerable periods of time, and a division was made between nobles and commoners in 1614. Only in Britain did medieval assemblies stemming from that called by Simon de Montfort in 1264, when he brought two knights and two burgesses from each shire to a meeting, lead to a bicameral system and to modern parliamentary institutions. This was largely the result of the inability of any outside nation to invade the country and disturb its institutions, the decay of the feudal order, and the strong central administration. The Parliament, rather than the executive, had become the true representative body. By the seventeenth century royal powers were being controlled within constitutional limits, and parliamentary approval was necessary for all laws and taxes. In most European countries the system of estates lasted considerably longer than in England, even into the twentieth century; thus, in pre–World War I Prussia there was a "three-class system" of voters: large landowners and wealthy businessmen, small businessmen and officials, and others.

Political development has included a move toward greater political equality. This has meant the gradual elimination of religious, property, racial, educational, and sexual disqualifications and the creation of fair electoral areas. But only recently has the principle of "one person, one vote" been established even in the older, more developed democracies such as Great Britain and the United States. Until 1975 property disqualifications still existed in Portugal where a minimum tax payment was required for a person to vote. But the belief that land is the basis for the suffrage or that there be no representation without taxation or that only those with a stake in the country should vote because the enfranchisement of others would endanger private property is no longer tenable. This is especially true since agriculture has ceased to be the dominant factor in modernized economies. Some countries exclude women, as did Switzerland until 1971. In 1966 Spain granted the suffrage only to heads of families and married women; some Moslem countries exclude women on the grounds that there is a constitutional difference between the sexes and that a woman fulfilling her natural destiny ought not to be involved in political decision making, but rather with domestic matters. But with larger numbers of women obtaining higher education, entering the labor force, living in urban areas, and living more independent lives, they are becoming a major political force. Separate provisions are made for racial groups in South Africa, New Zealand, and Rhodesia. Illiterates may be excluded from voting, as in Brazil and Portugal, but it is now rarely urged that the more highly educated should possess greater electoral weight, as John Stuart Mill argued and as was allowed in Britain until 1948. In medieval times different ages were fixed for the attainment of entry into the different classes of society; that for the upper-class knight, fixed at 21, gradually became the rule for all other classes. This age limit is now being lowered in an increasing number of states, including the United States, Britain, France, Germany, Israel, Sweden, and the Soviet bloc, which allow the vote at 18; but other states, such as the Netherlands, delay voting age until 23. The principle that an age of 21 is an index of maturity, both personal and public, is less obvious in societies where individuals mature at earlier ages. In some countries, as in Italy, the voting age may be different for the different chambers.

A Typology of Representation

The word "representation" is inherently ambiguous, and representative government may have different meanings. For some it is analogous to the activity of a lawyer acting on behalf of a client; for others it means that the representative approximates the characteristics of the represented. Some see the representative as embodying the declared interests of the represented; others view that person's function as acting on behalf of constitutents in the way he or she thinks most desirable.

The different attitudes on representation mirror the various views on the relationship between the rulers and the ruled. Samuel Beer in his *British Politics in The Collectivist Age* has proposed a typology of views on representation in Britain that is useful for comparative purposes. Beer suggests five major alternative views.

The first, the traditional conservative position, based on the desirability of order, degree, authority, and hierarchy, holds that the common welfare is represented by a monarch or a government charged with formulating a political program. The elected members of a representative body bind their constituents to provide taxation in return for the right to present grievances and argue the case for special and local interests, political formations being corporate in character, to the policy-making body.

The second, the traditional Whig or aristocratic view, is based on the idea of a balanced constitution symbolizing the differences of rank in a society. All social groups participate in the search for the common good. The government is acknowledged to be the directing body, but the lower chamber acts not only as representative of the corporate bodies, both local and functional groups, and therefore of a variety of different interests, but also, as Edmund Burke argued, as representative of the whole community. In this view, men of reason and judgment deliberate on affairs, without the need for a mandate from an electorate to guide or bind them. Hence the elected body can justifiably be based on an unfair "rotten borough" system.

The liberal view is the third type. It sees the national welfare and the common good as represented by a parliamentary assembly made up not of corporate bodies, but of individuals of the middle class; thus a property qualification for the franchise is emphasized though electoral areas are to be approximately equal. This view stresses the importance of individual deputies deliberating in a rational and civil atmosphere on matters of principle.

The fourth view, that of the radical, sees representation as based on the unified will of the people binding individuals together. This will, regarded as the ultimate sovereign in the community, is in practice the will of the majority, expressed either directly or through interest groups. The right of individuals and groups to influence government is acknowledged, and the nineteenth century, in which this view originated, witnessed the proliferation of voluntary associations and nationwide interest groups.

The fifth view embraces both conservative and socialist democrats. Modern conservative democrats may differ from modern socialist democrats in important matters: conservatives stress the organic character of society and the need for strong government, political leadership, and discipline, in contrast to the egalitarianism of socialists. Yet both see representation in terms of government based on disciplined political parties with social classes as basic units, though functional groups also have a role. Socialists view representation as based on classes not on individuals, since society is divided essentially into two classes. Party groupings of left and right logically follow from such a division. Members of the legislature will be bound on most major issues by party decisions, which frame political policies and make members largely party delegates. At the same time organized producer groups play an important role in advice, influence over decisions, and even some governmental representation. In this view the voter chooses between two alternatives presented by the competing parties, selecting a government that is strong and stable and that has responsibility for the formulation of policy.

The typology illustrates the difficulty of defining representation. Differences exist as to whether representatives are concerned with common needs of the whole community and common values, or with particular, special needs and individual wants. Acute differences also exist as to which individuals, groups, or parties are to be considered the representative and what kind of people ought to be chosen to act for others. The theory of A. V. Dicey that legitimate authority meant political power flowing from the people to Parliament and from Parliament to the government is no longer true in an era when Parliament is not necessarily the mediator between government and people and when the executive power may claim to be the embodiment of legitimacy, as did Charles de Gaulle in France.

Is the Representative a Model of the Represented?

It is clear that political representatives are in no sense duplicates of the average citizen. Parliamentary assemblies or government ministers are composed of members of an elite rather than average citizens; they are largely middle class, considerably better and longer educated than the average, wealthier, and with a high proportion of professionals. Indeed those responsible for nominating candidates may consciously choose individuals who are better educated and have a higher social status than the average. Tables 1 and 2, showing the occupa-

Table 1. Occupation of Members of House of Commons October 1974

	Conservative	Labour	Liberal
Professions:			
Barrister	55	32	3
Solicitor	12	9	1
Doctor/Dentist	2	6	—
Architect/Surveyor	3	—	1
Engineer	3	2	1
Accountant	9	7	1
Civil servant	7	7	—
Armed services	8	—	—
Teachers:			
University	2	25	1
Adult	1	15	—
School	9	38	1
Research and Consultants	16	15	—
Business:			
Director	38	2	—
Executive	23	15	1
Insurance/Commerce	22	2	—
Management/Clerical	6	4	—
Small business	2	4	1
White collar	—	10	—
Politicians	4	8	—
Journalist/Publisher	27	22	1
Farmer	23	—	1
Housewife	1	3	—
Local administration	—	4	—
Private means	2	—	—
Clerk	—	5	—
Miner	—	19	—
Skilled worker	2	45	—
Semi/Unskilled worker	—	20	—
Total	277	319	13

Source: David Butler and Dennis Kavanagh, *The British General Election of October 1974* (London: Macmillan, 1975), p. 214.

Table 2. Education of Members of the House of Commons
          October 1974

	Conservative	Labour	Liberal
Elementary only	—	19	—
Elementary plus	1	12	—
Secondary only	22	51	2
Secondary plus	5	49	—
Secondary and university	41	132	2
Public school only	59	6	3
Public school and university	149	50	6
Total	277	319	13
Oxford	80	52	3
Cambridge	75	28	2
Other universities	35	102	3
Total	190	182	8
Eton	48	1	2
Harrow	10	—	—
Winchester	7	2	—
Other public schools	143	53	7
Total public schools	208	56	9

Source: Butler and Kavanagh, *op. cit.,* p. 215.

tions and educational background of members of the House of Commons, clearly shows this preference.

Should the Representative Be Chosen by the Represented?

A major argument for systems of representative governments is that they not only allow voters to choose between competing people or ideas, but they also have an educative effect on voters and provide an intellectual training in the management of public affairs. For John Stuart Mill representative government allowed the less educated to choose educated representatives and to defer to their opinions. Moreover it is claimed that the suffrage is an indispensable natural human right.

Yet for long periods of history and still today in some developed and most undeveloped multiracial societies, the argument has been made that *virtual representation,* acting on behalf of others without their deliberate choice, may be more desirable and take more account of the real needs of the people than representation in which citizens have participated. Virtual representation meant for Burke a "communion of interests and a sympathy in feelings and desires" between the representative and those in whose name he acted. Virtual representation existed in Spain from 1942 until 1967, when the deputies of the Cortes were appointed by trade unions, municipalities, and professional organizations. Only after the constitutional change of 1966 were some Spaniards—heads of families and their wives—able to elect about one-fourth of the deputies; the others continue to be chosen by the government or official bodies.

Should Representatives Be Bound by Their Constituents?

In some systems with representation through estates assemblies, such as the Spanish Cortes or the Estates of the Dutch Republic (1581–1795), the *mandat impératif* bound the delegates who were instructed by their electors. Only in this way could the representatives be made responsible to the represented. But no modern representative system implies that legislators are bound by the electorate, or that they are simply spokesmen for group interests. The classic discussion of the problem was made by Burke in the statement to his constituents in Bristol in 1774; he argued that a member of Parliament was a representative, not a delegate. Burke maintained, "Parliament is not a congress of ambassadors from different and hostile interests, but is a deliberative assembly of one nation with one interest, that of the whole."[4] The representative, according to Burke, ought not to sacrifice his opinion, his mature judgment, his enlightened conscience to his constituents. Ironically, it was in the 1791 French constitution during the revolution that Burke detested so bitterly, that the principle that no binding instructions could be given by the electorate to representatives was made formal. In most systems, representatives have some degree of independence from constituents; binding instruction, the possibility of recall or referendum on the actions of a representative, or annual elections are rare. Paradoxically the possibility of recall exists in the Soviet Union where it may be used as an instrument for political control by the party leadership rather than by constituents. But in fact representatives, if not controlled by their constituents, may be bound by party discipline or influenced by the prevailing rules of the legislative body.

In the *Legislative System* John Wahlke has suggested a tripartite typology by which the role of deputies can be analyzed: (1) the trustee-deputy role, according to which deputies can see themselves as delegates of their constituents and be willing to accept instructions or act as they think necessary without seeking advice or consultation; (2) the facilitator-neutral role, with deputies consulting interest groups and others to different degrees and attempting to perform some services for constituents; and (3) the district-state or country role, with deputies deciding whether the interests of their own particular areas or that of the country as a whole should predominate in their actions.

Much of the difference in the behavior of deputies and in their perceptions of their role can be traced to the competitive nature of their constituency and to the safeness of their electoral seats. The high-minded Burkean trustee position is available only to those who, in a safe area, can afford the luxury of complete independence from their constituents. It is usually forgotten that Burke, after his eloquent oration, lost his own seat in Parliament.

Is There an Electorate Mandate?

A representative government is based on the consent of the governed, who approve the policies of the rulers at regular elections. But this does not imply that the governed approve of all activity of the government, that the government will implement every detail of its announced program, or that it will invariably reflect the interest of the governed. The case for representative government is that it does each of these things more satisfactorily and in greater detail than a nonrepresentative government that may also perform some of them. Through a representative system a government can be formed of groups having some claim on public approval. Voters can choose between competing candidates and programs, and a method is thereby created by which citizens may be related to government.

Parties may differ about the meaning of an electoral majority, some seeing it as approval for certain proposed policies, and others regarding it as a mandate to govern. The concept of a mandate does not necessitate that a party, if successfully elected, will carry out all its electoral proposals, but it does insure that some of those proposals will be enacted or introduced and that controversial proposals not included in the party's program will not often be presented. Vague though the concept of the mandate is, it does imply a general responsibility of the government to the people, while leaving the government wide powers.

Direct Participation

Representative government is inevitable in any society of any considerable size or population, for there can be no proper deliberation or common meeting in such a setting. In *Federalist Paper 14* James Madison drew the distinction between a democracy, in which the people meet and exercise the government in person, and a republic, in which they assemble and administer it by their representatives and agents. For Jean Jacques Rousseau the inability of citizens to participate directly in political affairs meant that they were really free only at election periods because the general will could not be represented and freedom entailed direct political participation.[5] Debates in the French Constituent Assembly of 1789–1792 made the point not only that proper deliberation was impossible over a large area and population, but that it was unnecessary to get the opinion of all citizens, because all did not have the leisure nor the education to judge wisely. Nevertheless during the French Revolution attempts were made to implement Rousseau's concept by preventing a representative assembly from being a conspiracy against the general good and by insuring that it legislate in accordance with the general will of the people. This meant frequent elections, holding debates in the presence of large crowds, and possible resort to insurrection. But in the case of Robespierre the voice of the people was equated with the dictatorial Committee of Public Safety and the use of terror.

In their *The Civic Culture* Gabriel Almond and Sidney Verba discussed three different types of citizen orientation to politics. In the *parochial type* most citizens are distinct from or unaware of political phenomena. In the *subject type* they are oriented to what the government does. Only in the *participant type* is there any considerable active orientation to politics. In fact, only in highly developed states such as the United States and Britain does the mutual trust of the people and their willingness to work together allow stable and responsible government to exist and provide opportunities for direct participation of some kind.

For John Stuart Mill the participation of the private citizen in public functions had a good effect on the moral education of the individuals.[6] But Mill conceded that opportunities for participation were rare and suggested that service on juries and on local assemblies were of great significance. Direct participation by the people in government has, however, taken a number of forms. Probably the most common is the referendum.

The Referendum

If specific issue or proposal is a matter of considerable significance it can be submitted to a direct vote of the people by *referendum*. For example, in Britain a historic precedent was set by submitting membership in the European Community to the people in 1975. A referendum can also be taken on constitutional changes, as is done in New Zealand where a referendum is required before an alteration of the electoral law can be made, or it may be necessitated by deadlock between the legislative chambers.

In some countries such as Belgium, Norway, and Sweden a statute must be passed authorizing each new referendum: since 1945 only four have been held in the three countries. Other countries such as Switzerland and Italy allow referenda by popular petition. The small number of signatures required by Switzerland has resulted in 122 being held since 1945. In the United States referenda have frequently been held in the states and local communities but not at the federal level. The referendum process is also available in communist countries, but has not been used for any significant purpose. Charles de Gaulle, who resorted to referenda on a number of occasions to gain popular approval for his actions, argued that a referendum is "the clearest, the frankest, the most democratic of procedures" since national sovereignty belongs to the people. The use of referenda for de Gaulle was not simply a method of settling major problems. It was also a method by which the chief executive could appeal for a vote of confidence to the people and could ignore the intermediary elective organs such as political parties, which de Gaulle regarded as engaged in political bickering and in producing political division. Table 3 lists the outcomes of the major referenda in France over the past two decades.

Table 3.   Six Referenda in the French Fifth Republic

	Electorate (in millions)	Votes (in millions)	Yes Votes		No Votes	
			Percent of electorate	Percent of votes	Percent of electorate	Percent of votes
Sept. 28, 1958	26.6	22.3	66.4	79.8	17.3	20.7
Jan. 8, 1961	27.1	20.2	55.9	75.2	18.3	24.7
Apr. 8, 1962	27.0	19.3	64.8	90.7	6.6	9.3
Oct. 28, 1962	28.1	21.1	46.6	62.2	28.2	37.7
Apr. 27, 1969	28.6	23.0	36.7	46.7	41.6	53.2
Apr. 23, 1972	29.0	17.5	36.1	67.7	17.2	32.3

The six referenda approved the new constitution, the policy granting independence to Algeria, the Evian agreement settling the Algerian problem, direct popular election of the president of the republic, and expansion of the European Community, and in 1969 rejected the creation of regions and the reorganization of the Senate.

De Gaulle's view, based to a large extent on a critical evaluation of parliamentary behavior, implies that a referendum will allow the expression of a will of the people that the multiplicity of parties, acting as intermediaries between the ruler and the people, may prevent from being heard. The referendum has been supported for allowing a real choice by the people on issues where party divisions are not clear, resolving political deadlock, and endowing a difficult decision with needed legitimacy.

But many others see a referendum as a device for transferring the government of a country from rule by intelligence to rule by ignorance. Writers like Walter Lippmann who see the impact of public opinion as a "massive negative" at critical times and the people as incapable of making correct decisions in important areas, especially in foreign policy, are hardly likely to agree that the referendum is a useful educative device.[7] "Foreign politics," as Alexis de Tocqueville said, "demand scarcely any of those qualities which are peculiar to a democracy; they require, on the contrary, the perfect use of almost all those in which it is deficient."[8] Moreover it is doubtful that resort to a referendum can be made on many occasions because the results largely depend on the way in which the question is put.

Other critics argue that not only does a referendum undermine the authority of the legislature, but it also can be a device to manipulate voters and allow politicians to escape making decisions. It is possible for a referendum to arouse divisive passions as the referendum on the Common Market in Norway did in 1972, and to obstruct or delay parliamentary action, as the referendum on the vote for women did in Switzerland until 1971. Referenda will often prevent rather than foster change; in Australia in 1973 the government was prevented from controlling prices and incomes because of a referendum, and in the United States tax increases have usually be defeated for the same reason. Referenda may sometimes be regarded as consultative rather than authoritative; in Sweden, for example, the government refused to accept the 83 percent majority in favor of continuing to drive on the left side of the road and crossed to the other side of the street.

Strictly speaking a referendum—the submission of a law or intended law to a direct vote of the people—can be distinguished from a *plebiscite*—an expression of the will of the people on a political issue. But in recent years the two terms have been used interchangeably. Since the Roman *plebiscitum*, which allowed the plebs a voice in public affairs, plebiscites have been used as devices to obtain approval of actions of governments. Thus the use of referenda and plebiscites could answer the rhetorical question asked by Rousseau of whether the body politic has an organ to declare its will: Switzerland has made use of the device since the fifth century.

Plebiscites became significant in the modern age as a result of the principle enunciated during the French Revolution that there be no annexation of territory without consultation of the inhabitants by vote. As a result of plebiscites held in Avignon, Savoy, and Nice, these territories became part of France.

But this device has often been used by dictators, including Napoleon I, Napoleon III, and Hitler to justify their policies and provide legitimacy for them on the ground that the authority of the leader comes directly from the will of the people for whom he is the guardian and spokesman. Thus Hitler obtained approval for the acquisition of the Saarland in 1935 and Austria in 1938.

Other Forms of Direct Participation

In addition to voting in referenda, the people may participate directly by means of ratification of the work of constituent assemblies, votes on constitutional changes and statutes, the initiative and recall, and public opinion polls.

Since the examples of the 1789 United States constitution and the 1793 French constitution drafted by constituent assemblies and submitted to the people for ratification, many similar instances have followed. Delegates to a constituent assembly can be elected by popular vote, as they were in France and Italy in 1946 and South Vietnam in 1966, or selected by officials, as in West Germany where delegates were chosen by the land parliaments in proportion to the strength of parties. Only occasionally, as in Israel, have constituent assemblies turned themselves into a legislative assembly instead of drafting a constitution. In democratic systems it is generally expected that the draft constitution will be submitted to the people for approval to endow it with legitimacy and lend it prestige.

Some systems also provide for popular initiation or approval of constitutional amendments or statutes. The most notable example in democratic countries is that of Switzerland, where the electorate must ratify both total and partial revision of the constitution, and where 50,000 voters may sign petitions asking for such revision. Amendments must be approved by a majority of voters in the country as a whole and by a majority of cantons. The Swiss electorate has approved a large proportion of the changes proposed by the Federal Assembly: of the 76 amendments proposed by the legislature between 1848 and 1960, 51 were approved by the people. In 1874 the people approved the total revision proposed by the legislature. But the legislature has been more reluctant to approve changes proposed by petitions of citizens: of the 45 proposed between 1874 and 1960, only 7 were accepted, and a proposal for total revision was defeated in 1935. The Swiss people cannot initiate legislation by petition, but on the demand of 30,000 citizens or of 8 cantons, the people can vote on legislation already passed by the legislature or on treaties. Of the 67 legislative referenda since 1874, only 25 have been approved.

The citizens of some countries may present petitions or bills for discussion in the legislature. But the *initiative,* as this practice is referred to, though sometimes protected by constitutional provision, is of little significance in modern systems. Moreover, initiators of such petitions and bills have often been interest groups, for it is almost impossible for ordinary citizens to combine to propose coherent legislation.

Provision is also sometimes made for *recall* of officials, as in some states of the United States and cantons in Switzerland, and in the Soviet Union.

Finally, governments and politicians may take account of the views of its citizens through public opinion polls and change their policies or attitudes accordingly. Gallup has cast its pall over many politicians. But many prefer the expression of views through interest groups, which possess knowledge and whose claims may be easier to assess than are public opinion polls. Valuable though the polls may be in ascertaining views on a given issue or person, a major problem is that these views are irresponsible in the sense that they are not necessarily linked with any intended action. Moreover it is not unknown for legislators to conduct their own polls for public relations purposes rather than to learn the views of their constituents.

The Problem of Majority Rule

Modern political practice is based on *majority rule.* This is the principle that the will of a body or group is best expressed through a majority of its members and that decision by a majority, rather than the will of a single individual, acclamation, or unanimity, should determine the outcome of political elections or disputes. Not until the mid-sixteenth century did the majority principle become the rule in legislative bodies. Some institutions such as the jury process still require unanimity in many countries and important constitutional or political action often requires a special majority.

The argument for majority rule is essentially that it represents the greater weight of the community involved, that the majority is more likely than a minority to be right, and, as James Madison argued, "it is less probable that a majority of the whole will have a common motive to invade the rights of other citizens."[9]

In systems based on political equality and on persuasion rather than coercion, the absence of majority rule would be undemocratic and would tend to favor special interests; moreover, the availability of an individual veto, as with the Polish *liberum veto* or the major powers' veto in the United Nations Security Council, can prevent any action from being taken.

The majority rule concept does not mean that the majority is always right. It does not imply the exercise of unlimited power or an unwillingness on the part of a majority to compromise or an inability of the minority to form a majority at some future time. The concept itself presupposes both that all will abide by its results and that opposition is allowed to exist.

Nevertheless the idea that political systems operate on the basis of majority rule is criticized from two different perspectives. One is that it produces undesirable results and the other that it is essentially unrealistic and irrelevant. The first criticism is directed against mass participation or influence in politics. It argues that Western democracies are governed by a public opinion that does not have the capacity for making rational decisions, that is vulgar and incompetent, lacking in initiative, impulsive, intolerant, and based on emotion not reason, aggression not harmony. It emphasizes the mistakes of majority decision—the people preferring Barabbas to Jesus—and the tyranny of majority opinion. At the worst it sees majority rule as leading to the politics of the street with mass movements appealing to fear and producing an atmosphere in which parliamentary rule is discredited. Aristocratic conservatives like Alexis de Tocqueville, Jakob Burckhardt, and José Ortega y Gasset, revolutionaries like Vladimir Lenin, the "Machiavellian" group of Gaetano Mosca, Vilfredo Pareto, and Robert Michels, and the students of political behavior have all pointed out the political inadequacies of the majority.

Political psychologists have suggested that mass democracy, at least in its present Western form, is characterized by alienation—the loss of a sense of self because people have lost control over their conditions of life and work—and by an anonymity in that social controls formerly in operation in small communities are absent and cultural values are disregarded. The result has therefore often been identification with a leader, since the mass would rather submit to a dictatorial regime than feel alone. Seymour Lipset and others have pointed out the authoritarian tendencies of some workers and explained them by a lack of education, a lack of participation in groups, economic insecurity and isolation, and by family patterns of behavior.[10] Yet criticism of the people as a gullible, destructive mob is not borne out by empirical studies of mass intervention; in the French Revolution mass behavior was essentially rational, and the main cause for revolutionary behavior was the high price of bread, not emotional rhetoric.[11]

The second criticism suggests that the problem is a false one, because all systems are really governments by minority and government decisions are responses to the articulated wants or pressures of social groups. The majority is always acted for; indeed, it is never a homogeneous entity. But much of the pessimism about the impact of the majority principle is based on the false premise that representative government entails a highly active electorate. The people as such do not enter the arena of politics; a whole electorate is rarely competent politically except to choose between competing political elites. An electoral majority chooses those who will govern and a broad outline of general principles rather than individual policies.

The Suffrage: Myth and Reality

The logic of political development has resulted in the extension of the suffrage to the whole adult citizenry. The case for such extension is based on both individual and social considerations. The vote has been claimed on the grounds that it is one of the rights all individuals should possess, that it is essential to full citizenship in a state, and therefore that it should be available to all except for those disqualified for certain reasons such as insanity, youth, or legal guilt for proscribed offenses. The vote is necessary for self-protection, allows the individual possessing it to be taken into political consideration to some degree, and provides an opportunity for government to be made aware of the views of citizens. According to the French saying, those who are absent are always in the wrong. It is a more dubious argument that the suffrage morally elevates those who possess it or that it is a potent "instrument of mental improvement," as John Stuart Mill hoped, or that it makes people more self-dependent.[12]

From the point of view of society, public affairs ought to be, as Aristotle, Mill, and Rousseau argued in different ways, a chief concern of citizens or a matter of duty. Ideally the suffrage ought to be exercised in the interests of the whole society rather than with an eye on private advantage. More pragmatically perhaps, it is a valuable method through which social groups and interests can be conciliated and compromises reached among all parts of the community.

But reality does not correspond to the anticipated picture of voters making a rational choice on the basis of an examination and understanding of interrelated issues, carefully comparing the differing views of the opposing political forces, and deciding between clearly defined alternatives. Political students are perhaps still too apt to project their own views and attitudes onto the electorate. It is not certain that human beings are political by nature, nor that participation in political decisions is necessary for their development. A series of voting studies in Western countries has shown that the level of political interest and understanding is low and that there is little intellectual appreciation of political issues. Less than one-third of the contemporary United States electorate has confessed to any real interest in politics, and only one-fifth of the United States electorate thinks it makes a "good deal of difference" who wins elections. Only 52 percent of the eligible electorate voted in the American presidential election of 1972. Similarly in Britain, in spite of a consistently high electoral turnout and great stability in voting for a given party, acknowledged interest in politics was limited to only 15 percent of the population. In Gaullist France 35 percent of the electorate claimed they held no political views. Many citizens do not understand the issues that concern the active or politically involved. After the 1958 Berlin crisis it came as a surprise that 63 percent of the American people did not know that the city was encircled by communist East Germany. Moreover, a number of recent studies in the United States have implied that democratic procedural norms such as tolerance and respect for civil liberties are more respected by the better educated than by the rest of the population, and that democracy is dependent on the adherence of elites to those norms.

Other studies have shown that only some 15 percent of United States voters have an understanding of political ideology or of the interrelatedness of major issues.[13] Many vote in ignorance or without any real involvement; they are often oblivious to contradictions between their own beliefs and those of the party candidates. Political knowledge tends to reinforce opinions already formed. Voting is likely to be conditioned less by political awareness than by membership in a social class, ethnic or religious group, family affiliation (80 percent of family members in Britain and the United States agree on candidates), parental image, and party identification, which appears to be the strongest determinant in voting and the most significant force for political stability. The theory of representative government holds that the citizen is both rational and active, that the electorate supports or opposes parties on the basis of their legislative programs or reacts to individual candidates on the basis of their identification with a party program. But these assertions have not been borne out by past studies of American behavior, which showed that the public knew little about the individual candidates and even less about issues, and tended to vote by party. A more recent study, however, argues that party loyalties have declined and that issues have greater significance due largely to newer entrants into the electorate.[14] It is apparent that the electorate as a whole does not have an understanding of ideological coherence, but instead habitually votes for the same party. Studies of voting in different countries indicate that the more educated and the wealthier members of society have more understanding of political issues than do the less well educated and the poorer citizens, and that they are more consistent supporters of the right than the less wealthy are of the left. Leftist supporters tend to cohere around their party, and this phenomenon is partly responsible for the greater discipline generally found in leftist parties than in those of the right.

What is the purpose of elections when voters have so little real understanding of political issues? Hopefully the electorate responds in a general way to the competing candidates and to the problems of the times. Upholders of the democratic credo express pessimism at the extent of electoral apathy produced by a feeling of the futility of political activity, by the view that discussion is not translated into political action, by the perception of inability to influence decision-makers, by the conviction that politics is overly abstract or unrelated to one's life, or by the belief that the whole political or economic system is wrong. The last of these views may lead either to apathy or to a vote for a purely negative protest party or for a revolutionary party; such action is part of what Hadley Cantril has termed "the politics of despair."[15] On the other hand some works by political sociologists have argued that widespread political participation, interest, and conflict may be harmful to democracies, because they may lead to intolerance and fanaticism.[16] In their view indifference to politics may indicate the stability rather than the insecurity of the system. But they accept too readily the position that ideological disputation is irrelevant to contemporary society or is dead. Too little zeal is usually a rationale for acquiesence to the status quo. Despite the survey methods and the voting studies, a strong case can be made, as V. O. Key has suggested in *The Responsible Electorate*, that the electorate responds to the great events, candidates, and conditions of the times, and renders a decision that is meaningful in the context of the political system. The fact that the European working class has remained solid in its support of leftist parties, except in those countries split by religious differences, indicates the rationality of its political behavior.

Who Votes and How?

In dictatorial regimes the ruler normally obtains over 99 percent of the vote, which itself is over 99 percent of the total possible electorate. Even in democratic countries with compulsory voting such as Australia, Belgium, or Greece the electoral turnout is never as high as this. In most developed political systems the poll varies between 75 percent and 90 percent in national elections in which voting is always heavier than in local or provincial elections.

Comparative generalizations about voting are difficult to sustain, but a few seem valid. A political or economic crisis will generally produce a large poll. Individuals or members of a group who are or will be affected by political action or whose religious and moral beliefs are affected are more likely to vote than those not affected. In any case, members of organizations vote more than do nonmembers, union members more than nonmembers. Married people tend to vote more than the unmarried, long-time residents more than new residents. Women vote less than men, and poorer women less than richer women. In both electoral participation and political understanding the young, the rural residents, and the lesser educated have the worst record. Abstention decreases with age but becomes high again among old people. Women tend to vote as do their husbands though they are generally more conservative; in Great Britain in 1959, when the Conservatives obtained a majority of over 100 seats, the Labour party still got a majority of the male vote. Paradoxically, the parties that urged the emancipation of women most strongly, the parties of the left, have benefited least from that emancipation.

The very poor and those who feel most alienated from society vote least, or vote for an extremist party such as the Communist party as a negative protest against the frustrations and injustices they experience. Those in insecure or hazardous occupations, such as mine workers, fishermen, or one-crop farmers, tend to be more extreme in voting. The same is true of minority groups, whether they are Catholics or Jews in a Protestant majority country, Indians in Sri Lanka, Andhras in India, Koreans in Japan, or Arabs in Israel. Economic growth of a rapidly developing nation, bringing accompanying problems of adjustment to new social conditions, has also led to increased voting for extremist parties.

Voting Methods

Citizens can be represented on either a functional or geographical basis.

Functional Representation

This implies representation through specific economic, social, or occupational groups. In the medieval period the assemblies consisted of representatives from the legally defined and hierarchical groups of estates: the lords spiritual and temporal, the clergy and the nobles, the burgesses or townsmen, and commoners; or, seen in another way, those who pray, those who fight, and those who work. The estates were regarded as collective bodies, the members of which had certain rights and obligations. After the consolidation of the power of the king, the estates either lost their significance and declined, as did the Estates General in France under Louis XIII and Richelieu, or became transformed, as did the British chambers, which began to represent citizens as individuals rather than as members of groups and occupations.

But the case for some form of functional representation is still argued by reformers of the left such as guild socialists and syndicalists, by pluralists, and by those advocating a corporate state. They all suggest that the increase in the electorate has meant less contact between territorial representatives and their constituents, and that there is a need for expertise in economic and social matters that parliamentary representatives do not possess. Functional representation is regarded as a meaningful concept because geographically oriented parliaments and parties are not sufficiently representative of economic interests. True representation is held to be always specific and functional, serving, in G. D. H. Cole's words, "certain purposes common to groups of individuals."[17] According to this view functional representation would provide both the necessary experts and a truer expression of the wishes of the community.

In spite of the practical difficulty of selecting appropriate functions and groups to be represented and allocating proper significance to the various occupations, many systems, including those of Finland, France, Germany, Italy, Indonesia, and the European Economic Community, have set up economic and social councils of different kinds. The Irish constitution provides for functional councils, and the Irish Senate contains representatives directly elected by functional groups, as do the upper houses of Peru and Paraguay. The complicated Yugoslavian system provides for a Federal Chamber composed of delegates of self-managing organizations and communities. Normally, however, such bodies are confined to advisory functions and limited in influence. Interest groups are better able to influence parliamentary and governmental activity through direct contacts or through membership in the hundreds of advisory committees that meet in all important policy-making areas than through an economic parliament. In some countries interest groups play a more direct role in economic affairs: the West German system of codetermination (*Mitbestimmung*) provides for worker participation in industrial management with representatives on boards of directors. To a lesser degree this also exists in Norway.

The device of functional representation has also been used in non-democratic systems. In the Soviet Union the system of soviets or councils, supposedly representative of the workers, has not been very meaningful. But in Yugoslavia the workers' councils in industry and the cooperatives in agriculture have genuinely participated in the management of affairs and the concept of worker management has been extended to social self-management.

The concept of functional representation was also purportedly implemented in authoritarian Portugal and fascist Italy; but the imposing theoretical scheme of representation through syndicates supposedly representing occupational groups and hierarchically connected into national syndicates and federations was largely ineffectual. Sukarno, while he was ruling in Indonesia, set up councils of functional groups and advisory bodies to represent public opinion.

The utility of functional representation is limited. It assumes that vocation is the chief determinant of behavior and interest and must form the basis for representation because all individuals will be considered members of an occupational group. The practical problems of deciding which occupations are to be represented, and to what degree, are incapable of equitable solution. Furthermore, the largest occupational group, the housewife, is always sadly neglected. Above all, functional representation tends to be divisive in character, assuming that insistence on group interests will lead to common policies. But there are many other opportunities for the interests of groups to be articulated and felt, while common policies are more likely to result from the compromises reached through systems of territorial representation.

Territorial Representation

A large variety of different methods are used for the purpose of territorial representation, whether in single-member or multimember constituencies. *Single-member constituencies* are relatively small geographic areas, usually approximately equal in population to each other and sometimes identical with administrative or political divisions, as in France, Norway, and Switzerland. The usual method is that the candidate with the highest plurality wins. This method has the great virtue of simplicity, tends to limit the number of parties, and occasionally fosters a two-party system. It may enable one party to gain an absolute majority and thus, in a parliamentary cabinet system, means that a voter may be registering his or her preference for a government as well as for a parliamentary representative. Logically it should lead to the formation of a strong government capable of taking the initiative and to the avoidance of coalitions. But it is also a system that is mathematically inequitable. A candidate may win by a minority of votes cast for the various parties in a constituency. The legislative majority may represent a minority of the population, thus distorting the opinion of the nation. A relatively small change in electoral opinion may produce a far greater proportional change in the distribution of parliamentary seats. Electors favoring a small party or a party with no local candidate are faced with the dilemma of either wasting their vote or casting it for the candidate they find least objectionable. Third parties are always underrepresented; generally their candidates take more votes from the weaker of the two major parties, thereby strengthening the incumbent. The inequities of this method are shown by the figures for Britain, shown in Table 4; this is the classic example of the single-member constituency with plurality decision. No one party has obtained a majority of the poll since 1935. A third party whose support is roughly evenly spread throughout the whole

Table 4.   British Elections, 1935–1974

Year	Percentage of total vote			Number of seats won in the house of commons		
	Conservative	Labour	Liberal	Conservative	Labour	Liberal
1935	50	40	7	387	154	17
1945	40	48	9	212	394	12
1950	43	46	9	298	315	9
1951	48	48.8	2.6	321	295	6
1955	49.8	46.3	2.7	345	276	6
1959	49.4	43.8	5.9	366	258	6
1964	43.4	44.1	11.2	304	317	9
1966	41.9	47.9	8.5	253	363	12
1970	46.4	43.0	7.5	330	287	6
1974 (Feb.)*	38.2	37.2	19.3	296	301	14
1974 (Oct.)	35.8	39.3	18.3	276	319	13

*Number of constituencies increased to 635.

country is condemned to failure. In the 1974 election the British Liberals with 18.3 percent of the vote obtained only 13 seats.

Similar distortions are produced in other countries such as Canada and India. In Canada between 1935 and 1957 the Liberal party had large majorities in Parliament but on only one occasion obtained a majority of the total vote. In 1974, with 42.9 percent of the vote, the Liberals got 53 percent of the seats. In India the Congress party obtained 75 percent of the parliamentary seats with less than 50 percent of the vote between 1952 and 1967.

To reduce inequity, some systems use the single transferable vote — as in Ireland and the upper chambers of Australia and India — preferential voting, the alternative vote, or a run-off ballot if no candidate has obtained an absolute majority. The two-ballot system in France can be seen, as Seymour Lipset has pointed out, as a functional equivalent to primary elections in the United States; both allow different factions to exist and interests in a party to be expressed within that party. At the French second ballot, the candidates with least chance of success retire, and there is usually a straight fight between a candidate of the right and one of the left. In general this system has reduced the chance for extreme parties to win, as Tables 5 and 6 show. At the second ballot in the 1962 election of the French National Assembly, there was a straight fight in 227 of the 369 contested constituencies; in 100 of these areas the Gaullists fought the Communists. In 130 other constituencies there were contests between 3 parties. In

Table 5.   French National Assembly, Election of 1973

Parties		First Ballot		Second Ballot		
		Vote in millions	Percent of vote	Vote in millions	Percent of vote	Seats won
Communist		5.1	21.5	4.4	20.6	73
PSU		0.7	3.4	0.08	0.3	3
Socialist		4.5	21.2	4.7	21.9	89
Left		0.6	1.4	0.8	3.8	—
Reformers		2.9	13.1	1.3	6.1	31
URP	UDR Independent	5.7	23.6	6.7	31.3	185
	Republican	1.6	6.1	1.6	7.7	54
	CDP Various	0.9	3.4	0.8	3.9	21
	Majority	0.8	3.3	0.7	3.2	14
Others		0.6	3.0	0.1	0.6	8

Table 6.   Groups in the Assembly, 1973

UDR	162 + 21 affiliated
Independent Republican	51 + 4 "
Centrist Union	30
Social Democratic Reformers	30 + 4 "
Socialist and Left Radical	100 + 2 "
Communist	73
Unaffiliated	13

the 1973 election of the Assembly there were straight fights in 339 constituencies. In 148 of these a Gaullist candidate fought a member of the Federation of the Left, and in 146 others a Gaullist fought against a Communist.

In *multimember constituencies* the most usual electoral system is some form of proportional representation, the chief advantage of which is to obtain more accurate parliamentary representation of electoral opinion. Taking the premise of proportional representation to its logical conclusion would imply viewing the whole country as one constituency, as in Israel, Monaco, or the Netherlands, with parliamentary representation being allocated to parties in proportion to votes received in the country as a whole. A less extreme version is the method used in Norway, where the country is divided into 20 parliamentary constituencies; Sweden has 28 constituencies, Denmark 23 districts, and Italy 32 areas. In France the multimember constituencies elected between 2 and 5 members. However, the Japanese system provides for 130 multimember constituencies, each of which elects 3 or 5 members, but each voter in each constituency has only one vote.

Proportional representation systems undoubtedly produce a more accurate representation of electoral divisions and insure some representation to minority groups, classes, or races. But they also inevitably produce or perpetuate a multiparty system, thus making coalitions of different parties necessary, with possible undesirable consequences for stable or effective government. In Israel 22 parties and groups ran candidates in the 1974 election; in Holland 14 parties obtained seats in the legislature. Proportional representation may also prevent the development of disciplined parties and may encourage factional groups in the parties and frequent and temporary party alliances. To some extent the success of the Nazi party in Germany can be blamed on the German system of proportional representation, which in the 1930 election allowed 35 national party lists including those of the People's Bloc of Inflation Victims, and the Vital Interests of Celibates. This system resulted in 21 cabinets, whose average life was 8 months, containing members of up to 6 different parties and often resting on minority parliamentary support. Every country using a system of proportional representation has at least four parties of some importance in its legislature. Frequently an electoral situation is produced in which a small group may hold the political balance of power, as the Radical party has done in Denmark and a center party in Sweden.

Occasionally, however, a system of proportional representation may produce a legislature in which one party has a majority. In Norway the Labour party obtained an absolute majority between 1945 and

Table 7. German Bundestag Elections, 1957–1976

	1957			1961			1965		
Party	Percent of vote	Seats won by PR	Seats won by direct voting	Percent of vote	Seats won by PR	Seats won by direct voting	Percent of vote	Seats won by PR	Seats won by direct voting
CDU/CSU	50.2	76	194	45.3	86	156	47.6	91	154
SPD	31.8	123	46	36.2	99	91	39.3	108	94
FDP	7.7	40	1	12.8	67	–	9.5	49	–
Other	10.3	11	6	5.7	–	–	3.6	–	–

1961. The proportional system introduced in Turkey in 1961 at first prevented any single party obtaining an absolute majority and led to a series of coalition governments; but in 1965 the Justice party managed to obtain 52 percent of the total vote and a majority of the seats in the legislature. Even more rarely a minority government may survive for a term in a multiparty system as in Sweden in recent years.

What is the most desirable electoral system? Electoral systems are methods, not ends in themselves; their value must be related to the political system as a whole. A single-member plurality system tends to reduce the number of parties and thus to increase the possibility of a strong government with a coherent policy and an ability to rule. A multimember constituency with proportional representation tends to result in a multiparty system, which produces reasonably accurate electoral divisions, but also tends to preserve those divisions and reduce the possibility of strong government.

The political effect of different methods of election can be illustrated by the West German system, in which half the members of the Bundestag are elected by direct vote, if they obtain a plurality in individual member constituencies, and the other half are chosen by a system of proportional representation, in which a citizen votes for a party and not for an individual. Thus every citizen can exercise two votes, one for an individual candidate in a single constituency and the other for a political party. The distribution of seats in the Bundestag is determined by the percentage of these second votes won by the parties. The different results produced by the two methods of voting is shown in Table 7. If the system were entirely based on candidates obtaining a plurality in single-member constituencies, the Free Democratic party, like other minor parties, would get no representation. In the 1965 election it was not placed first or second in a single constituency, but through the proportional representation provisions the FDP obtained 49 seats. An incidental characteristic of the German system is

	1969			1972			1976		
Percent of vote	Seats won by PR	Seats won by direct voting	Percent of vote	Seats won by PR	Seats won by direct voting	Percent of vote	Seats won by PR	Seats won by direct voting
46.1	121	121	44.9	97	128	48.6	108	135
42.7	97	127	45.8	78	152	42.6	101	113
5.8	30	—	8.4	41	—	7.9	39	—
5.4	—	—	1.0	—	—	0.9	—	—

that the Christian Democratic party deputies from single-member districts are more likely to deviate from the party line than are those deputies elected by proportional representation.

Electoral systems cannot guarantee political stability as the experience of France, which has tried a wide variety of systems in the last 80 years, has shown. But not surprisingly, regimes have tried to sustain themselves by manipulating the electoral system in a number of ways.

One way is deliberately to strengthen the regime or the dominant parties. Fourth Republic France, for example, experimented with a system of electoral alliances to handicap extremist parties, especially the Communist and Gaullist parties. And the French Fifth Republic hoped to weaken center parties by requiring in 1966 that those candidates for whom less than 10 percent of the electorate cast a vote in the first round be automatically eliminated.

Italy in 1953 provided that a single party or alliance getting 50 percent of the votes would obtain 65 percent of the seats in the Assembly. In Italy a party must get 300,000 votes on the national level to obtain representation, while in Denmark a party requires a minimum of 60,000. Each Greek government in the postwar period has tried to change the method of election before every new one. In British Guinea the system was changed to defeat the more radical and allow the more moderate political leader to become the first prime minister of an independent Guyana. The Catholic party in Belgium deliberately introduced proportional representation after the 1898 election in order to strengthen the Liberals and reduce the strength of the Socialists. To reduce the possibility of minor parties gaining some seats, the West German system introduced its "5 percent provision." This permits only those parties that obtain over 5 percent of the total vote over the whole country or that win at least 3 individual constituencies to share in the distribution of those seats awarded on the basis of proportional representation. The success of this device is illustrated in Table 8. Ten of the 14 parties running candidates in 1957 failed to obtain any representation, and since 1961 only 3 have obtained any seats. In 1969 the National Democratic party, often regarded as a neo-Nazi party, obtained 4.3 percent of the total vote and thus was unable to obtain any seats. In neighboring Liechtenstein to qualify for representation in the Landtag, a party must obtain 8 percent of the total votes in the whole country.

Another way regimes have tried to maintain themselves is by banning extremist parties from the polls or by imposing penalties on defeated candidates. Examples of the first include the banning of Com-

Table 8. West Germany: Elimination of Minor Parties

Year	Number of parties running candidates	Number of parties in Bundestag	Share of Electoral Vote in Country	
			Percent CDU and SPD	Percent CDU, SPD, and FDP
1949	14	11	60.2	72.1
1953	15	6	74.0	83.7
1957	14	4	82.0	89.7
1961	8	3	81.6	94.4
1965	10	3	86.9	96.4
1969	13	3	87.8	94.6
1972	8	3	90.7	99.0
1976	19	3	91.2	99.1

munist parties in 26 countries, among them West Germany, Greece, and Spain, and of the Nazi and Fascist parties in Germany and Italy.

An example of the second would be Great Britain where minor party or freak candidates are discouraged by making such candidates forfeit their monetary deposit if they obtain less than one-quarter of the poll. In the October 1974 election there were 2,252 candidates for the 635 seats, of whom 367 lost their deposits.

Perhaps the tactic for maintaining stability most familiar in the United States is the "gerrymandering" or the deliberate altering, of districts in size or area to make the desired result more probable. All systems weigh the desirability of equity against the advantages of weighted areas. In the United States legislative apportionment so heavily favors rural areas that a majority can be elected in the legislatures of 44 states with less than 40 percent of the population, while in 13 states a majority can be elected by one-third or less of the population. Until 1965 the state of Vermont had not altered the districts for its lower house since 1792, and mathematically 11 percent of its voters could elect a majority of representatives.

One final way regimes maintain the status quo is by limiting the number of parties participating in primary contests or general elections. This is done by requiring certain qualifications that a new or extremist party may not be able to meet. In some American states a large number of signatures or a certain minimal proportion of the electorate may be needed to place a candidate on the ballot, a requisite that may not be easily met by extremist candidates.[18] Past party affiliations of individuals may restrict their ability to run as third party candidates. A party may not be allowed to run candidates if it did not gain a certain minimal percentage of the vote at a previous election.

Notes

[1] Karl Mannheim, *Freedom, Power and Democratic Planning* (New York: Oxford University Press, 1950), p. 147.

[2] Charles A. Beard and John D. Lewis, "Representative Government in Evolution," *American Political Science Review* (April 1932), pp. 223–240; and Hanna Pitkin, ed., *Representation* (New York: Atherton, 1969).

[3] Thomas Hobbes, *Leviathan*, Book I, chap. 10.

[4] R. Hoffman and P. Levack, *Burke's Politics* (New York: Knopf, 1949), pp. 115–116.

[5] Jean Jacques Rousseau, *The Social Contract*, Book 3, chap 15.

[6] J. S. Mill, *On Representative Government* (London: Oxford University Press, 1954), ch. 8.

[7] Walter Lippmann, *The Phantom Public* (New York: Harcourt Brace, 1925); and his *Essays in the Public Philosophy* (New York: New American Library/Mentor Books, 1956).

[8] Alexis de Tocqueville, *Democracy in America, Vol. 1.* New York: Vintage, 1945), p. 243.

[9] James Madison, *Federalist Papers,* No. 10.

[10] S. M. Lipset, *Political Man* (Garden City, N.Y.: Doubleday, 1960), chap. 5; and Edward Shils, "Authoritarianism: 'Right' and 'Left'," in R. Christie and M. Jahoda, eds., *Studies in the Scope and Method of the Authoritarian Personality* (New York: Free Press, 1954), pp. 24–29.

[11] Richard Cobb, *Terreur et Subsistances, 1793–1795* (Paris: Clavreuil, 1965).

[12] J. S. Mill, op. cit., p. 274.

[13] P. E. Converse, "Politicization of the Electorate in France and the United States," *Public Opinion Quarterly* (Spring 1962), pp. 1–23.

[14] Norman H. Nie, Sidney Verba, and J. R. Petrocik, *The Changing American Voter* (Cambridge, Mass.: Harvard University Press, 1976).

[15] Hadley Cantril, *The Politics of Despair* (New York: Basic Books, 1958).

[16] B. Berelson, P. Lazerfield, and W. McPhee, *Voting* (University of Chicago Press, 1954).

[17] G. D. H. Cole, *Social Theory* (Philadelphia: Lippincott, 1920), pp. 49–51.

[18] Frank Sorauf, *Party Politics in America* (Boston: Little Brown, 1972), p. 215–216.

Chapter Six

Interests and
Political Parties

Groups play an important and sometimes an indispensable part in political activity by formulating demands, expressing political attitudes, and making claims, as David Truman said "through or on the institutions of government."[1] Groups may be concerned with pressing for concrete specific interests or material advantages demanded by their members, opposing intended action they find objectionable, expressing or articulating the views of some part of public opinion on public issues, or campaigning for new policies or a new society.

Pressures on rulers have always taken a wide variety of forms, from riots, acts of organized violence and rebellions, social movements, and political parties to the peaceful presentation of petitions and the seeking of redress of grievances or the ability to influence decisions. What is distinctive in modern times is the sustained nature of group activity and the prominent role played by groups in obtaining or preventing action, and in influencing decisions and policy.

It has often been argued that the expression of group interests is undesirable in itself and may be contrary to the public interest. Jean Jacques Rousseau argued that there should be "no partial societies within the state" because they were a danger to social and political unity; and Thomas Hobbes said that corporations were "worms in the entrails of natural man."[2] At the opposite extreme is the theory of Arthur Bentley who held that individuals combine into groups that then exert pressure, that there is no group without its interest, that society has no group interest as a whole, and that the function of government is to act as the conciliator of different interests in an attempt to create equilibrium. The legislative process is thus reduced to the play of group interests; *log rolling*, or mutual accommodation and support on issues in which representatives are interested, is its essence. The Bentley view need not be accepted in full to suggest that the activity of groups is both inevitable in and necessary to modern political life. Indeed they may be indispensable in helping run the state, as in the case of the British National Farmers' Union, which assists the Ministry of Agriculture in settling farm problems. The administration of the British health service is dominated by professional experts, and the Ministry of Health has frequently left the initiative to doctors or to medical organizations.

Nevertheless an undue concentration on group activity neglects the significance of the state and political institutions, the role of individual behavior and political will, and the political climate and culture of a community. Such a concentration, and the accompanying view of politics as the maneuvering of well-organized interest groups, leads to the belief, as expressed by Murray Edelman in *The Symbolic Uses of Politics*, that the masses must be content with "symbolic" satisfaction and that the vote is little more than a symbolic action providing psychological satisfaction to the voter but hardly affecting the distribution of "political goods." This is to see the activities of politics as little more than powerful associations reaching equilibrium by some automatic procedure or invisible hand. As Roy Macridis has pointed out, the group theory of politics cannot explain differences among groups.[3] This can only be explained in terms of other factors such as the multiple focuses of decision making, the diffusion of power, conflicting ideologies, the nature of political compromises, the party system, and the degree of consensus.

There is a wide variety and diversity of groups, though the vital characteristic of them all is, as David Truman said, some shared attitudes or interaction. Most groups have a formal structure and organization, but some are informal, such as the "Cliveden set" of British upper-class supporters of appeasement or the "Boston Mafia" of politicians of Irish background. Some are temporary bodies organized to fulfill one specific purpose and disbanded when that is achieved unless some pretext is found for continued existence; others are permanent bodies concerned with a continuing problem or interest. Some are concerned primarily with the interests of a number of related persons; others may be interested in a general problem or issue relevant to the whole society.

Specific interest groups are concerned with a multiplicity of subjects. Some, such as employers' organizations, trade unions or farmers' groups, are essentially concerned with the economic interests of members. Some, such as associations of lawyers, teachers, or doctors, are professional bodies. A multitude of organizations bring members together because of some common interest such as automobiles, athletics, or music; sometimes their concerns are of a public nature. Groups concerned with a specific matter or objective may be, in Samuel Finer's term, "promotional" rather than "self-oriented," in that their primary interest is a particular cause.[4] These groups will be civic, social, or charitable bodies interested in matters such as penal reform, divorce reform, mental health, or better education. Groups of this kind may feel strongly enough about their issue to become involved in political action, running candidates or trying to influence public opinion.

Group activity and influence may also be studied from the perspective of particular social forces or bodies such as the military, the bureaucracy, newspaper proprietors or editors, religious leaders, or university students, who have frequently been a source for the expression of political discontent. The role of the military, for example, has been considerable in both the developed and the less developed countries. The military has not only been an important avenue for upward social mobility in Spain, Latin America, and in many of the newer nations, but it has also been a force in politics in a number of ways. Sometimes it has acted as an interest group, attempting to influence policy, debating public issues, concerning itself especially with the amount and nature of the military budget, and occasionally issuing overt or veiled threats against the regime. Sometimes, as in Turkey, its members have acted as moderators in a complex political situation or as trustees to bring stability where irreconcilable divisions existed among political groups and have helped provide a transition to a system of free parties and elections. Sometimes it has seen itself as the only skilled, honest, organized group prepared to modernize the society and to act in the interests of the whole, as in China after 1911, the Middle East, or Thailand. The army "as the vanguard of progressive action," in Kemal Ataturk's phrase, has therefore been prepared to attempt coups and set up military dictatorships. The dilemma always faced by the military is how to endow its role with legitimacy and how to convert itself into a political body or prepare for a civilian regime.

Interest Group or Party

The distinction between an *interest group* — concerned to influence decisions on a limited number of issues — and a *party*, — concerned also to put up candidates, fight elections, and hold office — is not always as easy to make in practice as in a theory. Such separation was often not possible in Weimar Germany where some parties, such as the German Farmers' party and the Coalition of Victims of Inflation, were essentially interest groups. In the present West German regime the Refugee party has acted as little more than spokesman for the refugees from the East. The Japanese Sohyo (General Council of Trade Unions) is not simply an interest group but is also part of the radical movement of the left. The Japanese Socialist party is heavily dependent on Sohyo for financial support, provision of facilities, and recruitment of candidates. Many of the delegates to the annual conventions of that party are union officials, and many party candidates for local and national elections come from the union leadership. A postwar peace movement may be expressed by an interest group such as the Campaign for Nuclear Disarmament in Britain or by a political organization like the Communist party in France. In Scandinavia and the Low Countries there is a close relationship between parties and groups. An historical link has existed between NVV, the Dutch Socialist union federation, and the Dutch Socialist party. It is not easy in Sweden to distinguish between the Social Democrats and the trade union movement. In France relations between the General Confederation of Labor and the Communist party are close both in policy matters and in overlapping leadership; a similar relationship exists in Italy between the General Confederation of Labor and the Communist party.

In Norway, as Henry Valen and Daniel Katz have shown in their study *Political Parties in Norway,* the seven political parties tend to act as interest groups or are believed to represent them, and only the Liberal party is based on ideological lines; the Anders Lange party focuses primarily on lower taxes. Sometimes organizations of officeholders, such as the Association of French Mayors, play a significant part in politics. At times a group becomes the basis for a party; the French Union for the Defense of Shopkeepers and Artisans provided the major base of the French Union of Fraternity, which it created. In Britain the Anglican Church has been called, somewhat unkindly, "the Tory party at its prayers."

A more secular interrelationship is that between the Labour party and the trade unions. The British unions provide five-sixths of the membership of the Labour party through affiliation, supply 80 percent of the central income and over half of the total income of the party, provide 96 percent of the party's general election fund, aid individual constituency associations as well as sponsor candidates for office—some 180 in 1974, of whom 143 were elected. The unions circulate party statements to their local branches for discussion and information, use their journals for discussion of party actions and programs, form district organizations as political advisory bodies, and hold joint weekend conferences with the party. At the annual conference of the British Labour party, the unions have about 85 percent of the total vote, the three largest unions together almost possessing a majority. The Transport and General Workers' Union with 1,443,000 members, the Amalgamated Engineering Union with 1,048,000, and the General and Municipal Workers' Union with 795,000 send delegates to the conference, which has representatives from 6,328,000 members. But the unions are not united in a solid front nor do they uphold any one particular political point of view against the representatives of the constituency parties. Since there is an important left-wing element in the trade unions, every important issue has divided them as it has divided the constituency parties. Of the 25 elected members of the National Executive Committee, the controlling body and administrative authority of the party, 12 are chosen by the unions who can also determine the voting of 5 of the other 13. Usually every large trade union has a representative on this central body of the party organization.

Group Effectiveness

The behavior of groups is the outcome of the demands and interests of their members. But it is also a response to the amount of state activity and the functions performed or planned by government, as well as a reflection of the degree of political participation in the community.

The effectiveness of groups in the arena of politics depends on a number of factors. It depends first on the nature and size of the group, its cohesiveness and internal unity, the degree to which it speaks for all interested in a particular function, activity or issue, the degree of its sustained organization, and the amount of interest its members have in issues that affect them. When an organization such as the Federation of British Industries suffers from internal divisions and the rivalry of other business groups, it is less successful as an interest group.

The Swedish Federation of Labor, which includes almost all wage earners, the British Medical Association, which includes 80 percent of all doctors, or the German Federal Union of German Employers Associations and Federation of German Industries, which are strong federations of business and industry, are likely to be powerful and influential groups. But Mancur Olson in his *The Logic of Collective Action* has provided the salutary warning that it does not necessarily follow from the premise of rational and self-interested behavior that individuals in large groups will necessarily act to advance the common objectives or that groups will act in their own self-interest; it is also not necessarily true that a small group is more likely to provide itself with a collective good than is a large group.

A group advocating temperance will have stronger convictions and a more intensely concerned membership than an automobile association, which chiefly provides convenient services for its members. A group that is homogeneous or whose members or supporters feel strong loyalty to it is likely to be less politically neutral than a group whose members experience cross-pressures or hold a diversity of opinions. A group that has affinity with others may obtain support by a process of mutual aid. The divisions among French interest groups between home distillers and commercial distillers, road haulage and rail transport, secular public schools and private Catholic schools, increase the number of people interested in the policy at issue but reduce the potential effectiveness of organized pressure.

The behavior and impact of groups will depend secondly on the political culture of the community. In a unified system such as that of the British interest groups will tend to be nationwide and disciplined as are the political parties. On the other hand, in Continental Europe, where a number of subcultures based on political ideologies or religious convictions exist and differing views are held on the nature of justice, interest groups tend to reflect and reinforce those divisions rather than try to broaden their appeal.

Many studies have suggested that members of groups are more likely to be politically active and informed than are nonmembers, and that members, even if passive, and organizations, even if lacking any considerable political content, still have a political impact more significant than individuals acting alone. But success of the groups may also depend on the opportunities available to them to articulate their interests, the degree of permitted freedom and tolerance in a society, and their ability to use the media of communications.

A third important variable affecting group effectiveness is the quality of leadership. Much of the value of a group may stem from its use of professional staff and agents and from its permanence or full-time activity. But equally, much may depend on the social composition of the members of the groups, the nature and background of the leaders, and their relationship with government personnel. If the leaders of groups come from similar economic and cultural backgrounds, educational institutions, or occupational bodies, or mix in the same social world as members of the political elite, they are likely to have an easy entrée into the avenues of power. Old Etonians and graduates of Oxford and Cambridge in business groups will find their counterparts in the British civil service and political offices. Engineers in the French *grands corps* will have studied at the École Polytechnique as have many industrialists with whom they are in contact. And about 15 percent of the top management of France studied at the Grandes Écoles together with top political decision makers.

A fourth factor affecting group success is the willingness of political parties to respond to the declared interests of groups and the extent to which they try to obtain support from groups by proposing policies and choosing personnel acceptable to them. The Social Committee of the German Christian Democratic Union is composed largely of Christian trade unionists and its Economic Committee largely of business representatives. Members of the legislature interested in a particular subject may sometimes be appointed to the legislative committee dealing with that subject at the urging of an interest group. Interest groups may in fact attempt to influence the choice of political personnel at many levels and in the different branches of government.

Finally, group effectiveness is contingent upon the nature of the political system, the number and nature of activities performed, the structure of government, and the organs and personnel capable of making decisions. Where the locus of power in the regime is in the executive and the administration, as in Britain, interest groups concentrate more on influencing the administrative organization than on the legislature. Thus in recent years the British National Union of Teachers noticeably transferred its attention from a mixed concern with Parliament, public opinion, and the Ministry of Education almost wholly to the last, as well as engaging in more militant behavior. Efforts of groups may even concentrate on the more friendly opposition party, which they anticipate will gain power in the future; the British Road Haulage Association did this when it tried to influence Conservative policy on road services in 1948. In the United States where the power of the executive branch is not always so striking and its internal coherence or discipline not always so great, groups will be more active at both the legislative and electoral levels. Similarly, in the

French Fourth Republic groups actively cultivated individual deputies because of the power of parliamentarians over the legislative process, and influenced the choice of members of legislative committees. The existence of unstable coalitions and fluctuating party representation in those coalitions provided an additional opportunity for groups to influence the choice of members of the government. Not surprisingly for the Gaullist Michel Debré, the key figures in French interest groups were seen as among the "princes" governing the Fourth Republic.[5] The shift in the locus of power in the French Fifth Republic from the legislature to the executive has meant that groups have concentrated to a much greater degree on influencing the latter branch, including the ministerial *cabinet*, composed of civil servants and personal advisers, the body assisting the minister in his official activity.

In nondemocratic systems, groups perform functions different from that of articulating interests, which is their primary function in democratic systems. Zbigniew Brzezinski and Samuel Huntington, in their *Political Power: USA/USSR*, speak of the existence of social forces such as the demands of workers and peasants, the presence of various groups — workers, peasants, intellectuals, and scientists, — and the impact of groups concerned with policy matters such as the military, heavy and light industrial managers, agricultural managers, and state bureaucrats. In addition, struggles both for control of power in the party, state, and army, and over policy making have occurred between different party factions, central and regional party bodies, central and regional ministries and officials, groups of officials, different occupational groups, and different nationalities. In the Soviet Union, as in democratic systems, many groups exist that make claims on other groups in the society, and through and on the institutions of government.

The Activities of Groups

Political decisions and the achievement of political harmony and relative equilibrium result from tension among the common interests, the centripetal forces of political institutions, and the centrifugal forces of interest groups. These groups will participate in the process by which politicians, civil servants, or even the judiciary influence or resolve issues. Their methods of participation vary from the crass and venal to an impersonal concern with the public welfare as a whole.

At one extreme is the method of bribery or covert corruption. The bribery of politicians by foreign business as in Japan, Holland, and Italy, where American manufacturers have tried to sell their planes and equipment, is an example. More open or legitimate methods include direct monetary contributions, subsidies, or aid to legislators. Politicians or civil servants may be found lucrative jobs in industry later in their careers. British trade unions subsidize members of Parliament, sponsor candidates, or contribute to party funds; business organizations dangle lucrative directorships. The Italian farmers' federation, the *Federconsorzi*, has subsidized the Christian Democratic party and is said to influence some 200 parliamentary votes. Parliamentarians may be members of or hold office in an interest group and may therefore concern themselves with the subjects in which the groups are interested. In Sweden some leaders of interest groups expect to become government officials such as governors of provinces or directors of central administrative bodies later in their careers.

Groups may also play an indispensible role in a political system by providing decision makers with information, writing memoranda, or collecting statistics. Indeed, the very proposals made by government personnel may depend on the information provided by interest groups to members of both the legislative and executive branches. Groups employ lobbyists who not only scrutinize all proposals affecting their interests but also obtain access to deputies, especially those who are on special committees dealing with those interests. Groups are consulted on government legislation and administration regulations, providing aid in the formulation, drafting, and amending of rules. At the preliminary stage of proposals they may give advice in hearings of legislative committees, as in the United States. Groups provide members of governmental advisory bodies, commissions, or inquiries, as in Britain where there are some thousands and in France where some two thousand committees obtain advice from group representatives. The number and significance of these advisory groups have raised the question of whether interest groups have in fact become responsible for a major part of administrative policy.

These advisory bodies are even more significant when their advice is normally accepted; in the French Fourth Republic the Service des Alcools, which fixed the amount and price of alcohol bought by the state, often accepted the advice of its advisory council, and in Canada advisory groups have frequently amended existing policies. Again in the French Fourth Republic, bodies set up to study problems were frequently places where organized interests could meet with and influence legislators. Groups may be represented, either directly or indirectly, on economic councils composed of experts from different areas of economic and social life; such councils provide advice to the executive or legislature or participate in the dissection of legislation and rules.

Another way groups participate is by mounting campaigns appealing to public opinion or holding demonstrations publicizing their views. This is sometimes done by groups advocating some social reform or reacting to some specific contentious political issue. But it is rarely true of groups interested in their own particular welfare, except in some unusual circumstance such as a threat of nationalization, which can be opposed as an attack on the right of private property.

Rather than mount an elaborate public campaign, groups usually seek to influence those governmental and nongovernmental persons, such as editors and columnists, whom they consider to be most important or relevant to their particular interest. The corollary of this concern with the political elite rather than with the public as a whole is that the interest groups may be regarded by government as the major "public" to be taken into account in the framing of policy. For example the German Soldiers' League, composed for former professional soldiers, has greatly influenced the selection of officers.

Groups may even be strong enough to dominate or control the decision-making process, as did the alcohol groups in France when they virtually imposed a veto on certain aspects of governmental agricultural policy. The Histadrut in Israel, the powerful trade union movement, plays an important role in both the economy and politics of the country.[6] And in postwar Austria opposition to proposed legislation by a major interest group in commerce, labor, or agriculture has frequently been regarded as a veto.

Governmental activities are often unworkable without the aid or cooperation of groups. To be successful the British National Health Service needed the assistance of British medical groups. The British Coal Owners Association helped draft the statute nationalizing the coal industry when it became aware of the inevitability of the legislation. Part of the political and economic stability in Sweden has been attributed to the 1938 agreement between the federation of employers and the major trade union organization, which contains the vast majority of trade union members. Unions in some countries not only engage in collective bargaining and mediation of labor conflicts but also play a large role in running the welfare programs of the nation. The German economic chambers perform some governmental activity such as granting licenses to businesspeople, shopkeepers, and artisans. In a corporate system, such as Portugal prior to 1974 or fascist Italy, groups have played a vital part in the management of affairs.

But a major problem stemming from the activity of interest groups is that they benefit only the organized and active. In *The Semi-Sovereign People* Elmer Schattschneider has argued that the "major flaw in the pluralist heaven is that the heavenly chorus sings with a strong upper class accent."[7] The mass of people, neglected by groups, can only be taken into account by the existence and effective functioning of a competitive party system.

A more recent criticism of pluralistic politics and of the view that the public good results from competition among private interests argues that American pluralism, whether termed creative federalism or countervailing-power relationship, has led not to coherent and direct federal control but to the parceling out of the power to make public policy to private parties. In this view interest groups have determined government policies in many areas: farm groups have fixed Agriculture Department policies, timber interests those of the Interior Department, and local developers the decisions of the Army Corps of Engineers. To counter and control this power of groups, Theodore Lowi argues there is a need for central government to exert its authority.[8]

Political Parties

Political parties are the major bodies through which political action occurs in developed and in most undeveloped systems. A country like Ethiopia in which no party organizations have yet appeared and where traditional structures continued until 1974 under the control of the ruler is now exceptional. Factions have existed since the days of Byzantium, and historians are familiar with the Renaissance division between the Florentine Whites representing the merchant class and the Blacks representing the nobility, and in literature between the Montagues and Capulets with their cliques and cabals. Equally familiar is the struggle between the Guelfs and the Ghibellines, the former wearing red roses, cutting their fruit straight down, and wearing feathers in their caps on one side, while the latter wore feathers on the other side of their caps, cut their fruit crossways and wore white roses. But organized and permanent parties are relatively new. In the eighteenth century the Earl of Halifax regarded parties as composed of low and insignificant men, George Washington spoke of their "baneful effects," and John Adams saw them as dividing the nation.[9] Many regretted with Oliver Goldsmith that Edmund Burke had given up to party what was meant for humankind. In authoritarian countries such as Franco's Spain parties were regarded as undesirable and no one could participate in the state through the mediation of a political party. Only since Franco's death in 1976 have parties been legalized, and then only if they are regarded by the government as neither subversive nor destructive of the political or social order. In neighboring Portugal parties were equally undesirable, and under the Salazar regime the government was supposedly guided by "the historic tradition of the Portuguese nation, and by the Christian conception of life and the family."

Only rarely has the constitution of a country taken account of the existence of parties. West Germany, Czechoslovakia, and Yugoslavia are examples. The West German constitution formally recognizes them and says they form "the political will of the people." The Czechoslovak Communist party is defined as "the leading force in state and society. In Yugoslavia the Communist party, because of its guiding ideology and political work, is declared the fundamental initiator of political activity.

In democratic countries governments have increasingly been regulating party electoral behavior and activity. In the United States, state and local governments regulate the nominating and election processes for party candidates. State laws govern the selection of party candidates by primaries or conventions and the conduct of elections. In a number of countries such as Sweden, Italy, Britain, and West Germany, the government contributes to the expenses of the parties, either to help their electoral campaigns or to assist them to perform their parliamentary functions. Some countries allow parties free broadcasts on radio and television during election campaigns and at regular intervals between elections, the amount of time allotted a party being roughly proportional to the support obtained at the previous general election.

Countries may also impose limits on the campaign spending of parties, either strictly as in Britain or more generously as in the United States. Though American congressional campaigns are not supported by public funds and there is no limit on total spending by a party candidate, there are now legal limits of $1,000 per individual supporter and $5,000 for each political committee. Under new rules federal funds helped finance the 1976 presidential campaign.

A political party is notoriously difficult to define accurately. It is not always easy to differentiate it from a faction, an interest group, a parliamentary group that may have a life of its own independent of electoral opinion (as in France), or from a political movement that may temporarily transcend a number of parties or groups (e.g., the Rally of the French People in France, the Rassemblement Démocratique Africaine, the National Union of Popular Forces in Morocco, and the National Front in a number of systems.)

The French political clubs, composed of intellectuals and civil servants, which started in the Fifth Republic, provided a new avenue of political expression outside of the old political parties, and attempted to influence informed opinion on the desirable policies and sometimes on the choice of candidates. The case of the All German Bloc, a party created to protect the interests of refugees from East Germany which largely disappeared in 1957 when the refugee problem was removed from politics, is an illustration of the difficulty of distinguishing precisely between parties and interest groups.

Essentially party signifies a group of people who hold certain political beliefs in common or who are prepared to support the party candidates, work together for electoral victory, attain and maintain political power. All party struggles, as Max Weber has said, are struggles for office as well as for objective goals, and there are a variety of incentives leading to association with a party.[10] Frank Sorauf, in his *Political Parties in the American System*, suggests seven such incentives: (1) patronage, (2) obtaining special treatment by the government, (3) career opportunities, (4) economic benefit, (5) personal rewards, (6) ability to wield influence, and (7) ideological gratification.

Some parties may be defined in terms of common convictions as with Communist or Socialist parties; some exist largely to win elections. Some coincide with economic class to a large degree, as do labor, agrarian, or conservative parties. Some are associated with a religious faith; the Popular Republican Movement in France, the Christian Democrats in Italy and Germany, the Christian People's party in Norway, three different Protestant parties and a Catholic party in Holland, Moslem groups, the Syrian Arab Resurrection party, the Jan Sangh in India, and Komei-to, the political arm of Soka Gakkai in Japan, are examples. Some depend on ethnic or racial connection, as does the Tamil Federal party in Sri Lanka, or the two major parties in Guyana—the People's Progressive party, which is largely confined to East Indians, and the People's National Congress, which is largely composed of blacks. Some, like the Scottish National Party, are based on nationalism; others, like the Flemish Nationalists in Belgium, rest on language, or on historical association, as did the Radical party in France or on caste, as in India where the lines of Hindu caste have largely coincided with factions in the towering Congress party. Some, like the Mapai in Israel, began not as a cohesive body but as a confederation of economic, political, and ideological groups. Some, like the Liberal Party of Australia, are a composite of several distinct state parties. Some are particularly related or are strong in certain parts of the country as were the Dixiecrats in the South of the United States, the Liberals in Wales and Scotland, and the Democratic Labor party in the Australian state of Victoria. Some are held together by a clique, an attractive leader, or by patronage. Examples are Maurice Duplessis and the Union Nationale in Quebec, Bandaranaike in Sri Lanka, or Magsaysay in the Philippines. Some serve largely as a receptacle for those disenchanted by other major parties, as with the Social Credit party in Canada.

Definition of membership in a political party is equally varied, from the Leninist conception of a member as one who supports the program of the party and participates in a party organization under the control of the center, to the view of a member as merely a normal voter for the party. In Burma the military-led Lanzin party in 1966 had only 20 members but 99,000 candidates and 167,000 sympathizers. With delicate nuance, postwar Germany prefers to regard an individual who joined the Nazi party because of pressure put on him as a *"Mitlaufer,"* a follower or a nominal rather than a true Nazi. Membership in most parties is direct, but some parties also provide for indirect membership, especially through trade unions or youth organizations; indeed, most of a party's strength may come in this way, as in the British Labour party, where trade union affiliation constitutes five-sixths of the membership.

Functions of Parties

Parties can perform certain invaluable functions in political systems.

They are the chief mechanism of informing and influencing the electorate, linking together the electoral areas of the nation, and allowing public opinion to be made known through a choice of candidates or policy. The opportunity for opinion to be expressed in this way is more functional to a system than having political change produced by a revolution or coup d'etat, which may be the only alternative in nondemocratic regimes.

Parties are the chief means by which candidates can be selected and a campaign run. Other groups, such as business associations, labor unions, or cooperative societies, may sometimes sponsor candidates, but this will only be an incidental part of their activity, which is primarily concerned with other matters. Nominations are of crucial significance, for even in democratic regimes nomination may be equivalent to election in a considerable number of constituencies. Local party activists who largely control the nominating procedures will thus determine the composition of the parliamentary party. Primary elections within a party to choose its candidates allow the different factions an opportunity to be heard and test their strength.

Parties serve as "brokers of ideas"[11] by selecting a certain number of the countless issues confronting a society in some order of priority and focusing attention on them in campaigns and elections, thus fixing the battleground for the political troops. They may serve as spokesmen for the divisive elements in a society, but they may also act as unifying elements in emphasizing common interests, aggregating wants, and attempting to conciliate the maximum number of citizens. In many developing countries there has been little continuous attachment of either voters or politicians to parties that cannot be regarded as aggregators of interests. In India this function is still performed in part by castes and village and small-city groups, which may be based on family alliances.

Though political leadership may be derived from many sources — the military, bureaucracy, religious organization, hereditary succession, and so on — parties are the major source for providing such leadership in developed and often also in developing nations. The leaders of the successful or majority party will normally become responsible for the conduct of governmental affairs and policy making, and party inevitably becomes linked with the governmental apparatus, in both democratic and nondemocratic systems.

Parties may take on an independent existence of their own, with a hold on the habits and emotions of adherents that is irrespective of candidates or issues to a large degree. Party becomes, in Graham Wallas' words, "an entity with an existence in the memory and emotions of the electorate, independent of their own opinion and actions."[12] Voting studies in a number of developed countries have shown that the strongest determinant of future electoral behavior is the party identification of an individual.[13]

In a democratic system revolutionary parties — those opposing the established order as such — act not as conciliatory elements in aggregating the largest number of common interests but as focal points of discontent and organized opposition. They often refuse to agree to the compromises required in democratic behavior. These parties may adhere to the political left, as do the Communist parties; to the right, as did the Nazi parties or the Poujadists in France; or to revolutionary nationalism as with the Aprista in Peru, the Revolutionary Nationalist Movement in Bolivia, or the Acción Democratica in Venezuela. In a nondemocratic system, revolutionary parties may be not simply the mechanism through which the political system operates, but the real core of the system itself, with power being exercised by party leaders rather than by governmental officials.

In those newer nations without any firm political habits or traditions, the party may be the chief force for modernization, shaping the government, providing the main link among the different social and economic groups, constituting the chief agency for political education and socialization, breaking down traditional behavior, and acting as the binding force in communities divided by groups based on tribal affiliation, religious denomination, or national origin. Some Latin American parties also act as a unifying element in their societies; the Latin American Popular Revolutionary Alliance party in Peru with its sustained organization including barber shops, soccer teams, and cafeterias is an example.

Democratic parties are not central to the life of citizens. But frequently they engage in nonpolitical activities, as in Sweden where a party may be connected with leisure activities or the boy scout movement, or in the Netherlands where there is a Catholic Goat Breeding Association. In Austria citizens may live their lives, from cradle to grave, within the frame of party-linked organizations, which include not only trade union and welfare groups but also stamp collecting societies, pigeon clubs, and weight-lifting associations; in the United States old-time bosses of the Democratic party were often the chief agencies of social welfare. But these activities are peripheral to the central concern and activity of democratic parties.

Nondemocratic parties or parties controlling a nondemocratic system are more likely to interest themselves in social, cultural, and moral matters as well as political ones, and to be highly disciplined, ideologically oriented, militant in behavior, and periodically engaged in purges of party members and leaders. The most familiar party of this type is the Communist party of the Soviet Union, which is the only party permitted, and which, according to the constitution, is "the vanguard of the working peoples" and "leading core of all organizations of the working peoples, both public and state." Its strict discipline is based on democratic centralism. But real power in the party and state is in the hands of the members of the party Secretariat and Politburo. The party controls the process of socialization and indoctrination from childhood on with a series of party units—the Little Octobrists, Young Pioneers, and League of Communist Youth—and with domination over the mass media, propaganda, the school system, manipulation of employment for the faithful and the dissident, and, in varying degrees of intensity, with terror. Membership in the party is regarded as a privilege, achieved, after a period of probation, by adherence to party rules in both public and private behavior.

Ideological Parties

Few today would accept as universally true the definition of party given by Burke: "a body of men united for promoting by their joint endeavors the national interest, upon some particular principle on which they are all agreed." Ideological parties most closely correspond to this definition because they are committed to a cause, to a set of interrelated beliefs and values, and to the implementation of some fundamental concept. In the post–World War II period in the Western world ideological beliefs were seemingly reduced in intensity with the increase in economic affluence and the decline in political tension, but the problems of Vietnam, Watergate, urban areas, race relationships, economic recession and inflation, and ecology have tended to ignite ideological fervor once again.[14] Parties, however, are less rigid in their commitment to and support of ideological concepts. They have become more solicitous about the interests of groups whose support they are attempting to attract and on which they may depend for information and advice. Nevertheless, ideological parties are present in democratic as well as in nondemocratic systems, primarily to urge social change to foster political nationalism.

Probably the most widespread and inflammatory contemporary ideology is *nationalism*.[15] It arises from the view that the world is divided into nations, that there is a bond of fraternity, a feeling of identity and cohesion, and a sense of identification among individuals who compose a unit called the nation, which is larger than a clan, tribe, or group of tribes; it also supposes that one's chief loyalty is owed to that particular nation. The bond may be based on different criteria: a common history or memories, geography, language, race, religion, ethnicity, culture, national character, habit, or manifest destiny.

Politically nationalism requires that a nation express its self-determination by the creation or enhancement of a state endowed with sovereignty, with a territory, and with governmental institutions of its own, distinct from those of other states. Nationalism has accompanied the rise of democracy in the eighteenth and nineteenth centuries, been the expression of the sovereignty of the people, unified peoples in the nineteenth and twentieth centuries and been the basis for mobilization of the people, and provided a new political religion in the newer nations. A nationalist party has functioned in many ways: as unifying forces of disparate parts of a nation, as the maintainer of a state threatened internally or externally, as movement for independence against a ruler regarded as foreign or oppressive, as liberating force against colonialism, and as force for external aggrandizement, economic protection, irredentism, or imperialism.

Nationalism is present in all parts of the world and in nations at different stages of development.[16] The Communist systems, theoretically believing in the brotherhood of the human race, have not escaped national rivalries; Rumania, for example, claiming north Bukovina and Bessarabia from the Soviet Union, while Transylvania is claimed by Hungary and the Dobruja area by Bulgaria.

Left and Right

Parties advocating political and social change run in a spectrum from left to right. The ideological left-right metaphor results from the arrangement in a semicircular hall of representatives according to their self-determined place in the political spectrum in the French Council of 500 established in 1798. The terms "left" and "right" still allow people and parties to place themselves in a contemporary spectrum, suggesting a general thrust and direction rather than specific policies.

In Britain the left would be those members of the Labour party advocating the nationalization of the means of production, greater spending on social services, and high progressive taxation. The centrist Liberals call for decentralization and individualism and also humane social laws. On the right the Conservatives want a reduced income tax and oppose any further nationalization but would not automatically denationalize those enterprises already under public control or dismantle the national health service and public building programs.

In France, where *sinistrisme,* or leftism, has a strong emotional penumbra, the "leftist" is a revolutionary critical of the Communist party, which has seemed to endorse a common platform and political relationship with the Socialist party. The right includes social reformers as well as conservatives. In West Germany the party of the left, the Social Democrats, does not contemplate further nationalization but has extended the principle of worker determination in industry. In Sweden the left wants controls of industry through ownership of capital by labor groups and approximate equality of incomes through high taxes; the right accepts the social system but calls for incentives for private business and for lower taxes, and criticizes bureaucracy. A noticeable characteristic of European right-wing parties is that their title rarely reveals terms like "center" or "democratic" or "republican" to portray themselves. The most conservative party in Portugal in 1974, for example, was the Center for Democratic Socialism, and the name of the Danish right-wing Liberal party is Venstre (left).

Parties of the Right

There are today few important and permanent groups believing in a right-wing ideology. In the prewar period, fascist or Nazi parties, or like-minded bodies such as the Iron Guard in Rumania, the Arrow Cross in Hungary, and the Endek party in Poland, attracted substantial support by their violent anticommunism and by their appeal to those distressed by the decline of traditional values and authorities, political disorder, or national humiliation. Oversimplifying political issues, these parties appealed to the emotions of race, blood, or nation, directing these feelings against individual or national scapegoats, and were prepared to use ruthless methods to attain their ends. Thirty years after the war, neo-Nazi groups have remained small in Germany, Austria, and Italy. France has seen the rise and disappearance of right-wing groups such as the Poujadist movement. In Norway the right-wing Christian party draws its strength from the backward areas of the country; in Belgium the Walloon Popular Movement arose largely to protest against the closing of marginal coal mines. The Japanese right wing has little intellectual content but has stressed action and violence, militarism and imperialism. The Jan Sangh in India has emphasized those concepts familiar in fascism: the leader principle, racial or cultural superiority, an aggressive nationalism, symbols of greatness, national solidarity, and the exclusion of religious or ethnic minorities from membership of the nation; one particular interest of the party is the protection of the holy cow.

More frequently the right-wing parties are traditional and moderate conservative organizations that accept the existing political institutions, economic system, authority structure, prevailing beliefs, and inequalities and privileges, advocate order and stability, and do not equate change with progress. In the contemporary world they accept the liberal consensus and support policies for full employment, a welfare state and social services, and redistributive taxation. Probably the most successful of these has been the British Conservative party, which has been in office 66 years in the last 100.[17] Of its 13 million voters, 54 percent come from the working class as do 30 percent of the one and a quarter million working members of the party; only one member of the working class, however, is a Conservative Member of Parliament.

Parties of the Left: Socialist Parties

The heritage of the left has been split over a number of issues, especially on whether the movement should be primarily syndicalist and interested in working conditions or involved in parliamentary and political activity, and on the desirability of revolution. Since the Russian Revolution of 1917 the major split in the left has been between the Communist parties, primarily faithful to the views and policies of the Soviet Union—at least until recent years—and Social Democratic groups concerned with social reform rather than revolution, and considerably less prepared to support the activities of the Soviet Union.

The fate of Socialist parties in postwar Western Europe has been a mixed one; they have had some victories in Scandinavia and in England but also political defeats in these countries and in France and Italy as well. The French Socialist party may be able to supplant the Communist party as the major left-wing force, but its Italian counterpart has been unsuccessful. Religious inhibitions, especially among Catholic voters, have been overcome by Socialists in West Germany but to a lesser extent in Holland and Belgium. Social Democracy remains a dominant political force in contemporary Western Europe. By 1975 Socialist parties had obtained first place in 10 of the 15 most recent elections in those countries that have free elections—though only in Austria did one receive over 50 percent of the vote—and Socialists in that year occupied 125 of the 231 cabinet positions compared with 69 of the 206 positions in 1955.

The basis of socialism has been opposition to capitalism, both as revulsion against the inhumanity of the industrial system and as criticism of its waste and inefficiency; it has appealed to all those wanting a fundamental change in the structure and nature of society. Not surprisingly, the question has been asked if a political ideology protesting against the evils of nineteenth-century industrial society is still meaningful in a society characterized by a desire to obtain full employment, minimum wage policies, social welfare programs, and some regulation of wages and prices.[18] Socialists no longer naively believe that society is divided into two major hostile groups whose antagonism will inevitably increase with time. Some Socialists may consider themselves Marxists, but almost all are social democratic in outlook favoring mixed economies, the rule of law, and fundamental freedom.

Socialist parties have been perplexed by a number of factors. Many of the proposals for social change have been implemented by nonsocialist governments. Relations with Communist parties and appeals to *"sinistrisme"* have varied in warmth. To some extent there has been a north-south split among European Socialist parties on this issue. Most of the northern parties tend to see all forms of communism, no matter how revisionist they may seem, as Stalinist in reality and regard proposals for socialist-communist alliances, made since the original "popular front" proposed in 1935 by Georgi Dimitrov, then Secretary of the Comintern, as likely to lead to communist domination. In the southern countries, still in transition to fully industrialized societies, with large Communist parties and a labor movement influenced by those parties, there is a greater belief that Communist parties are changing in character and are prepared to abide by the rules of a pluralistic political system. The need to win votes and elections has resulted in heterogeneous political appeals and a reorientation of programs. The major source of socialist strength comes from trade unionists and their families, but only in Sweden do they constitute an absolute majority of the electorate. Socialism is a good example of Charles Péguy's maxim of the change from *mystique* to *politique* when politicians seek to translate their ideals into practice.[19]

In Sweden socialist doctrine was increasingly qualified until in 1944 the party declared that socialization was not an imperative doctrine. The German Social Democratic party in 1959 radically revised its basic program, declared that free enterprise and free competition were essential features of a socialist economic policy, and proclaimed that it was the "party of the people" rather than the party of the working class and that its members could hold differing beliefs and ideas. Similarly other Socialist parties have renounced adherence to old fundamental doctrine. The Dutch Socialist party renamed itself "The Party of Labor." In addition, French and Italian Socialist parties, because of their lack of a parliamentary majority, have the problem of deciding whether to participate in coalition governments with nonsocialists or to remain intransigently outside of the governing process.

Yet socialism remains as a symbol, as an invitation to a crusade, as a concern for the poor, as a deeply emotional experience, as a fellowship to create a new society, the informing characteristic of which would be economic, social, and moral equality, the reduction or elimination of privilege, and a brotherhood that nonsocialist systems cannot provide. Inequality remains in existence externally as well as internally, and special problems arose for Western Socialist parties when, like the French in Algeria, the Dutch in the East Indies, and the British in East Africa, they were obliged to act as colonial governments and maintain law and order, and realized that the international solidarity of the working class is a fragile and tenuous concept.

Though the premise of socialist doctrine is the possibility of the rational control of environment and the use of land and a deliberate choice of economic priorities, profound differences exist among adherents over the nature and degree of public ownership of resources. Moreover, the fear of statism, of the abuse of power, and the fear that the exercise of power may lead not to social justice but to inhumanity and to greater stratification haunts socialists who, in any case, approach the exercise of power with considerably more reservation than do their opponents. All systems, developed and developing, plan to some degree. To favor planning is not necessarily to be a socialist, because all countries desiring higher production, social security, fairer distribution of income and property, and a favorable balance of trade will plan.[20] It is not surprising that the loudest call for socialist ideas or aims now comes from the newer nations whose major ideology is nationalism and a stress on national unity.[21]

In Latin America populist movements have often seemed to exist as substitutes for socialist organizations. Usually led by members of the middle class, the military, intellectuals, or by charismatic leaders such as Juan Perón in Argentina, Getulio Vargas in Brazil, and Haya de la Torre in Peru, these movements have had a popular mass base, often urban inhabitants who have recently been removed from their rural background. Nationalist, usually anti-American, and sometimes violent in direct action, the strength of populist movements has resulted from the absence of a strong organization of the left. But they rarely contain any coherent doctrine or ideology. Inevitably the movements become less extreme if they capture power and introduce considerably less change in economic and political conditions than the mass supporters had originally anticipated.

Communist Parties

The strongest modern ideological appeal, other than that of nationalism, is that of the Communist parties. Often they have been able to claim the heritage of "leftism" and the revolutionary mythology; in France those departments voting Communist today are those which voted left in 1849.

All Communist parties are organized in the same fashion, with centralized leadership and vertical communication from the Politburo and Central Committee down through regional, sectional, and local organizations to factory and neighborhood cells that are based on occupational or geographical factors and that recruit members, engage in militant agitation, and elect members to the higher party levels. The principle of "democratic centralism" insures that all will accept a decision once it has been made. For the member the party is a community and a way of life in which he or she participates. To the highly disciplined and militant political organization are always connected a whole variety of front organizations, party schools, and frequently parts of the union movement. But the leaders of Communist parties have remained those who control the central party organization. This control has often lasted unusually long periods as it did with Maurice Thorez "the son of the people" in France for 34 years, Palmiro Togliatti in Italy for 38 years, and Palme Dutt in England for over 30 years. In power the leader has been virtually unrestrained. This is clear in the case of Joseph Stalin, who controlled all avenues of political power, and equally clear in the case of Mao Tse-tung, who for 30 years dominated all party organizations and bypassed them at will, working through other groups, especially the army, to maintain his control.

In Western Europe, where there are 23 Communist parties with about 2 million members, the French and Italian parties are the most important examples of strong, highly organized, disciplined, and well-financed parties. The French party, with a membership of half a million and with 23,000 cells, has regularly gained about 20 percent of the vote at national elections. Essentially Stalinist in nature until

recently, interpretations of its role have varied between that of revolutionary vanguard and counter-community to that of popular tribune,
government party, and participator in coalitions.[22] The Italian party—
with over 1.5 million members, some 40,000 cells, 50,000 officials, agricultural cooperatives, national, regional, and factory newspapers and
magazines, publishing houses, movie, real estate, and business interests—is a particularly powerful force, sharing in the governing of over
1,000 communes, controlling 6 regions and 40 of the 92 provinces
and obtaining 34.4 percent of the vote and 228 out of 630 deputies,
and 33.8 percent of the vote and 116 out of 315 senators in the 1976
elections. In 1976 a Communist became speaker of the Chamber of
Deputies, and some others became committee chairmen. The party at-
tracts support from a wide variety of groups and all geographical
areas, using appeals of different kinds, sometimes exploiting the discontent caused by specific domestic problems, sometimes trading on
national traditions, urging the socialization of the means of production yet also defending the rights of the small farmer, evoking the
past revolutionary glories but also appealing to the future, attracting
large numbers of intellectuals but using them chiefly for their prestige
or to sign appeals.

Tactically, Communist parties have used parliaments as places for
propaganda rather than for serious policy proposals, and parliamentary representatives have been under strict control of the leaders.
They have been prepared to enter the government when it suited
them, as the Italian party did from April 1944 until May 1947. But
the strength of parties such as the French and Italian have helped
produce government paralysis. The policies of other parties have been
partly determined by the Communist threat, in the substantive policies
they propose, in the changing of electoral laws, and in the government coalitions formed.

Yet disciplined though the Communist parties are, this has not prevented the emergence of factional and doctrinal disputes, often between the older and younger generations. Differences occur over internal policies, relations with the Soviet Union and with China, the
changing atmosphere of the Cold War, collective leadership and party
democracy, and alternative tactical positions on government coalitions
or electoral alliances with other parties. Western Communist parties
have proposed joint actions with Socialist and even Christian Democratic parties, claiming that their intention is to achieve power
through parliamentary means and avowing they will respect the tradi-

tional freedoms and existence of other parties. This course has been urged most strongly by the Italian party, based on the views of Antonio Gramsci, the founder of the party; the objective of the party according to Gramsci, is "the dominance of the working class" not the "dictatorship of the proletariat," and this view has been supported by the late leader Togliatti's advocacy of "a national road to socialism." A contrary position is that expounded by theorists like Frantz Fanon, Régis Debray, and Herbert Marcuse and groups influenced by them who challenge the existing Communist parties, discount the revolutionary potential of the working class, which they regard as upholding the existing system, and argue that other groups, such as the peasants, *lumpen proletariat,* and students, will spontaneously produce the revolution.[23]

The Communist movement has become increasingly divided by the issue of polycentrism and the possibility of emancipation from domination by Moscow. Splits in the movement had occurred in the past: in 1903 between Bolsheviks and Mensheviks, after 1917 over the Russian Revolution, and between Stalinists and Trotskyists. But until World War II for all Communist parties the needs of the Soviet Union took precedence over national needs and policy. The example of Yugoslavia in defying Soviet policy, the revelations about the tyrannical, paranoic behavior of Stalin by Nikita Khrushchev in 1956, the emergence of a powerful Communist China as a challenge to the Soviet Union's hegemony of the Communist movement, the independence of Rumania in international affairs, and the increasing nationalism in Eastern Europe all encouraged the concept of *polycentrism,* the view that Communist parties should be relatively independent and autonomous bodies not controlled by the Soviet Union or China. Communist parties have increasingly accepted this position, opposing Soviet hegemony and refusing to recognize Moscow's "guiding role." The Italian party has even proposed "Eurocommunism," a bloc of parties within Western Europe and the North Atlantic Treaty Organization. The Soviet invasion of Czechoslovakia in 1968 was condemned by a number of Communist parties, East and West, which rejected the Soviet argument that it intervened on the grounds of "proletarian internationalism." Younger Communist party leaders, who do not have the same unconditional loyalty that their predecessors had to the Soviet Union, have been disturbed by the revelations of labor camps and mental institutions for dissenters in Russia. Increased trade between Eastern Europe and the West has also meant loosening of ties to Moscow and the Council for Mutual Economic Assistance (Comecom) trading bloc.

Christian Democracy

After the French Revolution social reform movements developed outside the structure of the church and often remained opposed to the Christian religion. In the nineteenth and early twentieth centuries social Christian movements remained small and rarely received support from the ecclesiastical hierarchy.

Christian Democracy emerged as a major political force in Continental European politics in the postwar period.[24] Based on allegiance to the principles of Christianity, on the philosophy of "personalism," and on the autonomy of the family, community, and classes against state centralization, it appealed to a variety of groups, none of which has wholly agreed with the program of a Christian Democratic party. Following the lines of the papal encyclical *Quadragesimo anno* of 1931, which proposed corporate organizations in industry and the professions instead of class conflict, Christian Democracy favored the creation of economic and social committees and works councils. In actual practice it has embraced a wide difference of political opinions and positions; the Italian party has split into a number of factions, political and personal. Its strongest support has come from women and older people.

Though Christian Democracy emerged as a religiously oriented force prepared to support social and economic reform to a greater degree than religious organizations had hitherto done, its lack of a coherent, systematic policy, apart from support of religious education, precludes it from being regarded as a major ideological trend. The dilemma for a Christian Democratic party was shown by the fate of the Popular Republican Movement (MRP). It gradually evolved from an ideological social reform group to a center party interested in office during the life of the French Fourth and Fifth Republics until its formal dissolution in 1967.

In most countries—Germany, Austria, France, the Benelux nations, and Italy—the role of the Christian Democratic parties has declined or become more difficult for a variety of reasons. They have not been able to increase their base of support; the distinctiveness of Catholic social thinking has declined; the non-Catholic parties have deemphasized anticlericalism; the climate of opinion resulting from the Vatican Council of 1962–1965 made change more acceptable; the hold of the Roman Catholic Church on women as they become more liberated has lessened, and issues such as divorce, abortion, and contraception have risen; the influence of the parties over Catholic unions such as the Confederation of Italian Workers' Trades Unions has been reduced; and finally, after 30 years in power, the parties have set a poor example. The Christian Democrats' image is that of a party of barons and factions, built on patronage, that attempt to accommodate all groups and interests. This is tainted by corruption; they have been held responsible for economic difficulties and mismanagement and for lack of social reform, and they only just managed to fight off the Communist party's challenge by obtaining a plurality of votes and seats in the 1976 election.

Party Organization

For some analysts, comparative discussion of different party ideologies is less significant than differences in organization and structure. Maurice Duverger, in his *Political Parties,* and others have envisaged three chief possible types of party organization: the clique, the mass party, and small dedicated extremist party. Each of these deserves some comment.

The Clique

The party as an aristocratic clique with politics thus revolving around shifting personal alliances and groups was common in the era when the franchise was limited. It was the typical situation in Britain between 1689 and 1832; even at the end of the nineteenth century the Liberal party was still dominated by the aristocratic Whigs who controlled the Cabinet. Similar relationships may exist in less developed systems such as Iran, where politics is largely based on family and social ties, and in the newer nations, where parties may remain largely a collection of politicians without any significant organization. Parties can therefore fragment or dissolve on an important dispute on policy or personality. The dismissal of Khwaja Nazimuddin in 1953 split the Pakistan Muslim League and the dismissal of Solomon Bandaranaike in 1952 led to the defeat of the Ceylonese United National party.

In the developed countries, this type of party—the "cadre" party or "party of individual representation" as Sigmund Neumann called it—may consist of a group of important figures influential in the local areas of the country. It will be small, decentralized, lacking in discipline and cohesion, both inside the legislative body and in the country as a whole; it will have no real program or ideology and will be held together by the scent of political office. France in particular has had a large number of center parties of this type; the prototype is the Radical party, which was split into at least six factional groups all competing for power, and all available to hold office.[25] In the Fourth Republic, between 1946 and 1958, 9 of the 21 prime ministers were Radical Socialists.

The Mass Party

The increasing extension of the suffrage and the effect of class divisions led to the rise of the modern party, "the party of integration."[26] In this type, largely illustrated in developed systems by twentieth-century European Socialist parties, there is a large mass organization dominated by professional leadership, exercising central control over branches and units organized horizontally throughout the country, and with internal party discipline inside and outside of parliament. Table 1 shows the organization of one such mass party, the British Labour party. In developing nations mass parties have been created or mass support courted by elite groups seeking either to achieve certain objectives and the implementation of ideological convictions or to maintain or extend their control.

Table 1.   British Labour Party Organization

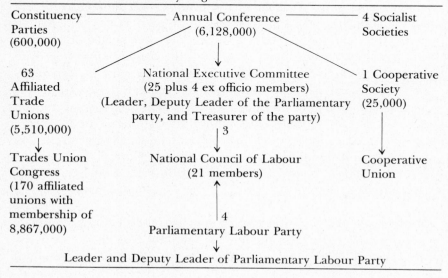

In mass parties there is always tension and struggle for influence among the different groups, the party leadership and the parliamentary representatives, the central organization and local constituency bodies. Party conferences, purportedly the place where party programs are debated and framed, are more realistically places for political contacts rather than forums where political decisions are taken or where the leadership gets advice from delegates. Generally the leadership dominates all debates, though it may offer concessions to critical delegates and may in fact use the conference to strengthen its own position.

The real power will normally lie in the parliamentary leadership of the party if the parliamentary members agree to accept decisions and show discipline and cohesion, as in Norwegian or British parties. This discipline and cohesion may be cemented by judicious use of patronage. The record of the British Conservative party between 1951 and 1964 when it was in power shows that 94 honors—in the form of offices, judicial appointments, diplomatic posts, governships, and titles— went to members of Parliament, and that there was a strong probability that any loyal Conservative member of Parliament would receive some honor. Parliamentary cohesion of the Labour party members of Parliament is virtually complete, and the conscience clause of the party, which allows Parliamentary members to express differences of opinion and to abstain on an issue about which they have conscientious scruples, suffers from the limited degree of elasticity allowed to conscience.

In presidential systems such as the United States, political leadership is likely to be disputed and diffused between the president or opposition presidential candidate and other leaders of the party in the legislature. In the United States power in the parties is more diffuse than in Britain, not only because of the rivalry between the president and congressional leaders but also because of the federal system. It is valid to talk of a two-party system even though half the states are dominated at state and local levels by one party. But the two parties are essentially loose groupings of individuals and local and sectional interests. Centralized control in the British sense is lacking as is ideological agreement in the two parties. The national party leadership competes for influence with the party hierarchy that ascends upward from the precinct, district, county, and state level to the national level of committees, clubs, and other related groups that are concerned as much with patronage and personnel matters as with political issues. Within Congress party members are rarely united on issues, but a number of key party personnel such as the Speaker of the House, majority or minority leaders, and the whips help provide some leadership. But again, the powerful chairmen and ranking members of committees may not always accept the position of the congressional leaders. The president is obliged to meet regularly with the congressional leaders in his search for legislative support. Though he uses a variety of methods of persuasion, including patronage, that support is not always forthcoming.

The British system is quite different. For example, in the cabinet system of Britain in 1945, Clement Attlee, the leader of the parliamentary party who had become prime minister, could successfully rebuke Harold Laski, the current chairman of the National Executive Committee of the Labour party, for attempting to interfere in the decision-making process of the government. But despite the theory of party democracy and election of officials, the mass organization rarely participates in the choice of leaders. Thus the leader of the parliamentary Labour party, elected by members of Parliament, has become recognized as the national party leader, and the main formulator of policy, often staying in office for lengthy periods of time. Leaders, once chosen, can expect considerable continuity in office; on his resignation in 1976 Harold Wilson had served 13 years as Labour leader, 8 of them as prime minister. In a rare exception, the Liberal party in Britain decided in 1976 to allow its constituency associations, instead of its parliamentary members, to choose its leader.

It is apparent, as both Robert McKenzie and Leon Epstein have shown in their studies of British parties, that the members of mass parties play a small role in the political process.[27] In the Conservative party the representatives of the mass party at the annual conference have little influence over the formulation of policy, and almost all motions are passed unanimously. Arthur Balfour was not the only leader to feel that he would sooner consult his valet than the party conference. No Conservative government feels itself bound by the conference decisions, and both policy and the chief personnel of the party organization are under the control of the party leader who is now elected by the Conservative members of the House of Commons rather than selected by an inner elite group.

Though the Labour party annual conference in theory can decide on specific proposals and though there is real, meaningful debate at it, the leadership, though sometimes defeated, usually dominates the debates, may formulate compromise resolutions, and will decide which recommendations are to be included in the election manifesto. More-over, when the party holds office the government may not accept the views of the party. In spite of both a recommendation by the National Executive Committee and a vote of a special Labour party conference, as well as of the General Council of the Trades Union Congress, that Britain should leave the Common Market, the Labour government did not accept this view in the 1975 referendum.

The struggle for power within the party may revolve around the nomination procedure. The West German electoral process shifted power to nominate candidates from the central party organizations to local officials and interest groups. The Christian Democratic Union or-ganization consistently refused Konrad Adenauer's demand for a fed-eral party list of candidates that would have given the national leader-ship a greater voice in the nomination process. The order of the names of candidates in the list proposed by the Government Alignment party in Israel is devised after intense bargaining among the leaders of the various factions and groups within the general coalition, since the can-didates at the top of the list will certainly be elected. In other propor-tional representation systems, such as in Italy, this power of the party leaders may be slightly reduced by the opportunity voters have to ex-press a preference among the party candidates.

Internal struggles for power within a mass party are also well illus-trated by the example of the Congress party in India and the Socialist party in Japan. For a time the core of all Congress party activity was the central election committee, which had most influence over the choice of candidates for both Parliament and the state assemblies and which added to the authority of the national leadership of the party, deciding in advance its choice of the national chief minister of a state and allotting nominations to provide a legislative majority for the des-ignated leader. But in the 1960s, when the committee no longer pos-sessed a common will or an agreed leadership, political power was fragmented and other party organs and personnel entered the arena.

The Japanese Socialist party is divided into at least six factions that run parliamentary electoral campaigns and that compete with both the party organization as a whole and with candidates of other fac-tions in the 130 multimember constituencies of the Japanese electoral system. This competition is reinforced by that between the party members in the Diet supported by their factions and the party organi-zation. The position of the Diet members has been reduced in impor-tance since 1962, when they were no longer accorded automatic representation at the party convention; at that convention there is now greater representation of the local branches of the party, and the outcome of debate is now less predictable.

Yet a strong central leadership will usually impose its views on the party organization. This was illustrated in West Germany in 1966, when the leadership of the Social Democratic party decided to form a coalition with the Christian Democrats, though seven of the eleven party organizations in the Länder and almost one-third of the party deputies disapproved.

The Extremist Party

Extremist parties are akin to the extremist ideological groups already dealt with. Dedicated to the overthrow of the system, they are based on small cells or militant groups and subject to strong discipline and acceptance of the policy of the leadership, which is difficult to displace.

Relations between the party organization and parliamentary group differ from those of the previous two types. In parties of the first type, such as the French Radical Socialists, the parliamentary group is virtually autonomous; each deputy, in control of a local constituency area, tends to act independently of his or her parliamentary colleagues or the leadership. In parties of the second type, parliamentary leaders tend to dominate the policies and activities of the party. But in extreme ideological parties, the party organization tends to dominate the group and tightly control parliamentary representatives in a variety of ways, which may include financial dependence, voting discipline, and possible expulsion for differences from accepted policy. Parties try to obtain harmony through a number of devices: by party caucuses at which parliamentary and nonparliamentary leaders can meet, by organization of the executive committee of the party to include parliamentary representatives, by allowing the executive committee to attend meetings of the parliamentary party, or by overlapping of the leadership of the different groups.

Organizational Similarities Among Types

The writings of Gaetano Mosca, Robert Michels, and Vilfredo Pareto among others have suggested that the differences between the different types of party organization and structure are less significant than the essential similarity.[28] In all parties, as in all groups, leadership is oligarchic, difficult to control, and often securely in command of the organization even when subject to election. It controls committee memberships, party newspapers, and educational programs as well as the party programs. But the law of oligarchy is not always cast in iron as Michels thought. In Norway party leaders are dependent on their members because of the custom of policy discussion at all levels in the party, the decentralized nomination procedure, and the democratic system of election, which means nomination as parliamentary candidates by provincial organizations and election as members of the party's national committee by the national congress, which also adopts the platform of the party. Yet even in Norway party unity is established by the platform, which is largely the position of the leaders. Leaders control the planning for the national congress and the agenda, speakers and officers chosen, as well as the lines of communication and information. Moreover the long continuity in office of Norwegian leaders suggests substantial control over the organization.

Notes

[1] David Truman, *The Governmental Process* (New York: Knopf, 1951).
[2] Jean Jacques Rousseau, *The Social Contract,* Book 2, chap 3; and Thomas Hobbes, *Leviathan,* Part 2, chap. 29.
[3] Roy Macridis, "Interest Groups in Comparative Analysis," *Journal of Politics* (1961), pp. 25–45.
[4] Samuel Finer, *Anonymous Empire* (London: Pall Mall, 1958).
[5] Michel Debré, *Ces Princes Qui Nous Gouvernent* (Paris: Plon, 1957).
[6] Michael Curtis and M. Chertoff, eds., *Israel: Social Structure and Change* (New Brunswick: Transaction, 1973), pp. 249–277.
[7] Elmer Schattschneider, *The Semisovereign People* (New York: Holt, Rinehart and Winston, 1960), p. 35.
[8] Theodore Lowi, *The End of Liberalism* (New York: Norton, 1969).
[9] A. Ranney and W. Kendall, *Democracy and the American Party System* (New York: Harcourt Brace Jovanovich, 1956), pp. 118–120.
[10] Max Weber, *From Max Weber,* H. H. Gerth and C. Wright Mills, eds. (New York: Oxford University Press, 1946).
[11] A. Lawrence Lowell, *Public Opinion and Popular Government* (New York: McKay, 1913), p. 105.
[12] Graham Wallas, *Human Nature in Politics* (Boston: Houghton Mifflin, 1909), pp. 82–84.
[13] A. Campbell et al., *The American Voter* (New York: Wiley, 1960); and David Butler and D. Stokes, *Political Change in Britain,* 2nd ed. (New York: St. Martin's Press, 1974).
[14] Daniel Bell, *The End of Ideology* (New York: Free Press, 1962); and Chaim Waxman, ed., *The End of Ideology Debate* (New York: Funk & Wagnalls, 1969).
[15] Barbara Ward, *Nationalism and Ideology* (New York: Norton, 1966).
[16] Rupert Emerson, *From Empire to Nation* (Cambridge, Mass.: Harvard University Press, 1960).
[17] T. F. Lindsay, *The Conservative Party, 1918–70* (New York: Macmillan, 1974).
[18] Stuart Hampshire and Leszek Kolakowski, eds., *The Socialist Idea: A Reappraisal* (London: Weidenfeld and Nicolson, 1974).

[19] Charles Péguy, *Notre Politiques et sociales* (Paris: L'Amitié Charles Péguy, 1957).

[20] A. Schonfeld, *Modern Capitalism* (New York: Oxford University Press, 1965).

[21] E. Kedourie, ed., *Nationalism in Asia and Africa* (New York: Harcourt Brace Jovanovich, 1970).

[22] Ronald Tiersky, *French Communism, 1920–72* (New York: Columbia University Press, 1974).

[23] Frantz Fanon, *The Wretched of the Earth* (New York: Grove Press, 1963); Régis Debray, *Strategy for Revolution* (London: Cape, 1970); and Herbert Marcuse, *One Dimensional Man* (Boston: Beacon Press, 1964).

[24] Mario Einandi et al., *Christian Democracy in Italy and France* (University of Notre Dame Press, 1952).

[25] Francis de Tarr, *The French Radical Party: From Herriot to Mendès-France* (New York: Oxford University Press, 1961).

[26] Sigmund Neumann, "Toward a Comparative Study of Political Parties," in Neumann, ed., *Modern Political Parties* (University of Chicago Press, 1956), p. 404.

[27] Robert McKenzie, *British Political Parties* (New York: Praeger, 1964); and Leon Epstein, "British Mass Parties in Comparison with American Parties," *Political Science Quarterly* (March 1956), pp. 97–125.

[28] Gaetano Mosca, *The Ruling Class* (New York: McGraw-Hill, 1939); Robert Michels, *Political Parties* (New York: Free Press, 1949); and Vilfredo Pareto, *Mind and Society* (New York: Dover, 1963).

Chapter Seven

Party Systems

A still useful method of comparing political regimes is to investigate the nature of the existing party system. Chapter Five examined the impact of electoral methods on the number of parties. A single-member plurality system may help foster and preserve a two-party system. But the opposing two parties may be different in different constituencies, as in Denmark and Canada. There are in fact few regimes with a national two-party system. A single-member system using a second ballot if one is needed to produce a majority in any constituency (as in France of the Fifth Republic) tends to lead to a multiparty system. Proportional representative systems almost inevitably produce or preserve a multiplicity of parties. But the number and kind of parties in any given regime is only partly the result of the electoral method; more important is the nature of the society, economic divisions, religious and ethnic affiliation, cultural diversity, and political differences over internal and external policy. The example is clear of France, which has experimented with eight different electoral methods between 1876 and the present, and has not been able to reduce the multiplicity of parties at any particular time.

The Two-Party System

A two-party system can be said to exist when:

(1) there are only two parties sufficiently strong to share the major part of the electoral vote and to exercise political control, though other parties may exist and obtain some seats in the representative assembly; and (2) the major parties alternate in the exercise of power. If the latter condition is not present—as in West Germany where the Socialist party did not exercise power at the federal level until the 1967

coalition, in Japan, where the Liberal Democratic party has dominated postwar politics, or in some parts of the United States where one party traditionally wins—the regime cannot exactly be termed a two-party system. Perhaps the term "one and a half" party system might be applicable in such circumstances.

The great advantage of the two-party system is that it can produce both a party with an overall parliamentary majority, on which responsibility can be placed, and a powerful opposition, of which the majority must always be conscious. Since the parties attempt to attract a sufficiently large number of voters to obtain a majority, it is probable that they will be moderate in opinion and action.

Underlying the existence of the two-party system is the premise that there is a dualism in human behavior and in political orientation such that individuals are attracted either to passion or to reason, to order or to change, to right or to left, to hierarchy or to equality, to conservatism or to liberalism, and that they therefore fall into two basic personality groups. Individuals developing personalities with liberal or conservative tendencies are then attracted to parties that support or resist change. But this theory of political dualism, exemplified by nations in which socialist groups are opposed by a coalition of nonsocialist groups, is immediately challenged by the very moderation forced on the parties in their effort to obtain electoral support, which may lead them to adopt very similar political positions. In addition, the split in the left-wing movement already analyzed inevitably forces the Social Democratic parties toward the center in order to seek further support.

The classic example of a two-party system and an accompanying strong government structure is that of Great Britain. In the 1966 election, 617 of the 630 successful members of Parliament came from the Labour and Conservative parties, which together obtained 89.8 percent of the vote, and the candidates of both parties fought 234 head-to-head fights. However, the October 1974 election witnessed striking gains for regional parties; the 2 major parties, although they obtained 596 out of 635 seats, polled only 75.1 percent of the vote.

Britain has been fortunate both that class and economic divisions have approximately corresponded to religious differences while the culture has been more homogeneous than in most other countries, and that the extreme left-wing movement has remained weak. Thus a party system based on Anglicanism and nonconformity was transformed into one based on agricultural interests and commerce, then into one divided between agricultural and manufacturing interests, and finally into one based on opposition between business and labor. Each major party has been based on a major social force or forces, but each has also been a national party. Each has been moderate, has been tolerant of other groups, has had a tenure of office, and, except on the Irish question, has avoided unconstitutional means or threats of action. Yet even the classic British model is subject to modification for at least two reasons. In the period from 1914 to 1966, coalitions or minority governments existed for 21 years, due to the two world wars, economic depression, and the presence of a relatively strong third party, the Liberals. Moreover, one party has dominated politics for almost 40 years. The Conservatives remained in power from 1923 until 1964 except for 7 years of Labour government and 9 years of coalition government in which they formed the majority element. The Conservatives have always captured England, while the Labour party has retained control of the Celtic fringes of Scotland and Wales. In addition, the joint share by Labour and Conservative of the vote has declined in recent years; in 1974 it was 59 percent of the electorate and 75 percent of the poll.

What distinguishes the British two-party system and makes it a model for some political scientists is the political discipline and coherence provided by it. This coherence is evident in a number of ways:

1. The pattern of voting is similar over the whole country and regional variations have been slight, though again the successes of the nationalist parties in 1974 offer some exception to this trend, as Table 1 indicates. In 1964, 91 percent of all British constituencies showed a swing to Labour, and in over half of them the swing in voting was within 2 percent of the national average. In 1966, in 608 of the 630 constituencies, there was a swing to Labour, and in over half the swing was within 1 percent of the national average.

2. An incumbent candidate has little political advantage over a new candidate. An attractive candidate, local issues, or a good local organization have little influence over the outcome. Voter identification with party is the strongest determinant in voting behavior, and the voter is voting for the party and its leaders rather than for individual candidates. However, in the present era where mass communication, television, and advertising campaigns have been shown to make a personality more compelling, short-run factors have tended to upset the equilibrium to a greater degree. Moreover, the emergence of new issues and the reluctance of the two major parties to deal with them in the 1970s has led to a decline in party affiliation.

3. Since the party that can control a majority in the House of Com-

Table 1. Nationalist Strength in Scotland and Wales, 1970 and 1974

Party	Scotland			Wales		
	1970	(Feb.) 1974	(Oct.) 1974	1970	(Feb.) 1974	(Oct.) 1974
Nationalist						
Votes (in percent)	11.4	21.9	30.4	11.5	10.7	10.8
Seats	1	7	11	0	2	3
Labour						
Votes (in percent)	44.5	36.6	36.3	51.6	46.8	49.5
Seats	44	40	41	27	24	23
Liberal						
Votes (in percent)	5.5	7.9	8.3	6.8	16.0	15.5
Seats	3	3	3	1	2	2
Conservative						
Votes (in percent)	38.0	32.9	24.7	27.7	25.9	23.9
Seats	23	21	16	7	8	8
Others						
Votes (in percent)	0.6	0.5	0.3	2.4	0.6	0.2
Seats	0	0	0	1	0	0

Source: Iain McLean, "Devolution," *Political Quarterly* (April–June 1976) p. 221.

mons forms the government, coordination is established between the legislative and executive branches, members of the government are invariably chosen from Parliament, and a coherent program becomes possible. A real political crisis occurs only when a group within a party changes its allegiance, as in 1886, 1916, 1922, 1931, and 1940, over differences of policy or personnel.

4. All members of the parliamentary party support the agreed policy of the party on all occasions except where dictates of conscience will not permit them to abide by that policy. Some qualification of this has arisen recently because the two major parties have been internally divided on a few important issues, especially on the Common Market. However, voting discipline of members of Parliament traditionally has been almost complete. Individual members who defy party discipline are reprimanded by the leadership, not appointed to an official position, and may not be readopted as a party candidate at the next election. Though control by the national organizations over nominations is limited, the local party activists who do control nominations are generally loyal to the party leadership and are likely to reward those candidates they consider equally loyal to the leadership.

5. The political leaders ·cement relationships between the parliamentary group and the party organization and therefore control the

policy and activities of the party as a whole, insuring continuity and integration.

By contrast with the British situation, the American two-party system has been criticized for lacking this national coherence and strong national machinery, discipline, and unity. Critics attack the dependence on coalitions of factions for electoral purposes, the concern with balancing the demands of special personal interests or those of sectional and ethnic groups, and the lack of clear alternative electoral programs. Indeed at the local level there is sometimes only one important party, which may be divided by factionalism. J. A. Schlesinger, in fact, has suggested that the United States party system can be differentiated into five categories based on the degree of interparty competition in the states. These categories include (1) competitive states, (2) cyclically competitive states, (3) one-party cyclical states, (4) one-party predominant states, and (5) one-party states.[1]

The British and American party systems operate in strikingly different fashion. The deferential behavior that Walter Bagehot and others have seen as typical of Britain and that makes party organization hierarchical and class ridden is vastly different from American behavior, which has been less deferential but also more corrupt and more likely to be boss dominated. American parties, less ideologically oriented, less disciplined, and less cohesive than the British, are in essence temporary coalitions bound together for electoral purposes, sometimes every two years, and almost always for the quadrennial presidential elections.

There are few other examples of a working two-party system. In Uruguay politics has been dominated by the Colorado and Blanco parties; the country was ruled for 90 years until 1958 by the Colorados, supported largely by the urban middle class, and from 1958 until 1973 largely by the rural Blancos. But as in the United States, factionalism has existed within the parties; in the past there were seven organized factions, which presented their own lists of candidates for seats in the legislature. The total party vote decided which of the two parties obtained a majority on the executive body, the National Council, and the factions shared in the allocation of membership in the Council according to their relative electoral strength. The Uruguayan two-party system has been in reality a multiclass or group system rather than one based on class differences. Similarly in Colombia, since 1957 two major parties have shared the legislative and executive positions since only these two are allowed to contest elections, though factions in each of the two can present alternative candidates.

An unusual variant of a two-party regime was the postwar *proporz* system in Austria, which existed until 1966. In that system the two dominant parties, the Christian People's party and the Socialist party, were so closely balanced in the legislature (see Table 2) that they entered into coalitions in spite of ideological differences between them, sharing cabinet positions, patronage, and most administrative positions in proportion to their voting strength in the country. The concepts of majority and minority had no relevance except in the distribution of government positions.

Similar conditions presently prevail in Luxembourg. There the two dominant and almost equally balanced parties are the Christian Socialists and the Socialists (see Table 3). In a six-party system, the two major parties have formed coalitions during most of the postwar period.

The two-party system has been praised for producing stability and compromise since each party seeks the widest political support. But it may also produce the exact opposite if the two parties are divided by acute differences, as they were in prewar Austria and postwar South Africa. The two-party system is successful only if the political culture is one in which both parties are prepared to accept each other as alternative governments, and if they are not committed to fixed ideological positions.

Multiparty Systems

In a multiparty system no one party is able to obtain majority control over the legislature. There have been rare exceptions in the past such as the Congress party's domination of politics in India, the Liberal Democrats' absolute majority in the lower chamber in Japan, and the Gaullist combination in France that constituted a majority in 1962 and 1967. Almost by definition a multipary system leads to coalitions and possibly to government instability, though the number of parties is not in itself a cause of disequilibrium. Coherent policy becomes more difficult to obtain as each party stresses its own interests or those of one

Table 2. Austrian Elections, 1949–1975

	Seats in Legislature								
	1949	1953	1956	1959	1962	1966	1970	1971	1975
People's	79	74	82	79	81	85	79	80	80
Socialist	67	73	74	78	76	74	81	93	93
Others	21	18	9	8	8	6	5	10	10

Table 3. Luxembourg Elections, 1959–1974

	Seats in Legislature			
	1959	1964	1968	1974
Christian Socialist	21	22	21	18
Socialist	17	21	12	17
Liberal	11	6	11	14
Communist	3	5	6	5
MIP.	—	2	—	—
Social Democrat	—	—	6	5

section of the population, and political responsibility remains more ambiguous than in a two-party regime in which strong responsible government is obtainable. But a multiparty system does not necessarily lead to governmental instability.

Stable Multiparty Systems

A number of systems have shown government stability for the most part: Switzerland, the Scandinavian countries, the Netherlands, Israel, and Germany. The model is Switzerland with at least nine parties, of which three share about 75 percent of the vote and four parties about 90 percent (see Table 4). All Swiss federal governments are coalitions composed of members of the four major parties, while members of the other parties may be included in the coalitions of the cantons into which Switzerland is divided.

Table 4. Swiss National Council, 1955–1975

Parties	Seats					
	1955	1959	1963	1967	1971	1975
Social Democrat	53	51	53	51	46	55
Radical Democrat	50	51	51	49	49	47
Conservative-Christian Social	47	47	48	45	44	46
Farmers', Traders', and Citizens	22	23	22	21	21	
Democrat	4	4	4	3	2	21
Independent	10	10	10	16	13	11
Liberal Democrat	5	5	6	6	6	6
Communist	4	3	4	5	5	4
Evangelical People's	1	2	2	3	3	3
Republican	—	—	—	1	7	4
National Campaign	—	—	—	—	4	2
Progressive Organizations	—	—	—	—	—	1

The Scandinavian countries witnessed considerable instability in the prewar period: Norway had ten minority governments and Sweden eleven ministries and two extraparliamentary governments between 1911 and 1936. In the postwar period the Labor parties of these countries, gaining 40 percent of the vote, have usually been pivotal to the coalitions formed, since there has been no single dominant right-wing party to oppose the Social Democrats. The Scandinavian systems can be regarded as two-bloc systems, pro- and anti-Socialist, rather than two or multiparty regimes (see Table 5). The division into two blocs was clearly shown in 1965, when the Norwegian non-Socialist parties fought the election on the assumption that they would form a coalition government if they won. In Sweden the Social Democrats have been the dominant party since 1932, while in Norway the Labor party won every postwar election until 1961 and remained in office until 1963 when a four-party anti-Labor coalition was formed; it thus occupied power for 33 of the last 40 years. In Denmark minority governments have alternated with coalitions. Finland with seven parties has mainly had non-Socialist coalitions; governments have sometimes included Social Democrats although Communists were excluded during the 1948–1966 period.

In Germany, with a three-party system, in which two parties have increasingly dominated the political scene but neither is capable of ruling alone, coalitions have been organized around the leading Christian Democratic party until 1969 and around the Socialist party since then. From 1949 to 1976 there have been only five chancellors in the country. Stability has been obtained but tension has not been eliminated because of the possible defection of the minor party from the coalition.

In other multiparty systems one party has dominated or a bipolarity has occurred with a number of parties grouped around a leading party. In Finland political bipolarity was established although eight parties were present. In the French Fifth Republic the UNR and other Gaullists had a stable legislative majority in 1962, though eight parties were represented in the National Assembly. The Gaullist attempt to polarize French politics has had considerable success. In the second ballot of the 1973 election for the National Assembly, Gaullists and Communists opposed each other in straight fights in 142 constituencies, while in 167 others a Gaullist was faced with a single candidate of the non-Communist left. In the same way in Israel, where until 1977 the Mapai was the leading party with about 35 percent of the poll and constituted the core of alliances of parties of the left, and in Eire where Fianna Fail has been the strongest party, coalitions have generally been formed around the leading party as a pivot. Indeed the Mapai dominated the Jewish *yishuv* (community) in Palestine since 1935 and the state of Israel since its creation in 1948 (see Table 6). The party always had a majority of the cabinet positions, including the prime minister's post and the major ministries, controlled the His-

Table 5. Political Stablility in Scandinavia: Seats in the Legislature

Norway, 1957–1973

	1957	1961	1965	1969	1973
Labor	78	74	68	74	62
Conservative	29	29	31	29	29
Liberal	15	14	18	13	2
Center	15	16	18	20	21
Christian People's	12	15	13	14	20
Socialist People's	—	2	2	—	—
Communist	1	—	—	—	—
Socialist Election Alliance	—	—	—	—	16
New People's	—	—	—	—	1
Anders Lange	—	—	—	—	4

Sweden, 1958–1973

	1958	1960	1964	1968	1970	1973
Social Democrat	114	111	113	125	163	156
Liberal	40	38	42	34	58	34
Conservative (Moderates)	39	45	32	41	51	
Center	34	32	35	39	71	90
Communist	5	5	8	3	17	19
Citizen's Front	—	—	3	—	—	—

Denmark, 1957–1973

	1957	1960	1964	1966	1968	1971	1973
Social Democrat	70	76	76	69	62	70	46
Liberal	45	38	38	35	34	30	22
Conservative	30	32	36	35	37	31	16
Socialist People's	—	11	10	20	11	17	11
Radicals	14	11	10	13	27	27	20
Independent	—	6	5	—	—	—	—
Single Tax	9	—	—	—	—	—	5
Schleswig	1	1	—	—	—	—	—
Communist	6	—	—	—	—	—	6
Liberal Center	—	—	—	4	—	—	—
Left Socialist	—	—	—	—	4	—	—
Center Democrat	—	—	—	—	—	14	
Christian People's	—	—	—	—	—	—	7
Progress	—	—	—	—	—	—	28

tadrut Labor Federation, the Jewish Agency, and most of the municipal councils in the country.

The postwar multiparty Japanese political system has been dominated by the Liberal Democratic party (LDP), which is more an alliance to oppose the Socialist party—with which it has since 1953
shared about 90 percent of the seats in the Diet and from which it is
divided on a variety of issues—than a coherent party. Like other Japanese parties the LDP has been marked by oligarchic control, internal
dissensions among competing factions based largely on personality
factors, and the struggle for office and influence; but it has exercised
power since independence. The ten factions or groups into which the
LDP has been divided are the core of political power. Loyalty to the
faction has usually transcended loyalty to the party itself or adherence
to political principle, and the selection of the prime minister has resulted from power struggles among the factions. But the strict party
discipline of members in the Diet has insured the ratification of the
decisions. Because of the prominence of a single party in the politics

Table 6. Israel Knesset Elections, 1949–1977

Party	1949	1951	1955	1959	1961	1965	1969	1973	1977
Mapai	46	45	40	47	42	45	56	51	32
Ahdut Haavoda	—	—	10	7	8				
Mapam	19	15	9	9	9	8			
Rafi	—	—	—	—	—	10			
Communist (Moked)	4	5	6	3	1	1	1	1	2
Communist (New)					4	3	3	4	5
Ha'olam Hazah (Meri)	—	—	—	—	—	1	2	—	
Civil Rights List	—	—	—	—	—	—	—	3	1
Free Center	—	—	—	—	—	—	2		
State List	—	—	—	—	—	—	4		
Herut	14	8	15	17	17			39	43*
Liberal (General Zionists)	7	20	13	8		26	26		
Independent Liberal (Progressives)	5	4	5	6	17		5	4	4	1
Mafdal (National Religious)		10	11	12	12	11	12	10	12
Aguda and Poalei Aguda	16	5	6	6	6	6	6	5	5
Democratic Movement for change	—	—	—	—	—	—	—	—	15
Others	9	8	5	5	4	4	4	3	4

*Now called Likud.

of the system, Japan like West Germany, may be seen as "one and a half" party regime.

Unstable Multiparty Systems

France and Italy provide the best examples and warnings of government instability. Between 1948 and 1975 Italy has witnessed 38 governments. In France from the liberation in 1944 until the end of the Fourth Republic in 1958, there were 26 governments with an average life of five and one-half months each, the longest—the Socialist government under Guy Mollet in 1956–1957—lasting 16 months. By contrast, in the Fifth Republic from 1958 to 1975 there have been 6 prime ministers, though there has been some ministerial instability.

In both countries internal differences have been sufficiently acute to prevent any single party from obtaining an absolute majority, either in the country or in parliament, and to insure that a large number of parties exist and gain some representation in the legislature (see Table 7). The parliamentary parties tend to engage in shifting alliances, not necessarily corresponding to any divisions outside the legislature, but depending on personal and political factors as well as on differences on economic and religious issues, the nature of the regime, foreign affairs, or nationalism. Instability is magnified by the fact that few of the parties have disciplined organizations to control the behavior of their parliamentary members.

The presence of strong organized Communist parties with which the other parties will not collaborate or will ignore in practice further reduces the chance of stability. After a short postwar period in which Communists were members of coalition governments in France, collaboration ended. In the Fourth Republic no party was prepared to enter into electoral alliances with the Communist party. In the National Assembly the party was denied committee chairmanships or an equitable role in the legislative hierarchy. French prime ministers often did not accept support from the Communists on a vote of confidence. One consequence of this situation was that government coalitions were pushed more to the political right than was the parliamentary assembly or the electorate. Only in the last decade have there been electoral arrangements made between the Communist party and other parties of the left in both legislative elections and the 1974 presidential election. In Italy the Communist party has not been put into isolation to the same extent, and the party has collaborated with other left parties both in the legislature and in the labor movement. In both countries the right has been very changeable, parties

Table 7. Italy and France: Legislatures

Italy: Chamber of Deputies, 1963–1976

	Percentage vote in country			Number of seats in the chamber		
	1963	1972	1976	1963	1972	1976
Communist	25.3	27.2	34.4	166	179	228
Socialist	13.8	10.7	9.6	87	61	57
Democratic Socialist	6.1	5.4	1.2	33	29	15
Republican	1.4	2.9	1.1	6	15	14
Christian Democrat	38.3	38.8	38.7	260	267	263
Liberal	7.0	3.9	.4	39	20	5
Monarchist	1.7	9.2	6.1	27	56	35
Neo-Fascist	5.1	9.2	6.1	27	56	35
Others	1.3	3.8	3.2	4	3	13

French National Assembly, 1951–1958

	Seats and Electoral Percentage		
	1951	1956	1958
UNR or Gaullist	57(20.4)	16(4.2)	189(26.4)
Independent	125(12.3)	95(14.1)	132(23.6)
MRP	85(12.8)	71(10.6)	57(7.5)
Socialist	94(14.9)	88(15.0)	40(13.8)
Left Center	—	18(5.7)	22(5.7)
Radical	82(11.2)	56(13.6)	13(2.0)
Communist	93(25.9)	145(25.6)	10(20.7)
Other Left Wing	6(0.1)	4(1.6)	2(1.4)
Extreme Right	—	52(12.1)	1(3.3)

appearing and disappearing equally quickly in France. In the parliamentary game required in this political situation, the center parties have the advantage of political maneuvering and skill, often uniting moderates of both left and right against the two extremes. Between 1924 and 1940 the French Radical Socialists, the key central group, led 16 governments. Of the 169 years from the French Revolution to the Fifth Republic, there have been governments of the left or right in only 32 years. Coalitions of the center achieve compromise and support the regime, but the price paid is *immobilisme,* or lack of action.

One-Party Systems

This type of regime is characterized by the party in power either dominating all other groups, trying to absorb the political opposition, or in the extreme case suppressing all opposition groups regarded as counterrevolutionary or subversive of the regime as forces dividing the national will.

One Dominant Party

In some countries one party has emerged as the controlling force, as may be seen in India and Mexico. In India the Congress party has held regional and sectional interests together, has tried to absorb village politics, and has performed the essential functions of obtaining consensus and integration.[2] Since independence in 1947, it always possessed an absolute majority in the legislature, (though not over 50 percent of the popular vote since 1952), obtained around 70 percent of the seats until 1967, and remained the only party with a strong nationwide organization (see Table 8). But its power, and the consequent danger to Indian democracy stemming from an inability to develop a credible alternative to the party, has been limited by at least two factors. The Congress party has been split into factions cohering around the struggle for office rather than ideological conviction. Also, the strength of opposition parties in some of the states into which India is divided provides a potential countervailing power against the central government. The decline in the fortunes of the Congress party at the 1967 elections has, however, introduced an element of

Table 8. Indian Lok Sabha (House of the People):
Number of Seats and Percentage of Vote, 1957–1967

	1967	1962	1957
Congress	275(39.8)	356(45.0)	371(47.6)
Communist	41(9.1)	29(10.0)	29(8.9)
Swatantra	44(8.3)	18(6.4)	−(−)
Jan Sangh	35(9.0)	14(6.3)	4(5.9)
PSP	13(2.8)	12(6.8)	19(10.3)
DMK	25(3.7)	7(2.3)	2
Socialist	23	6(2.7)	7
Ganatantra Parishad	—	4(0.3)	7
Republican	1	3(1.0)	7
Akali Dal	3	3(0.8)	—
Jharkhand	—	3(0.5)	7
Ram Rajya Parishad	—	2(0.6)	—
Forward Bloc	2	2(0.4)	3
Moslem League	—	2(0.4)	1
Revolutionary Socialist	—	2(0.2)	1
Hindu Mahasabha	—	1(0.4)	2
Others	49	25(12.3)	34(19.4)

fluidity and possibly of instability into the system, which led to authoritarianism between 1974 and 1977 when the party was defeated at the election in 1977.

In 1928 the Institutional Revolutionary party (PRI) was created in Mexico as a combination of regional political machines. It sponsors candidates and organizes electoral campaigns. It includes interest groups based on labor and peasant issues—and therefore balances interest groups and reconciles them—as well as a popular sector that normally wins the majority of the party's seats. Though the Communist party is illegal, other minor parties exist. But any real opposition exists and most political action occurs within the PRI itself, which has won every election since its formation. The purpose of a presidential campaign in Mexico is not so much to obtain votes, since the outcome is already known in advance, but to allow the people to see the future president.

A number of regimes are characterized by the existence of a dominant party and a number of other parties that appear to be permanent minorities with little chance of capturing power, either singly or in collaboration. This situation has been treated on page 176 as a "one and a half" party system. A variant of this situation has been the Burmese regime since 1962, in which the Lanzin is the only national party but has had to contend with two Communist parties and several ethnic dissident groups that command a certain following and control part of the territory of the country. Josef Silverstein has suggested that this can be classifed as a "one-plus" system.[3]

Absorption of Other Parties

It is a familiar experience, especially in a new system, for the party in power to attempt to restrict opposition parties or to absorb the political opposition as the Jeffersonians tried to do in early American history. In Burma the Anti-Fascist People's Freedom League at the beginning of the regime was a composite group including even the St. John's Ambulance Brigade for a two-year period. In Kenya the African National Union, largely led by members of larger tribes, absorbed the KADU (Kenya African Democratic Union), which represented the small tribes; the leader, President Jomo Kenyatta, preferred to keep opponents within the party to outmaneuver and neutralize them. In Egypt President Gamel Abdul Nasser did not allow any party to coexist with the Arab Socialist Union, the single mass movement permitted. In Spain under Franco the National Front or National Council

of the Movement was supposed to absorb all groups who had in common opposition to communism and support for the caudillo; opposition political parties were illegal although the regime tolerated some
groups such as the Christian Democrats and the Socialists. In Brazil
all political parties were dissolved in 1966 into one government party,
the National Renovating Alliance.

A number of African and Asian countries have tried to create unity
out of diverse pluralism by a one-party system, although sometimes,
as Ruth Schachter has pointed out, parties in West Africa do provide
for internal differences.[4] In Senegal a number of different groups
were included in the Progressive Senegalese Union; in Benin,
formerly called Dahomey, the Unity Party is essentially a coalition of
two factions. The Democratic Party of Guinea has tried to absorb
leaders of the chief tribes who might be focal points of dissension,
while in Gabon the opposition was taken into the leading party. In
most of the newer nations of the world that are not ruled by military
dictatorships, one-party regimes exist; in 1965 11 of the 13 countries
set up in West Africa since 1957 had such regimes. By 1975 only Bot-
swana, the Gambia, and Mauritius in black Africa had more than one
party in their systems.

A number of arguments have been proposed to explain or justify
the establishment of one-party systems. One argument is that such a
system is necessary to obtain national unity and to reconcile conflicts.
Since popular sovereignty is the basis of the regime, unanimous decisions, cohesion, and the subordination of all to the general interest is
held to be necessary; opposition in a new state is therefore looked on
as synonymous with sedition.

Some argue also that liberalism is inappropriate for the new nations
because there must be popular dictatorship led by a single party,
which can express the common interest of all classes. The party will
not be related to a particular social class, religious conception, or specific form of political system in this view, but will direct all organs of
state and seek to obtain complete identity of interest between the various economic, social, and cultural groups in the nation.

The argument is sometimes proposed that representative government and parliamentary supremacy are undesirable since voters become the slaves of elected representatives and these deputies are in-
clined to act for special interests. Democracy, Julius Nyerere has
argued, is government by discussion and the process of discussion
does not require organized political parties. A single-party state may
promote democracy more effectively and be more closely identified

with the national movement and the patriotic movement than would a two- or multiparty system, which implies class society, factionalism, and self-interest. In fact in Tanzania, free general discussion is allowed and encouraged at the local level, while the single party, the Tanganyika African National Union, provides a choice among two competing candidates for each legislative constituency, and the executive committee of the party includes representatives of diverse groups in the country. Nevertheless there is only one candidate for president.

Another argument favoring a one-party system is that strong government is required in order to develop economically and to deal with disturbances that might result from that development. Since the state plays an important role in economic life and in providing employment, one party can perform political, economic, and social functions, controlling the extent and direction of change.

Finally, a one-party system is said to be needed because a strong regime is needed to defend the state against an external menace. This fear is directed not so much at the former colonial powers as at other African states that might encourage parts of the population to rebel against the party in power.

Though strong government may be essential for the political development of the new nations, some of the arguments presented above seem more specious than substantial. It is certainly not true that single parties arose to oppose the colonial rulers or that single leaders led that fight. It is not self-evident that a single party is indispensable for the solution of African economic problems. In practice, the actual operation of most of these systems has meant government subsidy of the official party, a small role for economic groups, censorship and severe limits on free speech, denial of elementary rights, prison for political opponents, and sometimes corruption. As in comparable European cases, the theory of the necessary ruler has been tainted by personal ambition, as with Kwame Nkrumah who styled himself "Osagyefo," the Victorious Leader, among other titles, and insisted on an oath of loyalty to himself.

Ideological One-Party States

The major examples of ideological one-party regimes are those of the communist countries, now that the Nazi and fascist structures ended with the war. The prototype for all communist regimes is that of the Soviet Union, though the pattern of imitation has varied considerably from close facsimile to deliberate divergence. Divergence is found in Yugoslavia where the Socialist Alliance, a mass organization of over 8 million of whom less than 10 percent belong to the League of Communists, contests elections by allowing at the municipal level a choice of persons in different professions rather than a choice of ideology.

The Communist party of the Soviet Union, containing 15.5 million members and candidates in 1976, is organized on the principle of *democratic centralism,* the theory that all will accept a decision once it has been made; members of each organization are chosen by those at the next lower level, though in practice cooption rather than election has been the manner of choice. Centralized leadership therefore arises through vertical communication from the small cells organized on both functional and geographical lines to the Central Committee, now consisting of 287 full and 139 candidate members, which directs party affairs and the party Congress, which lays down the guidelines of policy at its infrequent meetings. At the apex of the political pyramid is the Presidium or Politburo, a small group of top party leaders, which acts between meetings of the Central Committee. But since the emergence of Joseph Stalin in 1924 the real core of power has usually been the Secretariat, which, nominally acting between meetings of the Presidium, is really in control of the whole organization. Of the 11 current members of the Secretariat, 6 are members of the Politburo.

Though the doctrine of Marxism does not logically suggest a single-party state, all communist systems have been created with the Communist party as the sole party, with all others eliminated, liquidated, or absorbed. At most elections only one candidate can be proposed although several nonparty organizations can make nominations.

In communist systems the party has had a varying relationship with the government apparatus. In the Soviet Union political leaders have held differing views on the mixing of party and government responsibilities. At all times the party has controlled and directed the operation of government, has been the ultimate source of authority, the organization providing guidance and policy on all questions, the body criticizing the work of other organizations, the disciplined group instilling ideological enthusiasm in the citizen body. Nevertheless the state administration has an independent existence, exercising an influence on operations, especially in the fields of economic planning, production, and accounting. In Yugoslavia there has been a growing divorce between party and state functions, with the party confined to ideology and political concerns.

Yet members of the party apparatus, the *apparatchiki,* control both the key political positions and state institutions at the central and local

levels. Organizations exist only under party control. Almost all important leaders of the Russian Communist party since 1917 have had
purely political careers, though the number of those with engineering
training has increased in recent years. Moreover, for most of the existence of the Soviet Union, the real power has been in the hands of a
leader—Vladimir Lenin, Joseph Stalin, Georgi Malenkov, Nikita
Khrushchev, Leonid Brezhnev—who has controlled the party apparatus and who has only lost power when that control ended.

The history of the Soviet Union from the 1918 Revolution until the
death of Stalin in 1953 was the evolution from a one-party state in
which other parties were outlawed to a monolithic party that expelled
or ruthlessly liquidated factions or groups within itself and that finally
became utterly subservient to the views and will of Stalin himself. Indeed from 1939 until 1952 no party Congress was called, and the
Central Committee rarely met. Other organs, such as the Secret Commission of State Security set up in 1933 or the State Committee for
Defense created during the war, possessed greater powers than the
formal party or state apparatus.

No opposition parties are permitted but this does not inevitably
mean monolithic unity or a monopoly of power by one person or
group. Pluralistic pressures take a form different from that in democratic systems. These pressures arise not only from nonparty groups
such as the state apparatus, the secret police, army leaders, and control commissions, but also internally from contending factions within
the party based on personal loyalty to an individual or territorial
group or on shifting alliances in the struggle and maintenance of
power or on different approaches to the solution of problems.

In China the Communist party is regarded as "the core of leadership" of the National People's Congress and of the whole Chinese
people. In reality, until his death the party was dominated by Mao
Tse-tung, who eliminated dissenting factions, individuals, or potential
rivals for leadership. Mao sought to end the ideology, culture, customs, and habits of the past, making idiosyncratic use of Chinese literature and history for his political purpose. Believing that the party
was succumbing to bureaucratic behavior and that it was losing its revolutionary values of hard work, equality, and mass enthusiasm, Mao
in 1965 began the Cultural Revolution, which wrecked the party and
administrative apparatus and eliminated many leaders.

Revelations after Mao's death in 1976 made clear that Chinese
Communist party politics had witnessed not only policy differences be-

tween the pragmatic moderates favoring a more orderly administration and economic modernization and the radicals placing greater emphasis on class war and collectivism, but also divisions stemming from strong personal rivalries and conflicts among the political leaders, senior bureaucrats, and army commanders, and disagreements among the provinces of the country.

The experience of the party in Yugoslavia has shown that the party need not be monolithic in behavior. Successive reforms have been aimed at the creation of an organization that can resist the abuse or monopoly of power by individuals or factions and make the party more democratic. To this end the small executive committee was abolished, the authority of the larger Central Committee was restored, permanent committees of the Central Committee were created to bring it into contact with the party members, experts from outside the Central Committee and the party were used for consultation, and workers' councils were maintained as basic units of social relations.

In spite of the changes introduced in the communist regimes in the last decade, it is improbable at the moment that they will become transformed into two- or multiparty systems, for that would admit the possibility of an alternative government formed by an opposition party. Two-party and multiparty systems will invariably be synonymous with democratic or nondictatorial regimes, though they may not always lead to government stability. But one-party systems can rarely allow the luxury of free expression and opinion.

Notes

[1] J. A. Schlesinger, "A Two-Dimensional Scheme for Classifying States According to the Degree of Inter-party Competition," *American Political Science Review* (December 1955), pp. 1120–1128.

[2] Stanley Kochanek, *The Congress Party of India: the Dynamics of One-Party Democracy* (Princeton University Press, 1968).

[3] Josef Silverstein, "The Burma Socialist Program Party and Its Rivals: A One-Plus Party System," *Journal of Southeast Asian History* (March 1967), pp. 8–18.

[4] Ruth Schachter, "Single-party Systems in West Africa," *American Political Science Review* (1961), pp. 294–307.

Chapter Eight

Assemblies and Rule Making

Rules are the product of a diversity of organizatons, individuals, and procedures. In developed polities, legislative assemblies still constitute the most significant arena for the discussion, dissection, and approval of rules, though this is not always their most important activity. The function of making rules and statutes came relatively late in the development of parliamentary bodies. The oldest existing body, the British Parliament, representing major occupational or territorial sections of the nation, grew in strength as a result of insuring a supply of money for the king, partly for his military needs, in return for his readiness to hear and redress grievances. Even the signing of Magna Carta in 1215 was not so much an affirmation of individual rights or personal liberties as a desire on the part of the feudal barons to control the arbitrary behavior of the monarch and his wastage of money. Nor was it a unique event in European history. Frederick Barbarossa in 1183 granted the liberties sought by the Lombard cities, while in France provincial charters of liberties were granted after the reign of Philip IV.

Historically, legislation has never wholly been the result of parliamentary activity. British royal proclamations in the fifteenth and sixteenth centuries, through which monarchs issued public ordinances, were valid even before a statute in 1539 gave the force of law to such proclamations. Tudor paternalism insured that regulations were made on a wide range of subjects including the imposition of penalties for hoarding food, price fixing, and the closing of brothels in London. Not until the sixteenth century did statutes begin to replace royal proclamations and the use of the royal prerogative as the chief method of making general rules. Not until even later was the Parliament regarded as the embodiment of the will of the people and as the institution from which the government would be created.

To seventeenth- and eighteenth-century political thinkers the legislature appeared to be the preeminent political institution, "the supreme power of the commonwealth" in John Locke's words.[1] Though the place of the legislature is not so highly regarded today, it is yet not surprising to find in the Soviet constitution that the highest organ of state power is the Supreme Soviet, the Soviet of the Union and the Soviet of Nationalities, or to find in Yugoslavia that the Federal Assembly is the chief organ of power and of self-government.

Unicameral and Bicameral Chambers

Of the 144 nations in the world today, 122 have parliaments of one kind or another, and 47 of them have bicameral systems. In recent years there has been an increase in the number of those countries such as Denmark, New Zealand, Finland, Greece, Monaco, Turkey, the East European countries, and many of the newer independent nations that have unicameral systems. Second chambers have been created for a number of reasons. Some have been influenced by British practice, which in the fourteenth century divided the nobility and ecclesiastical hierarchy sitting in one body from the knights and commoners in the other. Some have resulted from the creation of federal regimes, in which the constituent units or minority groups have been given special or equal representation. But the essential case has always been that the formulation of legislation and policy issues ought to receive a second consideration, and possibly might be rejected or delayed, by a chamber different from the first in character and composition. A group of eminent individuals might thus ascertain the popular will and delay the program of the first chamber if it felt that this program was contrary to the will of the people.

Most first chambers are directly elected by citizens, though in some countries they are chosen by local chiefs or heads of families, or appointed by the governor in a colony or dependency.

Second chambers have been chosen in a variety of ways:

1. By general election—as in the United States, the Soviet Union, Australia, Italy, Japan—with different constituencies from those for the first chamber, and sometimes different qualifications of age or social group needed for the candidates or for the electorate.

2. By appointment by the executive, as in Canada or West Germany. In Canada, where appointments to the Senate are until age 75, almost all of the 102 appointees are members of the prime minister's party; between 1925 and 1963 about 45 percent of the senators had

previously been members of Parliament. The 41 members of the German Bundesrat are appointed by the state governments of which they are members or civil servants.

3. By election by some other body, such as by local authorities, as in France until 1958, or by provincial and city councils, as in Sweden where one-eighth of the Riksdag is elected annually. In the Indian Council of States, 226 of the 230 members are elected by the state assemblies, and some of the Swiss cantonal legislatures elect members of the Swiss Council of States. In Norway the first chamber chooses part of itself as the second chamber.

The Norwegian parliament, the Storting, is thus an unusual example of a body that is both a unicameral and a bicameral assembly. Legislation, which can be initiated only in the lower chamber, must be passed by each of the chambers, the Odelsting and Lagting, except some financial legislation that is discussed in the whole Storting. A veto by the Lagting can be overriden by the Storting, and it is usually to the latter that the cabinet is responsible.

4. By some occupational or minority groups as in Portugal until 1974 and in Yugoslavia until 1963. In the Portuguese Corporative Chamber members were appointed as representatives of the various economic, administrative, moral, and cultural associations.

5. By some mixture of these four methods or by some other process, as for example in Ireland, India, or Great Britain. In Ireland the Seanad is chosen partly by the prime minister, partly by the universities, and partly by deputies, retiring senators, and local authorities. In India the president chooses 12 of the 238 members.

The British House of Lords, the largest second chamber in the world with over 1,100 members, is produced by a number of different methods: inheritance of a hereditary peerage, appointment to a peerage or to a life peerage, holding one of the top 26 ecclesiastical positions in the Church of England, or appointment as one of the nine Lords Justices of Appeal.

Though a number of second chambers have the legal power to reject or delay legislation, the case for them to act as a restraining element on the supposed rashness of the first chamber is less clear now in an era of mass communication, universal literacy, and dissemination of information through the mass media than it was in the past. But second chambers still perform some useful services. They may be used to relieve the legislative congestion of the lower chamber and to amend bills. Joint legislative committees may be established, either to discuss legislation as in Norway and Australia, to study common problems as in the Netherlands, or to settle disputes about legislation where disagreement has arisen between the two chambers, as in Great Britain and West Germany. Second chambers may provide the forum for individuals, distinguished in various walks of life but unwilling to enter the arena of partisan politics, to comment on public affairs and government policy. In federal regimes they may provide an opportunity for the interests of the individual states or minority groups to be safeguarded, although in fact these interests are likely to be protected more satisfactorily by other bodies or in other ways.

Second chambers are more useful in aiding the work of the first chamber than in exercising strong powers of their own. The Senate of the United States is altogether exceptional in its prominent place in the political system and in the real legislative and executive power that it exercises. Some other second chambers such as the Swedish, Italian, or Belgian may claim equality since both chambers may examine legislative proposals at the same sitting. The French Fifth Republic originally tried to strengthen its Senate. The German Bundesrat has increased its power since the Federal Republic was established in 1949, organizationally because it contains a large number of civil servants from the Länder who are expert in the legislation with which they are concerned, and politically because it has increased the scope of its veto power over legislation; controlled in recent years by the Christian Democrats who are in a minority in the lower chamber, the Bundesrat has opposed and occasionally blocked the programs of the governing coalition.

Despite these examples, in most cases the second chamber remains a weak political force no matter what its theoretical power may be. Any political system with a parliamentary cabinet almost inevitably requires that the cabinet be responsible to the lower chamber only.

The Nature of Deputies

It is dubious that there exists a "political personality" type, possessing certain physical characteristics and propelled by certain psychological motives, such as a desire for power, status, prestige, or wealth as Harold Lasswell has argued.[2] Attempts to correlate the weight of legislators' brains with their legislative ability appear bizarre rather than useful. Nor is the degree of their introversion or extroversion a valuable categorization. The reasons for embarking on political or parliamentary careers are numerous and ambiguous. In a story by the novelist Saki a character enters parliament "possibly with the idea of making his home life seem less dull."[3] Others consciously feel the call to public service; some see it as the avenue to material advantage or to psychological enrichment through the exercise of power and the respect and deference paid to them.

Certainly, as was seen in Chapter Five, parliamentarians are not typical of their constituents, nor of the whole citizen body. Geographically—as shown in Italy and the United States Senate—they tend to come from smaller towns than does the population as a whole. Demographically, they are older and contain a larger proportion of males than the average of the population. Except in the Soviet Union where they constitute about a quarter of the legislative body, women form a small proportion of the political elite. Only 6 percent of the candidates of the two major parties for the 1976 election of the United States House of Representatives (54 out of 870) and only 6 percent of the Labour and Conservative candidates in Britain in 1974 were women. There is a greater proportion in Norway with 24 women members out of 155. Parliamentarians on the whole come from the middle or upper-middle class. In general they are well educated and reflect the parliamentary importance of the professions, business, and labor unions. An examination of the United States Senate showed that only 10 percent of its members had working-class backgrounds. In Britain there is a high preponderance, especially among Conservatives, of members from privileged educational institutions such as Eton, Oxford, and Cambridge (see Table 2 in Chapter Five). British Conservative members of Parliament include very few Jews, though Benjamin Disraeli is the patron saint of the party, and few Catholics. Among Labour party candidates the number with formal higher education has risen substantially; in 1974 61 percent had attended a university, 18 percent had been to Oxford or Cambridge, and 8 percent to the prestigious public schools. Probably the most highly educated group are the members of the German Bundestag, 30 percent of whom have Ph.D.s.

Lawyers form a numerous occupational group in the legislatures of the United States, France, Turkey, and some Commonwealth nations, and public officials are important in Sweden. The argument has been made, based largely on American behavior, that lawyers are particularly suitable to become members of the legislature because of their experience in verbal articulation, flexible attitude, and ability to understand the details of legislation. But a high proportion of parliamentarians are political professionals who have spent a large part of their careers in some kind of party, union, or political office, either local or national. The Israeli Knesset is largely a group of professional politicians. Over half of the United States Senate in recent years have been governors or congressmen. Almost 65 percent of the Italian Communist deputies are party or union officials; about 40 percent of British Labour party deputies are sponsored by trade unions or cooperative societies. Only in Socialist or Communist parties does any considerable number come from the worker class. A noticeable characteristic of the French Fourth Republic was that about a third of the deputies retained some local office on election to the National Assembly in 1956, and almost 60 percent of all incumbent deputies held some local office. About one-third of the chairmen of local councils in France were also parliamentary deputies. In the current legislature 52 percent of deputies and 55 percent of senators are departmental councillors. Civil servants and leaders of interest groups constitute 60 percent of the current Bundestag in Germany.

Parliamentarians vary greatly in age, social background, previous experience, and political ambition, and their parliamentary activity is largely explicable by these factors. Donald Matthews has shown that former congressmen adjust more readily to the norms of the United States Senate than do former governors of states. Members of parties, such as the British Conservatives or the French Popular Republican Movement in the Fourth Republic, have usually entered the legislative body relatively early and with little experience, thus hoping to be politically promoted within the legislature. Since 75 percent of British Conservatives are first elected before they are 45 years old, the chances of promotion are strikingly high; 25 percent of all British parliamentarians between 1918 and 1955 held some leadership post and of the 319 Labour members in 1976, 118 have held governmental positions. Unlike American representatives who must be residents of their districts in order to be candidates and who are normally closely identified with those districts, British representatives are frequently "carpetbaggers" in that they may have had no previous association with the constituency for which they have been chosen a candidate.

In all assemblies there are categories of people who are forbidden to be members. The most significant group that is sometimes excluded is the political executive of those countries whose regimes embody the concept of separation of personnel. This has usually been done in order to balance the power of the two branches of government, as in the United States. In Fifth Republic France ministerial membership of the legislature has been forbidden, and substitutes replace deputies who are appointed ministers; after the 1973 Assembly elections, 41 out of 490 members were substitutes. Ministers, however, are allowed to speak and debate in the Assembly, in an attempt to strengthen the power of the executive. By contrast, parliamentary cabinet systems, as in Britain, Scandinavia, and Germany, rest on the fusion between the two branches; ministers are the front bench members of the legislature in such systems.

Pressures on Deputies

The problem of the nature of deputies, whether they are to be regarded as representatives or delegates, has already been discussed in Chapter Five. Conflict will be perennial between the interests of the constituents of deputies and the general interest. It is clear that the behavior of legislators will be influenced in a number of ways, by their constituents, by their party, by the political executive, by outside groups, and by the legislature itself. The relative degree of influence of the different factors will depend on the issue involved as well as the personality and political prominence of the legislators.

The initial, but not necessarily most meaningful, responsibility of legislators is to their constituents: attending to mail from them and to the problems and grievances of local inhabitants, participating and speaking at local functions, and taking the needs and sometimes the opinions of constituents into account when performing parliamentary duties. United States congressmen pick their way warily through the thousands of bills and resolutions introduced into Congress every session, and are obliged to enter into the political game of lobbying, bargaining, and logrolling. At times groups of an unusual kind make demands on their representatives; in the past in some parts of Colombia members of Congress could not be elected without the support of bandits who were then accorded protection.

Fortunately for legislators the very diversity of needs and opinions in any constituency allows them considerable discretion, though it also means multiple and contradictory demands for their attention. In addition, the lack of understanding of issues by most of their constituents allows deputies flexibility they might not otherwise possess.

It is rare for any legislator not to be a member of or affiliated with a political party. Political independence may be worthy of admiration but rarely exists if the party is well organized and disciplined. Where discipline exists, the influence of the party is likely to be stronger than that of constituency because it may determine the actions of deputies, their votes on legislative and other proposals, often their place in the hierarchy of the chamber and the possibility of their becoming part of the assembly leadership or committee chairmen or *rapporteurs*. Party influence on deputies seems stronger than other factors such as social relationships or friendships. Party representatives participate in the bureau or organizational leadership of the parliamentary body, in allocating membership of committees, in determining speakers in debates, and in organizing the agenda and work of the body. Some regimes — West Germany and Fourth Republic France, Switzerland and Israel — have tried to get greater parliamentary stability and responsibility and have reduced the number of parliamentary groups by insisting on a minimum number for the formation of a group.

The degree of party influence will depend on the discipline and cohesion in the party, the degree to which ideological beliefs are shared, the nature of the competition between existing parties, and on the degree of control by the party leadership and central organization over the nomination of candidates. And discipline may vary widely from the virtual complete cohesion in the British parliamentary parties, where even occasional dissents can be subject to reprimand, to a party like the French Radical Socialists whose members are divided on every issue. Similarly the fact that the French Radical group is composed of key local figures — "notables," mayors, or presidents of departmental general councils — and that the party has no strong central organization allows them almost complete freedom of parliamentary action. Pressure on deputies comes mainly from political executives, especially if these are also members of the deputies' party. Patronage or the hope for future office may reinforce doctrinal agreement in the willingness of deputies to accept executive policy.

James Barber in *The Lawmakers* has suggested that party leaders obtain the support of party members in the legislature in more ways than merely by the promise or expectation of patronage or aid that will be distributed according to the degree of support for the party. They also use devices such as emphasizing the need for party unity or the sense of party loyalty, evoking memories of the previous electoral campaign, bolstering the self-esteem of members, stressing the prestige and respect to be gained by being associated with the leadership, and attempting to establish party cohesion as a norm. Sometimes, too, the parliamentary leader may be imperious, as were the celebrated "Czar" Thomas B. Reed and "Uncle Joe" Cannon, who were autocratic Speakers of the House of Representatives, and Sam Rayburn, who refused to allow a congressman on the taxation committee of the House unless he or she supported the oil depletion allowance.

Outside groups frequently provide information and advice for legislators. They also attempt to influence them directly and by subtle means. They may sponsor candidates, or help pay their expenses, as do the British trade unions, or they may invite the deputy to be a member of the executive board of the group. In a country like Israel where there are no local constituents since the whole country is the electoral unit, deputies still cannot ignore the pressure of interest groups.

There is an old French witticism: "There is more in common between two deputies, one of whom is a conservative and one a revolutionary, then between two revolutionaries, one of whom is a deputy and one who is not." Every assembly has an ethos of its own that binds its members and conditions their behavior. Its rules of the game, or "folkways" as Donald Matthews has called it, govern the operation of business, regulate the organization of the assembly, train deputies, endeavor to resolve and diminish conflict, and attempt to promote cohesion in as painless a fashion as possible.[5] Even the physical structure of the assembly reflects the political atmosphere. The small, oblong-shaped British House of Commons, with the opposing parties on opposite sides of the chamber and party supporters sitting on the back benches behind the leaders on the front bench reinforces cohesion and discipline. The French Assembly, with its semicircular seating and its tribune from which to speak, encourages oratorical display and political independence. The German chamber, with the government facing the other members, is a reminder of strong leadership.

To be successful, members learn the rules and abide by them. Samuel Johnson spoke of the "clubable man" and the "House of Commons man," Robert de Jouvenel referred to the French Chamber of Deputies as "the republic of pals," William White made note of the "Senate insider," and Sam Rayburn once said, "The way to get along is to go along."[6] The new senator, according to Matthews, serves a period of apprenticeship during which he is expected "to keep his mouth shut . . . to listen and learn."[7] Sidney Verba in his study of small groups has shown that leaders often conform to group norms more strongly than do their followers.[8] Both Matthews and David Truman have shown that the recruitment of party leaders in Congress has favored those moderates who have exemplified group norms.[9] Most congressmen readily accustom themselves to expected behavior;

newly appointed members of the Senate Foreign Relations Committee usually begin taking internationalist positions if they had not previously done so. Reciprocal trading of votes and logrolling lie at the basis of congressional behavior. Not surprisingly, only seven senators and eighteen representatives have been censured by their peers in the history of the United States Congress, and of these two senators and ten representatives were reelected after their censure.

Acceptance of the rules brings coherence and certainty, but it also carries the danger of conservatism, *immobilisme*, and even corruption. Accepted practice, as in the United States Senate with its filibuster process, seniority system, and senatorial courtesy procedure, or in the National Assembly of the French Fourth Republic with its activity based on an avoidance of serious problems and a reluctance to antagonize individuals or groups leading to a minimum of action, shows that traditional behavior is not always the truest wisdom in politics.

Types of Assemblies

The place and significance of assemblies varies from one regime to another. The variation may be classified according to the relative power exercised or the prominence of the role of the assembly in the system, ranging from weak to strong.

The Submissive Assembly

Although it has almost no power, the submissive assembly provides a platform for policy, made by individuals or groups outside the assembly, to be declared. By endorsing that policy it allows the appearance of popular approval, though it has no real representative or responsible function. This kind of assembly has little more than ceremonial significance, and its members are chosen or elected for their loyalty to the current ruling group. Opposition to or serious criticism of official policy is not tolerated, and there is no possibility of rejection of that policy.

Examples of the submissive are the Cortes in Franco's Spain, which acquiesced in the will of the ruler and had no control over the government, and the Supreme Soviet of the Soviet Union. According to the 1936 Soviet constitution the Supreme Soviet can exercise only those powers not exercised by the Council of Ministers, the individual ministers, and the Presidium of the Supreme Soviet, which acts for the whole body between regular sessions that have usually lasted three days.

The Assenting Assembly

Britain is the model of the assenting assembly. Such an assembly is the supreme legislative authority in the sense that it has the final will in the making of legislation. But in Britain the assembly is formally opened and closed, and can be dissolved, by the ruling monarch, the head of state who must consent to legislation though he or she now acts only in accordance with the wishes of the government. The members of the latter invariably are drawn from the members of the party, or very occasionally parties, controlling a majority in the House of Commons. Since the government controls a majority in the House, the assembly usually performs a supportive or assenting role and approves in general, though it often modifies, the legislative program and financial policy of the government if party loyalty and disciplined voting remain strong. However, if that discipline should break down and the government loses its majority, the government would probably be unable to control the assembly or even to exist.

The Coequal Assembly

Best exemplified by the Congress of the United States, the coequal assembly is elected separately from the executive. Its existence, organization, and procedures are not dependent on the executive. In the United States the exact relation between the two branches has varied through history, but the legislature has often claimed a position of equality. Its thorough dissection of legislation through its powerful structure of committees and subcommittees, now numbering over 170, its powers over finance, its approval of executive appointments, its participation in patronage, its considerable facilities for obtaining information through committee hearings and investigations with the aid of a large staff, now over 30,000, available to it collectively and to its individual members, provide it with power sufficient at times to balance that of the executive.

The Assertive Assembly

The assertive assembly tends to dominate the personnel engaged in and the nature of decision making to the degree that the executive can never be certain it will possess a majority for its policy. This type is best exemplified by the assemblies of the French Third and Fourth Republics, which not only provided the source for membership, in assenting assemblies, but also had real control over the existence and activity of governments and regularly overthrew them. The important system of committees, originally organs of criticism and of advice in the formulation of legislation, soon came to be used for control over government action and for challenge of executive policy. Lack of disciplined party voting meant that party leaders in the government could not automatically count on support of party members in the assembly, with the result that executive leadership could only rarely be exercised.

The Role of Assemblies

Assemblies play roles and exercise functions of different kinds. They may have the power to choose heads of state or members of the government, to make governments accountable to them, to control their own functioning, to pass legislation, and to inquire into the government's activities. Each of these deserves further comment.

Selection of Government Leaders

Assemblies sometimes are empowered to choose the head of state, who may be an honorific or symbolic figure as well as a politically powerful one. Hereditary monarchs by definition succeed by inheritance but the assembly may have the right to alter the succession. In republics the head of state may be directly chosen, as in France during the Third and Fourth Republics when both chambers together formed the electoral body. Other variations may be found in West Germany, where the Federal Convention composed of the Bundestag and an equal number of representatives of the Länder parliaments vote, India, which has an electoral college consisting of the two chambers and members of the legislative assemblies of states, Italy with a similar system, and Israel where the Knesset chooses. In the Soviet Union the Presidium—the guiding body handling legislative matters between parliamentary sessions, the chairman of which is regarded as the nominal head of state—is elected by the Supreme Soviet from its own members. In the United States the House of Representatives can choose the president if no candidate has obtained a majority in the electoral college, as happened in 1800 and 1824.

Assemblies may also choose or approve the choice of the head of or the members of the government. They may elect the political executive directly, as in the Soviet Union and communist Eastern Europe, though this has been a formal rather than a meaningful power. They may have power to approve the nomination of the political leader of the executive branch by the head of state, as in Japan or in West Germany where the chancellor must be approved by an absolute majority of the Bundestag; or they may approve the whole cabinet as in Israel, Ireland, and the French Fourth Republic, or agree to individual members of the cabinet, as does the United States Senate. In parliamentary cabinet systems, such as those of the British, Scandinavian, and Dutch, governments last only as long as they control a majority in the assembly, which also supplies most of the personnel who comprise the government. But this in fact means that electoral decisions and party divisions, rather than parliamentary action, have determined the fate of governments.

Some assemblies, especially the Senate of the United States, also have the power to approve the appointment of high officials, civil and military, who are nominated by the executive.

Enforcement of Accountability

Assemblies sometimes have the power to influence or control governmental behavior, or to make governments accountable to them. The old device of *impeachment,* by which ministers or judicial officials can be tried for misdemeanors or incompetence by an upper house after indictment by a lower, has been used only rarely in the past century. In England the last such trial was in 1805 and in the United States the most startling trial, that of President Andrew Johnson, was held in 1868, although the threat of impeachment led to President Richard Nixon's resignation in 1974. A more important device derives from the precedent set in 1782 when a British government resigned as a result of a defeat set in on a major vote in the House of Commons. The House soon began to regard itself as the embodiment of the sovereignty of the people. Gradually the principle of collective and individual ministerial responsibility to the lower house emerged not only in Britain but also in the older Commonwealth countries. In some countries, such as the Scandinavian countries and Belgium, the executive is formally responsible to the upper chamber also; in others, as in France, defeats in the upper chamber have been regarded as occasions for a government to resign.

But again, political reality does not always correspond to theory and precedent. Governments rarely fall or ministers resign as a result of parliamentary pressure only. In Britain no government has been created or fallen for almost a century through such pressure, and there is no modern counterpart to the fall of the government in 1866 on the question of whether the franchise should be based on rent or on rates. Electoral decisions and party divisions have determined the fate of governments. If party discipline is maintained a motion of censure against the government has little chance of being carried. Since 1855 there have been only 16 cases of resignation by a British minister because of parliamentary criticism of his activity. In Germany the chancellor remains in office until the Bundestag elects his successor by an absolute majority; rather than any parliamentary action it was the loss of support within his own Christian Democratic party that led to the resignation of Chancellor Ludwig Erhard in 1966, and it was a spy scandal that led to the resignation of Willy Brandt in 1974. Similarly in Italy most governments have fallen chiefly as a result of splits and internal struggles within the ruling Christian Democratic party rather than because of parliamentary revolt against the government.

Many opportunities are available for attacks on the government: votes of no confidence, motions of censure, interpellation procedures (see below), debates on the budget and on other major policy and legislative issues. But French and Italian experience shows the problem involved. France under the Fifth Republic requires that a motion of censure be signed by one-tenth of the members of the National Assembly, who cannot sign another such motion in the same session; to be carried, the motion must be voted by an absolute majority after a 48-hour interval. Between 1959 and 1975 there were only 22 motions of censure proposed, and after the only successful motion the National Assembly was dissolved in October 1962 by the president of the Republic, who refused to accept the resignation of the prime minister. In similar fashion, Italy requires that a motion of no confidence in the government be signed by one-tenth of the membership, and that there be a three-day interval before it is debated. Between 1948 and 1958, 235 such motions were presented to the Chamber of Deputies and 101 to the Senate.

Yugoslavia is the only communist country in which government accountability to the legislature has had any semblance of reality. This was illustrated in 1966 when the government of the republic of Slovenia failed to obtain a parliamentary majority for a bill and offered to resign over this policy issue.

Control of Members and Organizations

No contemporary parliament possessing any real power is appointed by a government, as Napoleon appointed his legislative body or as Franco appointed the Spanish Cortes until 1967. Most assemblies control their own organization and membership, and possess powers of expelling or excluding elected members, although they do not always have the power to fix the qualifications for membership since these may be set by a constitution or electoral statute. In the United States the House of Representatives has acted six times since the Civil War to exclude members on grounds such as polygamy, pro-Confederate activity, corruption, seditious statements in wartime, and improper use of official money. But the exclusion of Adam Clayton Powell from membership in 1967 raised the problem of whether these actions had been unconstitutional and beyond the power of Congress, and whether the courts could adjudicate the decisions of the legislature. Members of democratic parliaments are jealous of their privileges, such as free speech, freedom from arrest for certain offenses, and freedom from legal action for their utterances or reports while engaged in parliamentary activity, which they claim as necessary for the performance of their duties. The House of Commons created the device of the Committee of the Whole—the whole body minus the Speaker—in order to eliminate the possibility of monarchical influence through the presiding officer. To the same end, officials of various kinds are forbidden to be members of the legislature, though by convention exceptions are made for members of the political executive.

Parliaments meet for varying lengths of time. In democracies they may meet for three months, as in Switzerland or Finland, or for over six months as in Britain, the United States, Israel, and the Low Countries. Sessions in communist or dictatorial countries are perfunctory, as in Franco's Spain where the Cortes every December approved dozens, sometimes hundreds, of draft laws in days or even hours, or in Hungary where the assembly meets for ten days a year. Sometimes, as in the United States, Sweden, and Belgium, the constitution lays down the times at which the parliamentary session will begin or provides for emergency sittings to be called by the executive. In Germany the legislative body is legally in session all the time. Normally parliament has the legal right to fix the length of its own life and its sessions, but in most cases it is the government that decides the time of meetings, duration of sessions, times for adjournment and dissolution of the chamber, and the calling of emergency sessions. In France, where the legislature has the right to ask for a special session, Charles de Gaulle even refused to comply in March 1960, on the grounds that deputies were acting on behalf of interest groups, not in the general interest.

Legislation

All legislative policy making is, as S. K. Bailey wrote in *Congress Makes A Law*, "almost unbelievably complex . . . and appearing to be the result of a confluence of factors stemming from an almost endless number of tributaries."[10] The passing of legislation is a significant, though not always the most important, activity of assemblies. Though modern executives sponsor the initiation of most legislation, there is still a legislative role for deputies, including amending and subjecting bills to critical analysis as well as initiation of them. Even in Britain, where little time is available for nongovernment members of Parliament to introduce bills, they have managed to sponsor bills that concern special interests or groups or that deal with moral or personal issues such as divorce, sexual relations, or capital punishment, which governments are notoriously reluctant to touch. In Italy over half the bills in the legislature are presented by deputies.

All parliamentary bodies operate through some kind of *committee system*, to allow for the division of labor among members, to serve for the detailed examination of legislation, and to provide an opportunity for inquiries into the behavior of officials or for broad scrutiny into ministerial departments. Some countries, such as Denmark, Sri Lanka, and India, emulate the general British system of setting up an ad hoc committee for the discussion of one particular bill. Most countries, however, provide for permanent and specialized committees concerned with all legislation or political behavior in a given area. In the United States and Continental Europe these committees are powerful bodies, permanent, specializing in a given area of subject matter, and capable of competing with the minister in competence and understanding as well as putting ministers under scrutiny, investigating administrative activity, eliciting information, and examining witnesses. Indeed, even the British system has been qualified by the creation not only of a number of specialist select committees but also by a number of special legislative standing committees for given subjects such as Scottish affairs, Welsh affairs, agriculture, science and technology (see Table 1). Almost all bicameral systems provide for joint committees,

Table 1. House of Commons Select Committees, 1974–1975*

Function, Area, or Type	Committee	Year Established
	Public Accounts	1862
Public	Expenditure (6 Subcommittees)	1970
Expenditure and	Nationalized Industries	1956
Administration	(3 Subcommittees)	
Control	Parliamentary Commissioner	1967
	Science and Technology	1966
Special Areas	(3 Subcommittees)	
	Race Relations and Immigration	1968
	Overseas development	1973
	Consolidation (Joint)	1894
Legislative	Statutory Instruments	1944
	Statutory Instruments (Joint)	1972
Types	European Secondary Legislation: One	
	Subcommittee	1974
	Privileges	c1630
Internal	Selection	1839
Affairs of House	Procedure	1961
of Commons	House of Commons Services	1965
	(4 Subcommittees)	
	Members' Interests (Declaration)	May 1974
	Wealth tax (2 Subcommittees)	Dec. 1974
Ad hoc	Assistance to Private Members	Dec. 1974
	Rt. Hon. Member for Walsall N.	Jan. 1975
	Violence in Marriage	Feb. 1975
	Abortion (Amendment) Bill	Feb. 1975
	Cyprus	Aug. 1975

*There are also 3 special standing committees: the Scottish Grand Committee (the 71 MPs for Scotland), The Welsh Grand Committee (the 36 MPs for Wales), and, since February 1975, the North Ireland Committee (12 Ulster MPs plus British MPs appointed ad hoc).

either as permanent groups to study legislation, as in Norway and Australia, or as ad hoc groups to draft legislation where disagreement exists, as in West Germany, or to study common problems, as in the Netherlands.

In recent years since the death of Stalin, the Soviet Union has created a number of committees of the Supreme Soviet to allow the deputies more opportunity to participate actively in legislative activities, to study problems, make proposals, and even initiate some legislation as well as to check the operation of government bodies. Since the time for a session is so short, the committees may be convened between regular sessions to examine matters within their competence.

Inquiring into Government Performance

For John Stuart Mill assemblies were to serve as organs in which popular demands could be articulated and wants made known, as forums for the discussion of all opinions on public matters, and as mechanisms for watching and controlling the operation of government.[11] It was this possibility of control over government that led Count Cavour to say that the worst of chambers is always better than the best of antechambers.

Probably the most significant contemporary function of assemblies is the supervision over and inquiry into the performance and behavior of governments. This function can be performed in a number of ways: by debate, by questions, by parliamentary inquiries, and by control over finance.

Debate "A politician" said Oscar Wilde "is a man who approaches every question with an open mouth." The most prominent opportunity for a public political dialogue is debate on the general outline of government policy or legislation. Formal occasions may be available for a grand debate, as in Switzerland, where the Federal Council is obliged to present an annual report to the assembly, or in Britain, Sweden, and the Netherlands, where the monarch's speech to parliament, the statement of future government policy, provides the opportunity for a long discussion of that policy. At other times debates may be initiated by party leaders or individual parliamentarians, making parliament not only the principal forum for political discussion but also the place where government can be sustained or opposed. This is the case to some extent even in Eastern Europe, especially Yugoslavia, where some government legislation has been rejected. In the Soviet Union ministers are supposed to make "progress reports" to both chambers of the legislature, though these are somewhat less significant than is the United States presidential State of the Union message to Congress.

A major method used in Continental European countries has been the process of *interpellation*. This is a means of obtaining information from the government or debating issues and gaining publicity for private and local interests, as in Switzerland; it can also be a means of controlling the government, as in the France of the Third and Fourth

Republics. In the Third Republic some 60 percent of all ministries fell as a result of a defeat on an interpellation.

Where parliamentary party discipline is strong, debates are not likely to diminish the number of laws passed, reduce public expenditure or greatly alter governmental policy. Nevertheless parliamentary debates still provide the most effective opportunity for the criticism of that policy, for the bringing of political and constituency grievances to public attention, and for the gaining of political experience by the opposition.

The crucial factor in a parliamentary democratic system is the presence of a legal opposition that is not only tolerated but that may sometimes choose the subjects and the opportunities for debate and criticism and have an impact on governmental action. It is a sign of the change in communist systems that in the Eastern European countries there have been occasional demands for an opposition party. The existence of a legal and constitutional opposition—the term "His Majesty's Opposition" was first used in Britain in 1826—depends on its loyalty to the system and its acceptance of the rules of the political game. The minority agrees not to sabotage the work of government, limits its opposition to pacific political activity rather than overt action, and does not attempt to use the civil service or military as a conspiracy against the government. In the classic situation, that of Great Britain, the opposition tries to moderate or amend government policy and legislation, makes the parliamentary arena a forum for appeal to the citizen body, and attempts to woo individuals or groups to their viewpoint so that the government majority will disintegrate. It is kept informed by the government, especially on defense issues, is consulted on major policies, and helps formulate the parliamentary agenda and timetable. The official and paid leader of the opposition can always be seen as an alternative prime minister. But realistically the function of opposition has become increasingly difficult in an era when the multiplicity and complexity of government proposals makes effective informed criticism difficult.

Opposition, Machiavelli argued, is a necessary condition of liberty. But the example of Britain—with its responsible constitutional opposition based on the internal stability of the system, acceptance of the regime by all, and anticipated alternation of ruling parties by peaceful change—is now rarely imitated. In developed countries with extremist ideological groups, opposition may be less responsible and seek to achieve power by force. Among the newer nations of the world only a few, such as Sierra Leone and Israel, have meaningful, constitutional oppositions. In few new countries is the opposition represented in parliament, and rarely in African and Asian countries is there much regard for those parliamentary procedures that restrain behavior and induce collaboration in developed regimes. On the contrary, parliamentary behavior in many of the newer countries, as sometimes in postwar Japan, has been marked by walkouts, boycotts, sit-ins, and other forms of disruption by opposition groups.

Questions The asking of questions by individual deputies—a device introduced in Britain, where it largely replaced the presentation of public petitions to the House of Commons—has been useful in obtaining information from ministers, exposing abuses, and serving as an indirect means of criticizing government policy. Countries that have imitated the British example, such as the Commonwealth countries, Israel, Italy, Germany, and the Netherlands, have not made it an important device in controlling the operation of government, and both the number of questions allowed and the time available are limited, although the number of questions asked in Germany has increased substantially in recent years. In the British House of Commons oral questions, followed by supplementary questions, have provided real tests of the knowledge, competence, and verbal skill of ministers and have been effective in changing administrative behavior.

Inquiries and investigations Most assemblies provide for committees of inquiry to study specific issues related to legislative or administrative activity. Occasionally the work of such committees bears little relationship to their purported raison d'être. The most notorious example in recent years has been the United States Senate Subcommittee on Government Operations headed by Senator Joseph McCarthy, the nature of whose inquiries often were a flagrant abuse of the power of the committee. In many countries, including Germany, Italy, Turkey, and the Netherlands, committees are not allowed to carry out inquiries of a judicial nature. But in general special committees with power to make investigations, gather information, sponsor research, call witnesses, and subpoena documents have helped control the work of the executive and make ministers responsible to the assembly.

In countries with parliamentary cabinet systems, in which the executive is politically accountable to the assembly, committees of inquiry have not played any substantial role except where alleged misdemeanors have been suspected. But the role of specialized parliamentary committees has been substantial. This is illustrated in a parliamentary cabinet system by the experience of the British Select Committee on Nationalized Industries in getting some degree of supervision over those industries, and by the legislative committees of the French Third and Fourth Republics, which were sometimes powerful enough to challenge ministers themselves. In nonparliamentary cabinet systems such as the United States, committees have played a formidable role, even if not as great as implied by Woodrow Wilson when he spoke of the United States government as "government by the chairmen of the standing committees of Congress."[12]

The legislature may also seek to exert some control over the executive by requiring that the latter obtain advice from certain prescribed sources, especially if the advice is tendered publicly and as part of a coherent program. In a complex political regime such as the American one, marked by a dispersion of political power, some executive agencies may seek the aid of a legislative committee against other executive bodies with which they disagree.

But the executive may reduce the potential influence of the assembly by making extensive use of outside groups. Some groups may constitute committees of experts formulating written reports and recommendations for the consideration of the executive. Some groups gather together as consultative committees in which representatives of social and economic organizations exchange information with government officials. Others may almost be considered as administrators in effect, since the advice they tender to government is usually accepted. Governments in recent years have made increasing use of advisory committees, both to obtain information and to act as a channel of communication between administrators and citizens, a role that some fear may usurp the place of the assembly. They have also created committees of inquiry to investigate questions about which they have genuine doubts, to gather public support, and even to postpone embarrassing or difficult issues. Between 1959 and 1968, 170 such committees were set up in Britain.

Control over finance Much of the control of a political leader in a democracy depends on his or her ability to define the significant policy issues and to obtain finance. Financial control is the key to political responsibility; the ability to discuss or approve the budget and estimates, expenditures, appropriations, the tax system, tariff proposals, and accounting procedures, and to see that financial provisions have been executed has inevitably led to parliamentary debate, inquiry, and some control over government.

In systems such as Japan's, the government reports to the Diet at regular intervals on financial matters. In Israel the debate on the budget of the office of the prime minister serves as a major review of government policy. Some parliamentary appropriation committees and subcommittees have the function of fact finding, or investigating the use made of voted funds, as do the appropriation committees of the United States. Others can inquire into appropriations and accounts; the British Public Accounts Committee, aided by the comptroller and auditor general, and the United States General Accounting Office (GAO), headed by the comptroller general, are examples. The GAO looks into the affairs of public departments and agencies, as well as into the books of private firms on government contracts.

But the effectiveness of parliamentary control varies widely. In a system with a strong executive such as the British, the government controls the whole financial process, and no appropriation for the public services or increase in public spending can be considered unless proposed by ministers. Debates on finance are discussions of policy issues rather than a detailed examination of estimates. In the French Fifth Republic the government can raise money even if the budget is not passed, and a deputy cannot propose bills or amendments that would reduce public financial resources or increase public expenditure. In Germany budget expenditure or new expenditure requires approval of the federal government. But in the United States, as in France of the Third and Fourth Republics, the assembly and its financial committees exercise strong control over the approval of expenditure and estimates, frequently negate government policy or intention, and allow deputies to initiate proposals for revenue and expenditures.

But financial accountability may also be obtained through nonparliamentary bodies such as public audit groups that are concerned not only with the legality and regularity of government accounts but also with economy and efficiency. A prestigious body such as the French *Cour des Comptes* can make inspections, exercise some judicial functions, and make recommendations to government departments and state agencies about their efficiency. In Germany the commissioner for efficiency in the administration performs a similar function.

Parliamentary commissioner or ombudsman Many countries have recently become interested in the use of an official, appointed by the assembly, to oversee the way in which government officials apply the law and regulations and investigate complaints by citizens against public officials. The office of ombudsman originated in Sweden in 1809, and has been imitated in Finland, Denmark, Norway, New Zealand, Israel, and Great Britain. There are also separate commissioners for military affairs in Sweden, Norway, and West Germany who safeguard the fundamental rights of military personnel or assist in controlling the armed forces. Individual grievances are examined in Japan by an Administrative Management Agency, in Yugoslavia by a Bureau of Petitions and Proposals, and in the Soviet Union by a procurator general. In the Swedish system the Justice ombudsman, or JO, oversees not only the administrative bureaucracy but also the courts, police, state church, prison system, and social welfare services. Though appointed by the Swedish Parliament, he acts an an independent official, although he submits an annual report to that body. He can make inquiries, call for papers and documents, and make spot checks. Recently he has handled about 1,000 public complaints a year. He points out defects in the law or in existing regulations and proposes alternatives. Though he can order the prosecution of an official who has committed a misdemeanor, he normally tries to persuade erring officials to alter their action, and invariably his advice is accepted.

Undoubtedly the ombudsman has been an effective device in protecting the rights of citizens, in helping check excessive administrative or judicial power, in insuring freedom of speech and the press, in obtaining fair procedures and impartial decisions, in examining the validity of administrative actions, and in forcing officials to explain the reasons for their decisions. One of the most recent commissioners is the British ombudsman, created in 1967 as an officer of Parliament, who acts only on the complaints of the members of Parliament, confines himself to departments of state and some minor authorities, and has access to documents unless a minister forbids it as prejudicial to the interests of the state.

A variant of the parliamentary commissioner is the military commissioner who, as in West Germany, helps maintain civilian control over the armed forces by examining any complaints made by soldiers against their military superiors. The intervention of the German Bundeswehr ombudsman as a result of complaints in 1966 led to 8 prosecutions, 13 disciplinary measures, 43 educative measures, and over 1,000 changes in military rules or behavior.

Valuable though the work of the ombudsmen may have been in resolving disputes between citizens and government agencies, they have had little real influence or great impact on administrative activity. Another recent development, the executive ombudsman, a centralized officer handling complaints or expediting action, may be viewed as an alternative method of dealing with criticism of government actions.

The Competitive Struggle for Power: Legislature Versus Executive

The role and power of assemblies has declined in almost all countries in recent years. In a former age parliament was a body struggling against royal or aristocratic power, and trying to limit and control that power. In an age when government functions and activity are continually increasing, when the executive can claim to be as representative of the people as is the legislature, when the bureaucracy has grown substantially in both numbers and significance, when the complexity of both internal and international affairs often prevents members of the legislature from fully understanding issues, when the leadership of disciplined, organized parties has dominated politics, and when the mass media has tended to concentrate on the personalities of leaders, parliamentary control over the executive has declined.

Moreover, the inadequacies of contemporary assemblies have become increasingly noticeable, although parliamentary gladiatorial displays between the political leaders have tended to mask the fact that the reality of power lies elsewhere. Where the assembly has an important committee system that contains members who have come to possess some degree of expertise, have amassed information, and have a research staff available to them, it will maintain considerable authority. But most parliaments, with poor working facilities, inadequate library and research means, and little secretarial assistance, and sometimes without specialized committees, are less likely to have a similar impact. Interested outside groups have become aware of this transfer of power and not surprisingly are now more concerned with influencing the executive than the legislature.

In the continuing struggle between the two branches of government, the executive has a number of powers at its disposal. Five of them are discussed below.

Dissolution of the Assembly

In nondemocratic systems the life of the assembly is often at the disposal, or the whim, of the ruler. In 1965 the king of Morocco, exercising a constitutional power, suspended Parliament after deputies had voted against the government three times in succession. In democratic regimes the executive may be able to dissolve the assembly at its discretion, as in Britain, or under certain conditions, as in the French Fifth Republic where the assembly cannot be dissolved within a year following an election resulting from a dissolution of the assembly; it may also dissolve the assembly on the defeat of the government on a vote of confidence. Sometimes a limiting condition on executive action is the need to get the consent of the upper chamber, as was the case in France of the Third Republic.

But the threat to dissolve is not always a serious one, for the ministry may fear that it will not survive the election or may face even greater opposition. "May the 16th"—the occasion in May 1877 when President MacMahon dissolved the Chamber of Deputies only to see the ensuring election confirm the republican majority he had found undesirable—is still a meaningful symbol in French politics, reminding the executive of the effective limits of its legal power.

Executive Initiative over Legislation and Policy

The post–World War II political situation has clearly shown that the executive controls the formulation and initiation of policy to a very considerable degree, and often the parliamentary agenda as well. The constitutions of Italy, West Germany, and the Fourth and Fifth French Republics all made provision for the executive as the initiator of policy. The striking degree of executive control was evident in Britain in 1966, when the prime minister announced the name of the first parliamentary commissioner of administration before the legislation creating the office had been passed. The technical complexity of legislation and the need for economic planning and social services require the sustained activity, information, and research that the executive possesses or can obtain from its advisory groups, though this does not altogether remove parliamentary initiative. Executive control over initiation is particularly strong if the administration controls a majority party in the legislature. In Britain in 1965, 66 of the 82 general statutes passed were initiated by the government. In France between 1959 and 1971, deputies voted for 1,177 bills proposed by the executive and 120 proposed by deputies themselves. Recent constitutional changes illustrate the growing power of the French executive. The constitution of the French Fifth Republic allows the prime minister to commit the administration to a given legislative text, which is considered as enacted by the assembly without amendment unless a motion of censure is passed. Table 2 shows a similar picture in Germany. Of the 2,731 laws passed in West Germany between 1949 and 1972, 2,082 were introduced by the cabinet.

Executive dominance is particularly noticeable in the area of foreign policy, over which the assembly sometimes has little control. After agreeing to the 1955 Formosa resolution and the 1964 Gulf of Tonkin resolution, the United States Senate found it had granted more power to the president than it had originally envisaged. Assemblies may have the function of ratifying treaties, and sometimes this has been of great significance; the United States Senate in 1919 refused to ratify the Versailles Treaty and entry into the League of Nations, and the French Assembly defeated the important European Defense Community Treaty in 1954. Assemblies may use certain devices, such as the need to implement foreign policy by statutes or appropriations, or general debates on finance, to try to control the executive. Yet in general this control is limited. The United States Supreme Court in the 1936 case *U.S.* v. *Curtiss-Wright* recognized that "in this vast external realm (of foreign affairs) with its important, complicated, delicate and manifold problems, the President alone has the power to speak or listen as a representative of the nation." The American president has tried to escape senatorial control by making executive agreements rather than treaties. In Germany the legislature is given an important role in the approval of treaties, but it must vote on the entire text without amendment.

Executive Veto or Delaying Power

An additional limit on the power of legislatures is the possibility of the executive veto or delaying action. Some regimes, such as the French Orleanist monarchy (1830–1848), have provided for an absolute veto by the monarch. In most democratic systems the necessary approval of legislation by the head of state is purely nominal, and it is difficult to envisage any circumstances under which the head of state in Britain, Belgium, Germany, or the Scandinavian countries would refuse his assent to legislation. But in the United States the *presidential*

Table 2. Legislation in Germany: 1949–1961

Initiator	Bills submitted	Number passed
Cabinet	1319	1108
Bundestag	922	347
Bundesrat	54	21

and the *pocket veto* (by which a bill automatically fails if the president does not sign it within the last ten days of a congressional session), has been exercised 2,290 times as of 1976 and has played a significant role in control of legislation, since 2,201 of these vetos were sustained. In Eire the president may submit a bill passed by the legislature to a referendum under certain conditions. In Pakistan the president can veto any bill of the National Assembly; if his veto is overridden by a two-thirds majority in the Assembly, he can submit the disputed bill to a referendum. In Weimar Germany the president had the right to call for a referendum on a bill; in the present regime the German president can exercise a suspensive veto, as he did in 1953, when he suspended approval of the European Defense Community Treaty in order to allow the Federal Constitution Court to decide on its validity.

Delegated Legislation

The concept of the supremacy of parliament presupposes the primacy of statutes passed by parliament. But in all modern systems the executive is able to make regulations to implement statutes and to make delegated legislation that has the power of statutes. Only where the assembly legislates on matters of detail, as in Sweden, is there little opportunity to make rules.

In a number of regimes enabling acts allow the assembly to delegate to the government the right to act and make decrees in given areas. In France and Belgium *pleins pouvoirs* (full powers) allow decrees to have the status of statutes, as do ordinances in Germany. In the French Fifth Republic, the government is able to act by making *ordonnances,* the result of either a temporary or permanent delegation of powers in certain areas; it may also supplement by decrees the general principles of the *lois-cadres* (framework laws) passed by the assembly. Moreover, the assembly can delegate its powers to the executive even in those areas of "legislative competence" allocated it by the constitution. In India the executive has been given a constitutional right to make laws when the legislature is not sitting, though later legislative approval is needed. In most systems, such as the United States, Japan, or France of the Fourth Republic, the courts have allowed this exercise of executive power even when no such constitutional power exists, though the courts have occasionally challenged the validity of the exercise of the power. Some constitutions allow the executive to make laws when the legislature is not in session, as in India, Pakistan, Brazil, and Ireland; these laws often must later be approved by the assembly.

In other countries—Switzerland and Denmark, for example—regulations made by the executive have been allowed on the principle of compelling circumstances.

Clearly, abuses can and do arise by this legal use of virtually unchecked power. In 1933 the German Enabling Act gave Adolf Hitler formal power to make laws without consulting the Reichstag, thus allowing him to rule as a dictator. During the Algerian War, French governments repeatedly censored the press, making 265 seizures of newspapers in France and 586 in Algeria.

The obvious advantages obtained by the use of delegated legislation are those of flexibility, expert advice, speed, and the ability to act in an emergency. But parliaments and lawyers have been troubled that the making of such regulations and the inevitable exercise of discretion in amplifying statutes is in the hands of individuals who have not been elected to perform this function and over whom control is limited at best. Even the Select Committee on Statutory Instruments, set up by the British House of Commons in 1944 to insure that the ability to make delegated legislation is not abused, examines the form of the legislation rather than its merits in deciding whether to draw the attention of the House to it.

Emergency Powers

Increasingly, political regimes allow the executive to make ordinances or regulations in the case of emergencies or external or internal danger over which parliament has little if any control. A government may exercise emergency powers and then seek parliamentary approval, or it may act on the basis of a constitutional provision or law that allows such action. Governments may therefore act at their discretion or when parliament decides there is a crisis, and declare a state of siege or necessity. In many countries ordinary constitutional guarantees, including the right of habeas corpus, have been suspended during emergencies, as in Northern Ireland where for a time the government could order the arrest of any person or hold him or her without trial, subject to some limits.

Almost all democratic systems have made use of emergency powers; Britain used such powers during both world wars, while in India the Preventive Detention Act has become a part of its political life and the forerunner of the transformation of the regime to an authoritarian system that lasted between 1974 and 1977. The government of the French Fifth Republic has power to make special legislation or declare a state of legislative emergency, which in 1962 was imposed for a six-month period. The West German government can use enabling acts to act in crises and can also declare a state of legislative emergency at the request of the chancellor supported by the Bundesrat, the upper house. This is limited to a period of six months, but during the emergency state a bill that the Bundestag has rejected will be enacted if the Bundesrat has passed it. In Finland the constitution includes provisions for urgent constitutional amendment, allowing for quick enactment laws containing exceptions to the constitution.

The use of emergency law, or the creation of a "constitutional dictatorship," as it has been termed, has its dangers. Many have attributed the rise of Hitler and the weakening of the foundations of democracy in Weimar to the use over 250 times of Article 48 of the constitution, which allowed the president of the republic to take measures to restore order that were not subject to approval by either parliament or the courts.

The Passing of the Golden Age

It is apparent that parliaments are no longer the dominant bodies in political life. Rarely do they control the legislative program, act as a watchdog over government spending and the financial process, or control ministerial behavior. Parliamentary control over finance is rarely effective, partly due to the limited time available for consideration of financial matters and partly to the inadequate information possessed by the assembly. In democratic systems governments are created and fall as a result of electoral decisions, not as the result of parliamentary debate. The government is now responsible for the initiation of most important legislation, relying heavily on advice from groups and bodies outside parliament, and for planning the legislative program. Control by the government over the whole administration and civil service has reduced the possibility of any real ministerial accountability to the chamber. Above all, the power of the party organizations and machines in generating political leadership, managing public affairs, and creating disciplined political forces has reduced the possibility of independent behavior on the part of parliamentarians once a party decision on an issue has been made.

Assemblies no longer sit for only a few months in the year, recess on the days of fashionable horse races, or begin their daily deliberations in late afternoon. Parliamentarians are now paid for their services, though rarely handsomely, and the view that they are part-time amateurs who should not constitute a class of professional politicians is now rarely expressed.

But almost all political analysts are aware that the golden age of parliaments is over. To be effective they must be provided with more information on the formulation and execution of policies. This necessitates specialist committees knowledgeable enough to prepare legislation and to examine the ministers on their policies. But even the most enlightened of regimes are not always ready to accept this development, and parliamentary assemblies find it difficult to compete with the executive power.

Notes

[1] John Locke, *Second Treatise on Civil Government,* chap. 13.
[2] Harold Lasswell, *Power and Personality* (New York: Norton, 1948).
[3] Saki, *The Unbearable Bassington* (New York: Viking, 1943), p. 15.
[4] P. W. Buck, *Amateurs and Professionals in British Politics* (University of Chicago Press, 1963), pp. 52–54.
[5] Donald Matthews, *U.S. Senators and Their World* (Chapel Hill: University of North Carolina Press, 1960).
[6] Robert de Jouvenel, *La République des Camarades* (Paris: Grasset, 1914); and William S. White, *Citadel; The Story of the U.S. Senate* (New York: Harper & Row, 1957).
[7] Matthews, op. cit, p. 93.
[8] Sidney Verba, *Small Groups and Political Behavior* (Princeton University Press, 1961).
[9] David Truman, *The Congressional Party: A Case Study* (New York: Wiley, 1959).
[10] S. K. Bailey, *Congress Makes a Law* (New York: Columbia University Press, 1950), p. 236.
[11] John Stuart Mill, *Representative Government,* chap. 5.
[12] Woodrow Wilson, *Congressional Government* (Boston: Houghton Mifflin, 1913), p. 56.

Chapter Nine

The Political Executive

The core of political power in modern systems, both developed and developing, lies in the executive organ of government and in the administration that serves it. To govern, as a French prime minister with an unusual appetite for milk once said, is to choose.[1] It is the executive that must speak the language of priorities. For a brief era between the decline of absolute monarchies and the twentieth century, parliamentary supremacy was proclaimed, the functions of government were limited, and the power of the executive seemed to give way before the omnipresent hidden hand of Adam Smith, which brought economic and political equilibrium.[2] But the normal situation is that executive leadership is concerned, as Chester Barnard in *The Function of The Executive* has argued, with the determination of objectives, the initiation of policy, the manipulation of means, control over the instruments of action, and stimulation of coordinated action. These objectives and policies are implemented by the administration.

The role of the modern executive is great, and its prominence is a reflection of the increase in the activities of the state. This role is no longer limited largely to the maintenance of internal stability and external protection. It now includes the creation of a welfare service, the extension of social welfare to the whole population, and "the restoration of compassion," in Adlai Stevenson's words. Spending on social services is now the largest single item in the budgets of developed systems. The modern executive also has a prominent part in economic planning. Planning may be used to stimulate economic growth in the older democratic countries, to attain political objectives or for ideological reasons in the communist countries, and to symbolize independence in the newer states. This may include controls over prices and wages to check inflation or restore a favorable balance of payments account. It may involve the stimulation of economic growth, development of public works programs, ownership or sponsorship of industry, and reduction of unemployment to the lowest manageable level. It implies control over taxation and banking loans, over public spending and the total volume of expenditure in the community. A substantial part of the gross national product of a nation is spent on defense either directly or indirectly through expenditure on research and the development of technology, particularly on highly specialized products. The state has become increasingly concerned with the extension of education, not only because this is desirable in itself, but also because it provides the supply of competent people necessary in modern economies. In recent years developed states have become increasingly aware of ecological and esthetic problems and of the need to improve the quality of life in communities troubled by the magnitude and complexities of metropolitan areas.

Some neolithic political figures notwithstanding, government is generally recognized as a necessary positive instrument for the achievement of common purposes, the performance of social responsibilities, and the conciliation of conflicting interests, economic as well as political, in the public interest. Government wields legitimate authority, having the legal right to determine policies and employ coercion, and is thus differentiated from other bodies or individuals possessing power or influence. Moreover, many functions of government—the coercive powers of the police, the expropriation of land or the decision on a development plan, the enforcement of compulsory taxes, the imposition of a draft for the armed forces—are different in nature from nongovernmental functions. Nevertheless it is not always easy to differentiate between public and private activity.

In *The Scientific Estate* Don Price has argued that the impact of science in government has blurred the lines between government on one hand and business and the academic world on the other, between public and private interests, as well as between the executive and legislative functions. A habitual feature of democratic systems has been the collaboration between the press and other mass media and the government by which the former refrain from publicizing any news item that the executive thinks may be injurious to the national interest. In recent years trade unions in some countries such as Sweden have made a social compact with management and have established a voluntary incomes policy that may be as effective and realistic as the government policy itself in reducing the demands of labor.

To perform its activities the executive has at its command the abilities of civil servants, the military forces, and professional experts, the powers of appointment, delegation of authority, and the fruits of patronage. The last may be a mixed blessing, for executive leaders have been known to complain of the malignant fidelity with which their supporters, hungry for office, have pursued them. The indolent Lord Melbourne, preoccupied with the secular affairs of life and unwilling to concern himself with ecclesiastical appointments, was heard complaining, "God dammit, another bishop dead."

In addition, the executive may control or dominate the legislative process, may be given the right to make delegated legislation, and may have the power to make quasi-judicial decisions, as well as possess the ability to wield legitimate coercion while engaged in its administrative activity. The technological means and the scientific devices available to the government can provide unparalleled efficiency, but they may also be saddening to those who believe that liberty to some degree has always depended on governmental inefficiency.

Political Leadership

The executive branch of government is the major organization through which political leadership can be expressed. Leaders emerge either by displaying outstanding ability or by showing themselves competent to carry out a necessary activity. In his study of Oregon politics, Lester Seligman has shown that top potential leaders are recognized by their display of ability through a network of educational, occupational, and social relationships;[3] similar recognition has occurred in many systems.

The qualities required or deemed necessary in leaders, and the avenues from which they are likely to come, differ with time and place. Leaders have been drawn from warrior and priest classes, the social aristocracy, hereditary groups, the educated, the bureaucracy, as well as from the leadership of political parties. The search for the ideal political leader has been perennial. Plato appealed for a philosopher-king, Aristotle wanted the prudent man, David Hume the man of reason who could compare ideas. Woodrow Wilson sought the wise and prudent athlete, and William Gladstone, uncharacteristically, thought the political leader should be a good butcher. In recent years Harold Lasswell has written of the need for people with ability to make judgments based on a calculation of probabilities and capable of applying techniques to administer those judgments.

There are few personal qualities or character traits universally possessed by all leaders, and the nature of leadership depends largely on the functions to be performed and on the behavior of the ruled. Nevertheless leaders share some common characteristics. Empirical studies of different regimes have shown that leaders are higher in intelligence, education, and social class than the average and have similar professional, social, or educational backgrounds.

Higher education is a crucial key to entrance into political leadership. This is shown even in parties such as the British Labour Party. In the 4 Labour Cabinets between 1924 and 1950, 33 of the 61 ministers came from upper or upper-middle class backgrounds, and 32 attended universities including 18 who went to Oxford or Cambridge. Studies of the West German political elite have shown the similar significance of Heidelberg and the chief *gymnasiums*. In France the role of the *grandes écoles* and the École Normale Supérieure in providing the political elite has always been great. The École Nationale d'Administration is now even more influential. Included in the 2,500 people who have graduated since its creation in 1945 are 8 members of the 1976 government including the president, the prime minister, and the ministers of the Interior and Finance.

The Roles That Leaders Play

Leaders have different roles to play, which can be categorized as founding, implementing, and stabilizing a regime. Jean Jacques Rousseau stressed the significance of "the legislator, the engineer who invents the machine," who consciously founds a regime and lays down its basic principles or laws, and then has or should have no further right of legislation.[4] This kind of leader is likely to be caesarist in nature and, in spite of Rousseau, to remain in power. Such leaders correspond to the type postulated by Bertrand de Jouvenel in *Sovereignty* as "dux" the dynamic, activist, promoters of action, the leaders who can weld together a group of previously unconnected wills and who bring about purposive change. Sometimes founders see their role as requiring aloofness and a sense of distance, such was the case with Charles de Gaulle. More often founders stress closeness and a sense of identification with their people: the Irish leader Eamon de Valera said, "If I wish to know what the Irish want I look into my own heart."[5] They are prophets pointing the way to the future and ordering the new society.

After the regime is established, some executive leaders may inherit the mantle of the founder or attempt to implement his or her basic principles. An Inönü will follow an Ataturk, a Beneš succeed a Masaryk. Other leaders may provide for the continuity of the regime itself, for the institutionalization of cooperation by all participants, and for the bestowing of legitimacy on the system. These leaders lay down the rules of conduct, arbitrate differences, and constitute legitimate authority. Some are likely to be charismatic in nature or innovative in behavior, while others are concerned with stabilizing the system and providing the necessary adjustment. The charismatic innovator is the outstanding leader; the stabilizer adjuster is the person who possesses common sense to an uncommon degree. The first type sometimes has insatiable appetite for politics, as with Winston Churchill, or an overwhelming sense of self, as with Lloyd George. A strong leader like Benito Mussolini, with no real convictions or principles, can devote his energies to the perpetuation of his own success and power. But many leaders are concerned with ends beyond the capture and use of power for its own sake. In his *The Art of Politics* Rexford Tugwell, comparing the careers of Franklin Roosevelt, Fiorello La Guardia, and Muñoz Marin, argued that all had in common a strong will to achieve certain objectives, though each was sufficiently obscure to be interpreted differently by his supporters. Each was upheld by enormous popular enthusiasm, and each displayed remarkable virtuosity in employing flexible means to achieve his ends.

Some of these strong leaders have placed faith in their own destiny, as did Napoleon Bonaparte; others have claimed external authority, as did Otto von Bismarck, who claimed he was performing the work of God in making Prussia strong and in unifying Germany. A familiar charismatic figure is the Bonapartist style leader who stresses the desirability of strong leadership, force, and action, is contemptuous of parliaments and opponents, and appeals to and gains support from the majority of the people. In the newer countries the strong leader tends to be young. The older nations frequently turn to *patres patriae* in times of crisis. At 6 crises between 1871 and 1958 France called on men like Adolphe Thiers, Georges Clemenceau, Raymond Poincaré, Gaston Doumergue, Philippe Pétain, and Charles de Gaulle, whose average age was 73.

In normal times it is the stabilizer adjuster who, having acquired power by an accepted regular procedure, wields it on the basis of the authority in his or her office or position. The office may make the man who rules on the basis of what Max Weber called "rational-legal authority."[6]

Limits on Leadership

Political leadership implies the authority to issue commands and to order the behavior of others who will obey because they accept that authority as legitimate—whether it be a charismatic leader, head of a tribe, *pater familias*, or a police agent—recognize the symbolism associated with the orderer, are indoctrinated by the propaganda or skillful manipulation of the leader, or acquiesce for a variety of reasons including faith, habit, fear, and indifference. Some social psychologists, of whom Erich Fromm is the most eloquent, have suggested that people need the authoritative figure of the father to provide guidance, and that the powerful charismatic figure can be seen as a substitute for the traditional father-figures such as the parent, lord, or monarch.[7] The leader can use a variety of sanctions—legal, economic, social, or moral—by which to obtain compliance. But he or she cannot use coercion too frequently; all leaders have known that it is wiser to use honey than vinegar. They cannot even expect their orders to be executed automatically. Richard Neustadt, in his *Presidential Power*, pointed out the bewilderment of President Dwight D. Eisenhower, accustomed to military obedience, on finding that orders he had given had not been carried out.

All leaders are obliged in some measure to echo the cry of the French revolutionary when talking of the mob, "I am their leader, therefore I must follow them." The Georges in their study of Woodrow Wilson showed that the leader who cannot adjust to the expectations of others meets with frustration.[8] In his essay *Shooting an Elephant*, George Orwell has skillfully illustrated the dilemma that the ruled may dominate the actions of the rulers so that the official is compelled, unwillingly, to shoot the elephant to avoid seeming a fool.

Formal checks on executive power result from constitutional limitations on the number of terms or years an executive leader can serve. In three countries an individual can serve only one term as president. In eight others, including the United States, a president is limited to two full terms. In eleven nations a president is not eligible to run again for at least one full term, and six other countries impose limitations of different kinds.

But the most meaningful checks on the behavior of the executive result from the glare of publicity shone by a free press and from the presence of an organized opposition. Governments tend to operate on the assumption that anything official is secret by definition and are reluctant to reveal information or provide documents before inquiries.

Inevitable differences arise from the demand of the people to be kept informed on the one hand, and the obligation of government to rule efficiently on the other. If at one extreme the Wilsonian view of policy made openly is too naive, at the other a reliance on Official Secrets acts to prevent information or criticism is too constricting.

Only in a minority of regimes is there a responsible opposition that not only can be a restraining factor on governmental behavior and be an expression of loyal discontent, but also possesses a real chance to become the government in the future. Some opposition, such as that of extremist groups in democratic systems, is irresponsible in that its actions are not related to the performance or maintenance of the system. The essence of nondemocratic systems is the elimination of any real opposition or possible political challenge to the regime. In the new countries a combination of arguments, based on a supposed identification of the state, society, and the ruling party and on the view that criticism of government is both harmful and wasteful because it leads to governmental instability and a lack of concentration on necessary tasks, has accompanied, or provided a rationale for, the control of power by a particular individual or group. Edward Shils has pointed out that opposition may exist in the newer states if it has a strong territorial or regional base,[9] or if it has foreign support, as in the cases of Katanga in the Congo, the south Sudan in the Sudan, Kurdistan in Iraq, Nagaland in India, or Sumatra in Indonesia. Otherwise, it may take an extralegal form, as in many of the African nations, or exist within the ruling groups because the traditional sources of opposition — intellectuals, trade unions, commercial interests, the press — have little opportunity to express their views or be taken into account. The seemingly dominant single party in many of the new states has created an atmosphere of frustration and discouragement that has limited the will of opposition groups, already weak or lacking material support. The regimes are rare in which the executive is secure, is attached to constitutional government, and is prepared to allow the opposition to acquire power while the opposition, strong enough to be taken into account, does not challenge the validity of government orders.

For a constitutional regime to survive, it needs not only a responsible opposition but also a military establishment prepared to remain subordinate to the political executive and to act as its instrument. In many new countries and frequently in Latin America, the civilian authorities have been unable to control the military, which has often destroyed regimes or taken over power. Even in developed regimes the military has often presented itself as a model of order, efficiency, and obedience in politically divided countries. The Anglo-American countries have been fortunate in military leaders who have always accepted the principle of civil supremacy, and who, with rare exceptions, have themselves possessed political and diplomatic skill. But even in these countries the size and proportion of the national budget devoted to defense expenditure, the technological factors compelling unification or integration of the military forces and a centralized establishment, and the insecurity arising from the existence of nuclear weapons, have given rise to anxiety that the military may be gaining a considerable influence over the making of foreign and defense policy and that the sheer size and cost of military weapons may reduce the number of alternatives available and thus indirectly determine military and foreign policy.

Dignified and Efficient Executives

All regimes provide for what Walter Bagehot called "the dignified" and "the efficient" parts of the executive.[10] The latter includes the dominant figures or group responsible for the direction of government policy. In most contemporary systems a single person, whether president, prime minister, or secretary general of a party, has emerged as the key figure in such direction, and the focal point of political attention. His or her prominence is often strengthened by the institutionalization of the office and the growth of a staff, such as the Executive Office of the United States president, the Chancellery in West Germany, or the Cabinet Secretariat in Britain, which works under the executive officer's personal direction, providing information and helping with coordination. Frequently the executive's superior status is symbolized by a special house: the White House, 10 Downing Street, Hotel Matignon, or Elysée Palace.

The dignified part is performed by a ceremonial head of state, who is either the recipient of strong personal feeling on the part of citizens or is the symbol of loyalty and unity, and who provides the regime with stability, continuity, and tradition, but who does not possess real political power as a result of occupying this particular position. The ceremonial head may be the choice of the legislature, as in France until 1962, or elected by the people, as in Austria, or succeed by heredity as in Britain.

In some nations, such as the United States or Mexico, the same person performs both roles. But in most countries there is a separation of personnel, and the dignified function is performed by a constitutional monarch, as in Britain and the Scandinavian countries, or by presidents elected by the legislature, as in the France of the Third and Fourth Republics, West Germany, Italy, or India.

Throughout history the role of the monarch, as Harold Nicolson has shown in *Kings, Courts and Monarchy*, has varied. He or she has been medicine man, representative of god as in Mesopotamia, a god as in Egypt under the pharaohs, an incarnation of god as in Aztec Mexico, a *roi fainéant* as in ancient Japan, a warlord as in medieval Europe, a prophet as in Islam, an embodiment of state power as in the Europe of enlightened despots, an instrument of oligarchic power as in prewar Japan. Though in the contemporary world there are some absolute monarchies, as in Ethiopia until 1974 and Saudi Arabia, and other regimes, such as Iran, Morocco, Jordan, Cambodia, Yemen, and Afghanistan, in which the monarch exercises real power, most modern monarchies are constitutional in that the monarch reigns but does not rule. Beside being a symbol of the independence and unity of the nation, constitutional monarchs are largely limited in their functions to advising and encouraging the political executive whom they may also choose. For constitutional monarchs or their representatives to intervene in policy making or act in a partisan manner would be to provoke a political crisis.

But though the constitutional monarch, like the indirectly elected president, is not a figure with any substantial authority, a monarch who has been on the throne a considerable time or a president who is genuinely respected or has served more than one term may acquire wide knowledge and experience or have the ability to influence the political executive. The queen of England, meeting the British prime minister one evening every week, is able to present a continuing point of view to changing ministers. Even in an age when daylight, or the spotlight, has been let in on the magic of monarchy, it still possesses great prestige.[11] Similarly, the advice offered by a revered and trusted figure such as Vincent Auriol was likely to have some influence on the politicians of the French Fourth Republic.

The great advantage afforded by this differentiation of executive personnel is that the political leader remains the executive responsible for governmental policy while the ceremonial head of state acts as a nonpartisan figure in the interests of the community as a whole. A nonextremist opponent of the government may therefore attack or censure the political leader without seeming to be disloyal to the regime and the state. Where one individual is both the ceremonial head of state and leader of the political executive, political relationships tend to be less clear since disagreement with government policy may be construed as contrary to the national interest or to the stability of the regime, or even as an act of treason a view that is now taken in many of the newer nations. On the other hand, the political effectiveness of presidents who combine both roles may be enhanced by their role as head of state, as has often been the case in the United States where the prestige of the office and ceremonial occasions have been put to partisan use.

A more complicated problem arises when a double political executive exists and a president shares power with a prime minister or chancellor, as in Weimar Germany, France of the Fifth Republic, and eighteenth-century Britain where the prime minister emerged as a competitor for power with the king. The Gaullist Fifth Republic of France illustrates the dilemma. The ambiguous relationship between president and prime minister in the Fifth Republic has led some to regard it, like the Weimar Republic, as an "Orléanist monarchy" in which the government needs the confidence of both the president and parliament to survive. The president and the National Assembly are elected at different times for different terms and have policy-making powers, and the consequences are unpredictable if the president cannot manage to control a majority in the Assembly. An unusual double executive is in San Marino, where the Socialist and Christian Democratic leaders constitute joint heads of state.

In some developing countries the monarchical institution still remains as the undisputed executive power. Politics and administration revolve about the royal groups, families, or tribal leaders who have traditionally held power and exercised a variety of functions. Change is initiated from within these favored groups from which almost all political leadership is drawn and to which almost all political participation is restricted. In other countries where the traditional elites have been deposed in part or in whole and where the process of political modernization has begun, the political leadership is likely to be more charismatic or more military in nature. It tries to gain the conscious support of different groups in the society and attempts to implement goals pertaining to all. But these executives do not always have available the means or technical resources through which to achieve their ambitious goals. Moreover there may be no agreed formalized procedures through which action is taken, nor any agreed method by which political succession occurs. Political leadership may not be firmly institutionalized while real political participation is limited.

In developing countries that are more politically modernized than the previous nations, the institutionalization of the executive and the succession of political leaders is likely to be more secure. Political participation may be open to all, though leaders are drawn from the upper strata of society, the higher castes, or the military. Leaders act through political parties, which try to mobilize support for their doctrines or actions.

Executive Organs

The operation of executive organs is shaped by many factors, but a traditional and still useful method of comparing the behavior of those organs is by examining the relationship between them and the legislature. In nondemocratic systems the relationship is clear, with virtually complete executive control over the assembly, if one exists at all, or over the people. In the more developed democratic systems a number of different types of executive organization can be distinguished, though political reality sometimes makes it difficult to place a particular system into any other type. In general, classifications of five different types are often made.

Cabinet Government

The model for a cabinet government type of regime is Britain. For Bagehot "the efficient secret of the British system was the close union, the nearly complete fusion of the executive and legislative powers.[12] The fusion arises from the fact that political leadership is provided by the Cabinet ministers, a small group of leaders of the party controlling a majority in the House of Commons, who are drawn, with rare exceptions, from the two houses of Parliament. Members are almost never drawn from other professions, business, or academia. The members of the Cabinet, most of whom head a government department, are responsible collectively to Parliament for political decisions and governmental policy, for their legislative program and agenda, while individual ministers are responsible for the administrative conduct of their particular departments or for actions performed by them.

In Britain most members of the Cabinet are members of either of the two chambers when appointed; those who are not are immediately found a seat in one of the two chambers. But in some systems of this type, such as those of the Netherlands, Norway, France, and Luxembourg, a deputy must resign his or her seat on appointment to the government.

The legislative experience of cabinet ministers varies widely. In Britain over half the Cabinet ministers in the twentieth century spent 10 or more years in the House of Commons, and less than 10 percent spent less than 5 years before appointment. Of the 1967 Cabinet, 12 of the 23 members had been in the House of Commons for 21 years and 6 others had been members for 15 years or more. In the 1964 Conservative Cabinet 12 of the 23 ministers had been in the House for 19 years, and 7 others for 14 years. Hugh Dalton, one of the main leaders of the Labour party in the 1940s, gave salutary advice to an ambitious deputy: "If you have not entered parliament by forty, forget it." Very rarely does a backbencher, a parliamentary newcomer, move directly to the Cabinet, though more nonmembers of Parliament have been appointed to the Cabinet since 1916 than in previous years. On the other hand, in Canada, with a similar relationship between executive and legislature, some 35 percent of the Liberal party Cabinet ministers were appointed after less than seven years in the House of Commons.

The head of the government, and nominally all members of it, is appointed by the head of state, constitutional monarch or president of the republic. Though the head of state has some discretionary power and may prefer one individual to another, in most cases his or her choice is circumscribed. In Britain the choice is self-evident if one party has an overall majority in the House of Commons and if that party has an acknowledged and acceptable leader. If one or the other of these conditions is not present, some element of discretion arises out of an uncertain situation. In practice, the leader, once nominated by the head of state, chooses the other members of the government; this may be a personal choice or one shared with senior party leaders or, as in the case of the Australian Labor party, it may be the implementation of a decision made by the party caucus.

Though cabinet government has operated successfully in multiparty systems such as Eire, the Scandinavian countries, and the Low countries, this type of regime works happiest in a two-party system. A cabinet, composed of members of the politically united majority party, is able to control the initiation of legislation and the planning of policy, to make quick decisions and to obtain harmony with the legislature, while at the same time the opposition can act as a real critical force. Cabinet government is not a system of political equilibrium, but rather one of concentration of power in the executive. Parliamentary controls through the introduction of motions of no confidence or censure are rarely effective. The government stays in office until the next election or until it has lost control of its majority in the assembly. Though the power of dissolution is nominally in the hands of the head of state, in practice it is generally exercised by the head of government, though there may be political limitations on his or her power to act. The electorate is given the ultimate power of deciding between the opposing parties. An inestimable advantage of the cabinet government type of regime is that it provides in this way for a smooth transition of political leadership.

The pressure and complexity of government affairs have led to certain changes in the manner of operation of cabinet government. The cabinet has been regarded as the center of governmental coordination and of policy making, and as being collectively responsible for all decisions on major issues and the approver of all other decisions. But the seemingly great power of the cabinet and its control over all policy matters is qualified by three factors. Even in Britain the executive is not always united, and a de facto, informal hierarchy consisting of the politically most powerful individuals often exists within it. In addition cabinets have experimented with a system of overlords who have tried to coordinate groups of subordinate ministers and departments, usually unsuccessfully.

A second factor has been the development of a structure of cabinet committees, consisting of a small number of ministers under the chairmanship of a senior minister; such committees may be the real decision-making bodies in the areas with which they are concerned and their views may prevail in the cabinet as a whole, which has power of general supervision of the work of committees.

But above all the ascendency of the British prime minister is plain. Prime ministers have varied in talent and character, and in the nature of their interests, from a Lord Melbourne who could remain awake in Cabinet meetings only when suffering from insomnia, to a Harold Wilson who concerned himself with all major areas and said that a prime minister must know everything that was going on and must think about the problems of the administration as a whole and about long-term strategy. But all have been professional politicians who have acquired a reputation in Parliament, have normally had considerable governmental experience by serving in a variety of Cabinet positions, and have climbed, in Benjamin Disraeli's pithy phrase, "to the top of the greasy pole."

More than *primus inter pares,* a British prime minister is now in a position of being able to formulate policy and make decisions without consulting the whole Cabinet, as was shown by Anthony Eden in the Suez crisis of 1956. Harold Macmillan, prime minister in 1962, could dismiss a third of his Cabinet without warning or preparation; "dismissed like a pregnant parlormaid" was the comment of one saddened and embittered minister. The prime minister consults with individual ministers or groups of them at his discretion, decides what Cabinet committees to create, and establishes task forces and working parties. On his retirement in 1976 Wilson said of his 8 years as prime minister that he had presided over 472 Cabinet meetings and thousands of Cabinet committees, answered 12,000 parliamentary questions, read at least 500 documents every weekend, and attended 100 political meetings a year in the country. Elections largely radiate around the personalities of the prime minister and the leader of the opposition, so that they largely become a plebiscite on which of two individuals will head a government. In the 1964 and 1966 British elections the strategy and conduct of the Labour party campaign was closely in the hands of Harold Wilson. This has almost created a quasi-presidential system in which the prime minister draws support from the people, and the real check on his behavior is anxiety about the vote at the next election rather than the next vote in the House of Commons. Modern British political leaders have become skilled in using the mass media, especially television, as a direct link with voters, thus bypassing parliament and projecting themselves as national figures.

Presidential Systems

The presidential system is typified by the United States and countries such as Mexico, Latin America, and South Korea that are influenced by it. There is a single identifiable head of the executive, the president, who is also head of state, who is usually popularly elected, and who has general determination over policy. The members of the cabinet and of all executive agencies are appointed by him and are clearly in a subordinate position, though they may have their own sources of support. There is no collective responsibility of the cabinet and all ministers remain responsible to the president only. Nor does the cabinet aid in resolving the constitutional problems of a separation of powers, which might be reduced if the cabinet was composed of leaders of the legislature.

The American president is responsible for the control and coordination of government, and is aided not only by his cabinet and a multitude of other executive agencies, but also more personally by the Executive Office, which includes the White House staff, the Office of Management and Budget, the Council of Economic Advisers, and the staff of the National Security Council. He obtains from them the necessary information with which to formulate policy and secures advice from them on issues with which he ought to concern himself. Much of the business of government is reviewed and organized for the president by this personal staff, which in 1976 numbered over 5,000.

There is less harmony and more tension in this system than in a parliamentary cabinet system for two reasons. One is the inevitable rivalry between the executive and legislature, which share power and are jealous of their power; personnel are separated, though members of the administration may be questioned or make statements in committee hearings. The president can influence Congress through leadership of his party, his role as Chief of State, the prestige of his office, and his personal appeal. In the United States only a small percentage of cabinet secretaries have had any congressional experience. The executive cannot dissolve the legislature, which remains in existence for a given term. Equally, the legislature cannot obtain the resignation of a cabinet member since he or she is responsible to the President and not to it. In spite of the political rivalry between the two branches, they cooperate in the initiation and passage of legislation, in the making of appointments, in appropriation and budgetary issues, and in the making of treaties. Normally the president proposes and Congress disposes, though the legislature may be able to impose checks on effective policy. But in foreign affairs, because of the element of secrecy involved, the information available only to officials, and the activity of diplomatic agents, as well as the role of the president both as chief diplomat and as commander in chief, the executive is clearly the dominant power, formulating policies, negotiating treaties without the Senate being able to interfere, and bypassing the required two-thirds majority in the Senate for approving treaties by making executive agreements that do not need the participation of the Senate to be effective.

But one caveat is that the president may not be capable of controlling the whole of the executive. Some of the multiple centers of executive power, especially the regulatory agencies, may resist or thwart his policies. And if the system of checks and balances has prevented the likelihood of authoritarian government, it has also led at times to the weakening of effective government.

A second reason for difficulty is that the president may come from a different party than does the majority of the legislature, or he may be unable to command the support of his own party even if it does possess a majority. Nevertheless, the president is the leader of his political party and possesses different degrees of influence depending on his ability to control the party. The American system has not prevented strong leadership from being exercised, but the absence of executive control over a disciplined majority party in the legislature has necessitated the use of other forms of influence, pressure and appeals to public opinion as well as to the party, the use of patronage, and advantage taken of his access to the media.

Though the power of the presidency is great it is not unlimited. The president is not only obliged to share powers with Congress in a number of areas but is also dependent on the legislature for statutes and finance by which to implement policies. He cannot depend automatically on the support of the legislature, nor even on the members of his own party in it. There is no party caucus that binds the two branches together, nor any agreed party program that both support. In addition, Congress may limit the president's control over his own administration by approving independent action by subordinate officials, by its power of confirming the nomination of bureau chiefs, by its financial control over administrative programs, and by its creation of independent commissions not under the direct control of the president. Constitutionally, it has the right to impeach the president for treason, bribery, or other high crimes and misdemeanors.

In countries influenced by the model of the United States, the presidential system has not been altogether successful. Latin American systems have tended to become dictatorships, and only in a few countries such as Paraguay, Costa Rica, Chile, Brazil, and Peru have attempts been made over the years to limit executive power. Latin American dictatorships have been tyrannies tempered by assassination, for since the beginning of the nineteenth century, 30 presidents and ex-presidents and one president-elect have been assassinated in that area.

Almost all attempts in Latin America to limit presidential power or to require the collaboration of the legislature in certain matters have been unsuccessful. Constitutional restraints on executive power, such as the requirements that all official acts of the presidents be countersigned by a cabinet minister, or that ministers are responsible to the legislature and are expected to resign if censured by it, or that the legislature can appoint committees to investigate the conduct of the executive, have rarely been meaningful restrictions.

There are a considerable number of variants from the American model, as may be exemplified by the systems in Pakistan, Finland, Kenya, France, and possibly India.

In Pakistan, a less democratic presidential system than that of the United States, the system was consciously adopted as simpler to work and less likely to lead to instability than the parliamentary system, which required a much higher level of education, prosperity, and public spirit. The president possesses strong executive powers and appoints ministers who can take part in legislative debates but who are not responsible to the lawmakers. The assent of the president is required for all legislation, and he can refer proposed legislation to the electoral college for a vote if the legislature overrides his veto. The "basic democracy" of Pakistan created by General Ayub Khan was in reality a method of local administration, and every important local government body had a nonelected nominee of the president at its head.

In Finland the indirectly elected president is the holder of executive power, nominating and dismissing ministers, determining the general lines of foreign policy, and having the power to sign certain treaties without submitting them to parliamentary control. But though the president is the nominal commander of the armed forces and though he has the authority to dissolve the legislature, he does not possess as strong a control over the administration as does the president in the United States. He can influence the government and sometimes makes decisions contrary to government policy, but he is not the leader of a political party.

The Indian system too, while largely patterned on the British system, has some characteristics of the presidential type. Considerable powers are possessed by the president, in whom the executive power is vested and who is more akin, in theory, to the United States president than to the British constitutional monarch. He is chosen by an electoral college comprising the members of the two houses of Parliament and of the legislative assemblies of the states. But though the president has been a respected figure who has influenced policy on a number of occasions, he has normally avoided party politics, has not exercised any independent functions, and has been guided by the prime minister and the Council of Ministers in whom real power re-

sides. Indian practice is similar to other regimes framed on the model
of the British, such as the Irish, which make it obligatory for the president to exercise his powers only on the advice of a cabinet.

Though the Indian president can dissolve Parliament, can return
some bills to Parliament for reconsideration, can summon leaders to
form a government, can suspend governments in the states, and is the
nominal commander in chief of the armed forces, neither of the first
two presidents have been willing to compete for power with the Congress party or with Nehru or his daughter, Indira Gandhi, while they
held office.

The president of the French Fifth Republic, chosen at the beginning of the regime in 1958 by an electoral college of 81,000 consisting
largely of local councillors, is now elected directly by the people. In
neither case was the head of state chosen by the Assembly or by the
political parties. Originally the President was to act as head of state
and as national arbiter "far removed from political bickering," choosing the prime minister and concerning himself with some but not all
areas of government. But political events, especially the settlement of
the problem of Algeria, compelled Charles de Gaulle to intervene
more directly in the conduct of affairs, especially foreign affairs and
defense, and obliged him to ask for the approval of the electorate for
certain actions in a number of referenda in Bonapartist fashion. For
de Gaulle "it is the President alone who holds and delegates the authority of the state." His nominee, the prime minister, held office only
as long as he maintained de Gaulle's confidence: both Michel Debré
and Georges Pompidou were dismissed when they lost that confidence. The president regarded himself as responsible only to the
people, not to the legislature, which he could dissolve, nor to the political parties, which he regarded as destructive of national unity. His
own staff, including a Secretariat General, often duplicated and anticipated the work of departmental ministers and was sometimes responsible for the formulation of policy.

Nevertheless the prime minister is constitutionally given the power
to "direct" the action of the government, which "determines and leads
the policy of the nation" and which must have the confidence of the
legislature to which it is responsible. Government and legislature work
together, but with different functions and with separate personnel,
thus theoretically creating a balanced constitutional structure. This
separation of powers de Gaulle regarded as the basis of democracy.

The Fifth Republic, however, is even today after de Gaulle a regime
in which the president rather than the prime minister has been the

chief director of policy. He has unquestioned control over those matters, such as foreign, military, and defense affairs, which fall within
his reserved domain, and has intermittently concerned himself with
economic and social questions. De Gaulle used the referendum on a
number of occasions to seek popular approval for his policy decisions.
He interpreted the constitution in a highly personal fashion, refusing
to convene an emergency session in 1960 on rather specious grounds,
making use of Article 16 providing for emergency powers over a six-
month period, and making rather arbitrary use in 1962 of the provisions by which constitutional amendments take place.

The Gaullist regime, both during and after de Gaulle's own presidency, is not and has never been dictatorial, but it is one in which
strong executive powers, both presidential and governmental, have
been exercised, while the role of the assembly has remained a subordinate one, partly due to the unexpected situation of a Gaullist majority in it for some years. The Fifth Republic, in fact, is a regime somewhere between the British and the American, because the president
and the prime minister constitute a double executive. Such sharing of
executive power can only be successful and the system can work harmoniously only if the prime minister is prepared to accept the policy
of or subordinate his views to those of the president when differences
arise. In 1976 disagreement between the president and the prime
minister led to the latter's resignation. The conflict between the two
executives arose not only over specific policy issues but because the
prime minister opposed the president's intention to establish a more
"presidential" style of government and to reduce the scope of independent action by the prime minister.

Assembly Government

This type of system is the obverse of the first type. It is characterized by the dominance of the legislature over the executive, which has
little coherent control over legislative and financial matters and which
rarely has the real power, though it may have the legal authority, to
dissolve the chamber. It is the assembly rather than the government
which is the real decision-making body. Theoretically the Soviet
Union and other Eastern European countries have this type of regime. The Presidium of the Supreme Soviet, elected by the parent
body for a four-year term to exercise the functions of the Supreme
Soviet during the 11 months of the year it is not in session, is vested
with wide powers. It acts as the collective president of the Soviet

Union, having the right to quash legislation, convene the Supreme Soviet, appoint and dismiss ministers, appoint senior military officers, and conduct referenda.

But the regimes most characteristic of this type in democratic systems were the French Third and Fourth Republics, with weak political executives, constant cabinet instability—102 in the Third and 24 in the Fourth Republic—an inability in practice to use the procedure of dissolution, and few coherent, disciplined party organizations. Seeing itself as the true representative of the sovereignty of the people and deputies as embodying a part of that sovereignty, the French legislature established its superiority by preventing or making difficult any coherent or stable development of policy and by determining the creation and fate of governments. The leading figures of the chamber and the key members of legislative committees, the chairmen and *rapporteurs*, might be as influential as ministers in the shaping of legislation and policy and would be regarded as political rivals capable of replacing them.

Council Government

The struggle for political power almost inevitably results in a single person or group becoming the dominant political force. Systems of collective leadership, as in the Venetian "Council of Eleven" in the fifteenth century, are rare. They are also difficult to operate, as the Soviet Union has discovered; the Presidium of the Supreme Soviet, which has legislative, executive, and judicial functions, has never been the source of any important decisions. In Yugoslavia under Marshal Tito, there is a collective presidency made up of representatives of the country's six republics and two provinces, though Tito, in reality, dominates. The British Cabinet system is not one of collective leadership since the prime minister is clearly far more than *primus inter pares* (first among equals).

The most interesting example of such collective leadership is the council government system of Switzerland. The political executive, the Federal Council (Bundesrat) of seven, is elected for a four-year term by the Federal Assembly, the two chambers of the Swiss legislature, and the members are normally reelected if they wish to be. There is no formal presidential head of state, but one member of the Council acts as titular head of the country for a year. Each member is head of an independent department, and their continuity gives them great expertise and knowledge in the operation of that department, although there is no political solidarity. The Council is always a coalition, the members of which have for some time come from four parties: the Radical, the Catholic-Conservative, the Socialist, and the Peasant parties. Certain conventions govern its membership: no canton is represented by more than one member; the three cantons—Zurich, Bern, and Vaud—always get one each; and not more than five members may represent German-speaking cantons. Among the members of the Council there is usually a balance between Protestants and Catholics, between the large and small cantons, between the four languages spoken in the country, and between industrial and agricultural areas.

The Council is now the initiator and drafter of most legislation, has executive power over the administration of foreign and military affairs, promulgates laws, publishes ordinances and administrative decrees implementing the legislation, and exercises some judicial power in the area of administrative law. It is collectively responsible for its policies in principle, and its members normally stand united even when one of the four leading parties criticizes the government. In fact the decisions of each councillor in his or her department are usually ratified by the Council as a whole. Yet the Council is not a powerful body and tends to administer policy rather than formulate it. The Assembly cannot remove the government by a motion of no confidence, but equally the Council cannot dissolve the Assembly, which exists for a fixed term.

Other regimes that have tried to imitate the Swiss model have rarely succeeded. Uruguay, which in 1961 adopted a collegiate system, with a nine-member council made up of representatives of the two major parties, gave it up in 1966 in favor of a strong presidency. In Burma the Council of State, composed of a representative from each of the 7 states and 7 administrative regions and 14 others, is the nominal supreme policy making body, electing its own chairman who acts as head of state.

Chancellor Government

Another variant of the cabinet system, but distinctive enough to be regarded as a separate type, is the present West German system. Under this system the federal chancellor alone is proposed by the president of the republic, is elected by an absolute majority of the Bundestag, and is responsible to the legislature. The chancellor appoints the individual ministers, who are responsible to him and not to the Bundestag, though they are parliamentary deputies, and it is he who can ask for the resignation of a minister.

The prewar Weimar regime also provided for a chancellor democracy as well as for a president with certain strong powers, but the office never became a powerful one before Adolf Hitler. In the present regime the chancellor, partly because of the personality of the first incumbent, Konrad Adenauer, has been the real effective political leader, dominating the cabinet he has chosen and controlling the legislature, deciding ministerial disputes, and using the state secretaries of his office for advice and policy planning. Moreover, the chancellor is removable only by a constructive vote of no confidence, which entails the election of a successor by an absolute majority of the Bundestag before his removal can come into effect. This is difficult to obtain under present German conditions; it is possible only if the governing party is split but can find sufficient votes from another party to support an alternative leader, as in 1966 when Chancellor Ludwig Erhard was replaced by Kurt Georg Kiesinger. The only attempt at removal of the chancellor, then Willy Brandt, failed by a margin of two in 1972. The position of the chancellor is strengthened by his ability, if his motion for a vote of confidence has been defeated as happened in September 1972, to ask the president to dissolve the Bundestag or to issue a declaration of a "state of legislative emergency," which for a period of six months could enable government bills to become law if the Bundesrat had consented to them even if they had been rejected by the Bundestag.

The chancellor, according to the constitution, "determines the general policy of the government." On the other hand ministers are responsible for the conduct of their departments and can make decisions on concrete, individual matters. The relationship between chancellor and ministers and the reconciliation of the sometimes conflicting principles of hierarchical power placed in the chancellor, collegial or cabinet decision making, and ministerial autonomy have been more matters of empirical approach than conscious theory.

The policy of the chancellor is not always outlined in official instructions to ministers but may be understood through formal speeches or informal discussion. The chancellor is kept informed of departmental activities by reports on all subjects that raise policy issues. Not only does he personally appoint the ministers, but he also can and has altered the functions of ministries. In addition, Adenauer sometimes acted beyond his formal powers, but the limitation of his interests to foreign affairs allowed considerable authority to ministers concerned with internal affairs. The chancellor is assisted by a Chancellery of about 100, headed by a state secretary, a senior civil servant with special status. The chancellor may not directly intervene in the work of ministries, but the members of his Chancellery keep contact with those departmental officials who have similar functions, as well as collect information on matters with which they are concerned.

Though ministers can introduce legislative and budgetary proposals, no important decisions can be made against the wishes of the chancellor or, sometimes, the minister of finance. The government is a group of departmental heads rather than of policy makers, and ministerial office is not in itself a politically powerful position. The responsibility of ministers to the legislature is ambiguous. Although constitutionally only the chancellor and not the ministers are answerable to the assembly, in practice they are asked questions on the conduct of their ministries by deputies who may also move interpellations or even motions of censure on individual ministers. The legislature has retained a more considerable degree of independence from the executive than in the cabinet regimes, and a group of senior deputies, the Council of Elders, formulates the agenda of the assembly. But as in the other types of system, the legislative branch is clearly subordinate to the executive. The strong role played by the chancellor in the system has been restrained as much by electoral decisions, the operation of the federal system, the prominence of interest groups, the compromises resulting from coalition making, and the judicial review of the Federal Constitutional Court, as by the opposition of the assembly.

Notes

[1] Pierre Mendes-France, *Gouverner C'est Choisir* (Paris: Julliard, 1953).

[2] Adam Smith, *The Wealth of Nations*, Book IV, chap 2.

[3] Lester Seligman, "Political Recruitment and Party Structure: A Case Study," *American Political Science Review* (March 1961), pp. 77–86; and L. Seligman et al., *Patterns of Recruitment* (Skokie, Ill.: Rand McNally, 1975).

[4] Jean Jacques Rousseau, *The Social Contract*, Book 2, chap 7.

[5] Lord Longford and T. P. O'Neill, *Eamon de Valera* (London: Hutchinson, 1970), p. 467.

[6] Max Weber, *The Theory of Social and Economic Organization*, eds. A. M. Henderson and T. Parsons (Glencoe: Free Press, 1947), Part 3, sections 1–2.

[7] Erich Fromm, *Escape from Freedom* (New York: Avon Books, 1965).

[8] Alexander and Juliette L. George, *Woodrow Wilson and Colonel House* (Briarcliff Manor, N.Y.: Stein & Day, 1956).

[9] Edward Shils, "Opposition in the New States of Asia and Africa," in *Center and Periphery: Essays in Macrosociology* (University of Chicago Press, 1975), p. 428.

[10] Walter Bagehot, *The English Constitution* (Ithaca, N.Y.: Cornell University Press, 1966).

[11] Kingsley Martin, *The Magic of the British Monarchy* (Boston: Little, Brown, 1962).

[12] Bagehot, op. cit., p. 65.

Chapter Ten

Administrative Systems

All regimes employ a more permanent group of administrators than the transient politicians who occupy political office. The purpose of the group is to fulfill or enforce public policy. The role, size, and functions of administrators now occupy a significant place in political activity. While assemblies pass hundreds of bills each year, and the courts handle far fewer cases, the administrative bodies handle thousands of matters annually. The numbers involved in administrative functions have increased correspondingly. The growth of political participation and the greater demands of individuals and groups have resulted in more services and administrative organizations; public service is almost the fastest-growing area of employment.

At the origin of the United States administration there was a secretary of war and one clerk, a secretary of state and six clerks, and a Treasury that issued a one-page budget. By 1800 there were still only 64 clerks in the civil service. The United States federal government is now the largest spending body in the world and the largest American employer with nearly 3 million civilian employees; federal, state, and local officials number 14.6 million and account for 37 percent of the gross national product. In many contemporary European countries, the proportion of government employees in the total labor force is often as high as 10 percent. The increase in the numbers of civil servants in the United States, Great Britain, and France, is shown in Tables 1, 2, and 3. In many Western countries government is now the largest employer as well as the major investor and controller of enterprises, and its total expenditure is over one-third of the GNP. In Britain central and local officials numbered 1.6 million in 1975, and public enterprises accounted for about one-quarter of the economy. The concern of the state with economic, social, and cultural matters and with the implementation of social ideals as well as with the historic defense and diplomatic activities has meant not only that public expenditure has increased at a rapid rate, but also that the civil service is increasingly playing a managerial role in contemporary life.

The Administrative Process

Different views have been taken on the nature of the administrative process. For F. W. Willoughby certain fundamental principles and practices existed in all governmental operations in order to obtain efficiency and economy.[1] The view associated with Luther Gulick also stresses the objective of efficiency and is concerned with the technical problems of specialization of function and division of labor. Administration, according to Gulick, is concerned with implementing defined objectives by a number of activities such as planning, organizing, staffing, directing, and coordinating, reporting and budgeting.[2] More recent analyses by Herbert Simon and his school concentrate on administrative activity as the interrelationship of people in organizations, and pursue the problems of decision making and of behavior within those organizations. Simon and Chester Barnard have both argued that all organizations are systems of coordinated activities in which cooperating people perform formal functions to fulfill a common purpose and communicate that purpose to all concerned, and are also associated in patterns of informal behavior that maintain the common values in which they believe.[3] The task of the administrator is thus to provide the system of communication among the members of the organization as well as to implement the purposes and objectives of the organization.

The most commonly accepted view of the administrative function in modern systems is Max Weber's theory of administration as bureaucratic activity.[4] The word "bureaucracy" has often been used as a pejorative term, but it is also a neutral description of indispensable activity by a group of public officials arranged functionally on the basis of the activity to be performed, organized vertically by a hierarchical chain of command in ordered disciplined fashion, and territorially depending on the degree of centralization of the system. Weber suggested that the essence of bureaucracy was rationality and predictability of action. It is characterized by the distribution of activities in a rational way and the allocation of authority to command and a sphere of competence to act in a stable fashion and according to pre-

Table 1. Federal Civilian Employees in the United States

1816	4,837
1861	36,670
1901	239,000
1932	605,496
1941	1,042,420
1945	3,816,000
1952	2,600,600
1965	2,539,000
1974	2,893,000

Table 2. Civil Servants in British Central Government

	Nonindustrial Staff	Industrial Staff
1902	107,000	
1914	164,000	
1920	368,900	
1939	387,000	240,200
1945	704,600	665,300
1952	684,000	418,900
1963	688,100	359,300
1976	564,000	180,000

Table 3. French Civil Servants: Central and Local Governments

1914	468,500	
1922	594,600	
1936	681,700	
1947	1,000,600	
1956	1,102,400	(Central)
	64,800	(Local)
1962	1,310,000	(Central)
	62,500	(Local)
1975	2,668,000	

scribed rules. As a formal organization it requires the use of written documents and files, careful keeping of records, attention to detail, and routine and rigid procedures. The *merit system* implies that objective criteria such as achievement and seniority determine the selection and promotion of employees, while personal nepotism and ascription is reduced to a minimum.

Thus for Weber bureaucracy meant that qualities such as precision, speed, unambiguity, knowledge of the files, continuity, discretion, unity, strict subordination, reduction of friction and of material and personal costs are raised to the optimum point. For Robert Merton the bureaucratic structure induces officials to be methodical, prudent, and disciplined, and to maintain a high degree of reliability of behavior.[5] Bureaucratic behavior may therefore insure not only efficient or-organization, but also predictability and accountability.

Impersonal obligations of the office and relationships among officials who are constrained by mutually recognized sets of rules mean that an individual member of the organization occupies a known role and behaves in an expected way. Anyone who replaces that individual will perform the same role. The problem of succession is therefore less acute in bureaucracy than among political leaders. Holders of a given position are able to make decisions that fall within their competence, and all officials rest assured that their orders will be faithfully executed by their subordinates. In Western systems, to insure that officials act impartially and without fear of political domination, the civil service is usually a self-governing body with members whose rights are protected and who are given security of tenure and adequate pension allowances.

Even in the formal hierarchy of a civil service, some units are more prestigious and more influential than others. In Britain the Treasury and more recently the Civil Service Department, controlling the machinery of government and engaged both in financial oversight and economic planning, constitute the peak of the mandarin caste. In France the supremacy is clearly identified of the *Grands Corps,* which contains the intellectual and influential elite of the civil service and into which entrance is possible only for the most gifted students. The members of the *Grands Corps* — consisting of the *Conseil d'État,* the *Inspection Generale des Finances,* the *Cour des Comptes,* the prefects, and the diplomatic service — hold the key positions in the French administration, wield great influence over the conduct of affairs, and are regarded as a flexible reserve from which administrators in many services will be drawn. In 1964, 120 of the 200 members of the *Inspection Genérale des Finances* held high administrative posts in other units, as did 48 of the 210 members of the *Conseil d'État.*

Informal relationships among administrators may be as significant as the formal pattern of organization in many regimes. The formal chain of command is not always the way to expedite action or obtain coordination, and influence may be more diffused than the lines of authority suggest, as many students of human and industrial relationships have shown. Close relationships arise within groups whose members have been through a similar educational and training process or that have a sense of common purpose. If there is an "old school tie" network in Western democracies, there is a similar bond created in the Soviet Union as a result of association and training of administrators in technical schools. The French college system and the German system of pre-entry training for the civil service both tend to produce groups with a high esprit de corps. And from the Italian south, which is inhabited by only one-third of the population, come two-thirds of the members of the civil service, who are generally conservative and share the southern distaste for the industrial and more democratic north.

Bureaucratic Differences

Bureaucracies can be differentiated according to various criteria. They differ in the degree to which they embody the criterion of rational behavior. They differ on the nature and extent of functions performed, from the indispensable maintenance of law and order and demand for taxation to a system of total planning. In *Bureaucracy and Political Development* Merle Fainsod has suggested a useful model of five relationships of the bureaucracy to the flow of political authority that can be used for comparative analysis. In the first type, a representative bureaucracy is responsive to the political leaders and ultimately to the political will of the community. Initiative is taken with an awareness of the existing consensus, and change is conditioned by competitive party politics, as in the Western democracies. In the second type, a party-state bureaucracy exists in one-party systems. The state bureaucracy is dominated or controlled by the party apparatus, or both may be subordinated to a dictatorial ruler as in Stalinist Russia.

A third type, the military-dominated bureaucracy exists where the armed forces dominate the political executive. Inevitably it is most concerned with strengthening the military establishment and with inculcating military characteristics of discipline and authority, though it may also sometimes be interested in social change. Equally inevitably it will depend increasingly on civilian advice as its responsibilities increase. In a ruler-dominated bureaucracy system, the fourth type, the administrators serve as a personal instrument of the autocratic ruler or dictator. The influence possessed by individual bureaucrats will depend on the qualities needed by the ruler. In the fifth type, bureaucracies may rule either directly as colonial administrators or indirectly under a nominal ruling person or group.

Administrative Types

The nature of the administrative system is determined not by problems of personal management, but by the concerns of government, by social relationships, the general culture and ethical values, and often by history and tradition. The French tradition of state intervention from Jean-Baptiste Colbert on, for example, makes bureaucratic intervention in individual economic organizations less contentious than in the Anglo-American systems. The British civil service accepts the political pluralism, values, and bases on which ministers make decisions. In Britain it is exceptional for a civil servant to enter politics; in Germany the reverse is true. In Norway the civil service is acknowledged to play a prominent role but one that respects the consensus on political means and ends. There are differing degrees of politicization of the civil service: it tends to be high in Belgium and low in Holland and Sweden. In communist systems, apart from Yugoslavia, the senior civil service is an appendage of the party.

Since literacy is the indispensable requisite for administrative activity, the administrative structure has always been tied to the educational system and thus indirectly to social class. The early administrative elite of Europe was largely composed of clerics. But the nature of the desirable official and the qualities he or she should possess have changed with time and place. In Britain able and intelligent candidates are selected with little reference to their educational specialization on the premise that they can be trained on the job. This pragmatic approach implicitly denies there is a science of government or specialized knowledge that higher civil servants ought to possess.

By contrast, in Continental Europe government is thought of as a profession, and a specialized training is regarded as desirable for entrants, though a variety of approaches to training and recruitment exists. In France candidates for the higher civil service attend the *École Nationale d'Administration,* where a three-year course includes some practical work as well as academic study, largely in economics and politics. In West Germany, which except for its Foreign Service does not have the centralized recruitment or training that exists in France, candidates for the higher civil service are generally qualified in law and have some practical experience on the judiciary or in police administration and local government, though in recent years a training in economics has been encouraged.

If the German system has historically concentrated on producing jurists in the higher civil service, the British have sought intelligent generalists with a liberal arts education and with personal attributes such as "character" and "poise." Generalists of this kind have the advantage of being able to write clearly and precisely, but their lack of technical ability may make them unprepared for activities such as economic planning and fiscal policy, and job rotation has meant that many administrators perform functions for which they are unqualified. As a contrast, the United States civil service is marked by a much greater emphasis on experts, absence of job rotation, and by the ability of departmental heads to choose appropriate people.

The type of desirable civil servant is closely related to the manner of selection, as can be seen by a comparison of the British and American administrative systems. In the United States recruitment is open to all, including people from outside occupations, while Britain recruits almost entirely from those leaving school or university. The United States official may be recruited primarily for particular programs or activities and is often an expert in that field. The British official is selected by difficult examination on the basis of general intelligence and knowledge. The British civil servant remains in his governmental career, but it is becoming increasingly apparent that the British civil service lacks the wide range of contacts and the links with industrial managements and associations, local authorities and universities that are necessary in a complex society. The Fulton Committee report of 1968 proposed changes in the structure, recruitment, and organization of the British civil service, calling for great specialization and more modern management techniques. Much of the report has been implemented by creation of a Civil Service Department to recruit and to manage the civil service and to organize the machinery of government, by establishment of a Civil Service College to teach management techniques, and by elimination of the former division of the civil service into three major classes.

In European countries the ranks into which civil servants are divided correspond very closely to educational levels in the community. Britain, Germany, and Italy all have, or have had until recently, a civil service divided into three or four broad ranks, entry into which is dependent on passing an examination of university, intermediate, or matriculation level.

Behind the differences between the European and American systems lies an unstated difference of perspective on social relationships. In Britain the old divisions between the civil service classes, especially between the administrative, executive, and clerical classes, corresponded very closely to the divisions in the social hierarchy, though there had been increasing promotion from the second to the first class. Administrative divisions were widened by geographical separation since the administrative class was almost entirely located in the capital, while outside London the senior officials were members of the executive class. The senior members of the American civil service are not as socially different from their subordinates as have been their counterparts in Britain, though the latter have also tended to come from a middle or upper-middle class background. Greater opportunities for promotion and more lateral entrance have characterized the American system, and it is not uncommon for state and local officials to be appointed to federal positions.

In *The Job of the Federal Executive*, Marver Bernstein has pointed out that when new government agencies are created in the United States to carry out new programs, officials are often drawn from outside the government, and many come from the worlds of business, academia, and the professions. Their motives for entering government service are mixed, and among the chief reasons are the desire to perform public service, to pursue political objectives, to be concerned with stimulating activity, to improve their career prospects outside of government, to gain prestige or deference, or to occupy a place of power. All of these officials can be expected to favor the increase in size and in functions of their agencies. In the civil service of the United States there are currently some 1,200 appointed senior administrators who have academic, industrial, legal, or scientific backgrounds and among whom there may be considerable turnover. Senior administrative positions have not been as closed to scientists as they have been in Britain, and it is a familiar experience for scientists to initiate and publicly advocate policy.

Senior civil servants have been compared in other ways depending on their perceptions of their roles, their orientations to politics, the type of political minister with whom they deal, and their relationship to changing contemporary needs.

One view differentiates between the "classical" and the "political" bureaucrat.[6] The classical type, close to the model of Max Weber, tends to believe that an objective standard of justice, legality, or technical practicality can be used to resolve public issues and tends to be legalistic, illiberal, elitist, distrustful of politicians, and possibly undemocratic in outlook. The political bureaucrat recognizes possible differing interpretations of the public interest, advocates a preferred policy, and joins in a search for compromise with politicians, parties, and interest groups. The former type seems to be more common in Italy than in Britain or Germany.

A second approach is to compare the degree to which civil service patterns of orientation and attitudes reflect the political environment, relate to other elite groups, and support the stability of the system.[7] Dutch civil servants appear more opposed to political conflict than do the civil servants of most Western European countries. But, as with the British civil service, there is a mutual tolerance and great respect exhibited between the political and administrative elites.

Another analyst suggests that the impact on policy making of the civil service depends to a large degree on the nature and interests of the political minister, who may see his or her role in different ways: as the "initiator" of policy, as the "selector" among alternative policy objectives—the role most approved by civil servants—as the "ambassador" selling a department's policies, as the "executive" concerned with managing the department, as the "minimalist" who is uninterested in basic changes.[8] In each case the role of the civil service will relate to that chosen by the minister.

A fourth view compares two major types of senior civil servants: the traditional and the modern.[9] The traditional type—diplomats, prefects, military heads—tend to come from the upper or aristocratic class and have a literary, legal, or military training. The modern type—planners, heads of public enterprises and agencies, aides of ministers—are usually trained in economics, finance, and business administration. The size and influence of the traditional group are declining since technological and communication changes have reduced its significance, while that of the modern group, which relates more to business and labor organizations, consumer groups, and local politicians, has been increasing. In addition, in many Western countries a number of activities, such as planning, information gathering and dissemination, controlling atomic energy, and providing secret service functions, have been put under the direct control of the political head of the executive branch and its civil servants.

The Role of the Bureaucrat

The views that bureaucrats have historically taken of their role have varied, as S. N. Eisenstadt illustrated in *The Political Systems of Empires.* Some preferred to serve the rulers, dominate strata of the regime, or become passive tools of the rulers. Others have been critical of the objectives of the rulers and have either sought individual or collective self-aggrandizement or have tried to serve the polity as a whole rather than simply the rulers. In Prussia the bureaucracy saw itself as the guardian of the state and its law. The bureaucracy has often played a vital role in aiding the creation of political unity as in Meiji Japan, Prussia under Frederick William, the Soviet Union since 1917, and some of the newer nations.

The theory of ideal administrative behavior is that the administrator obtains all possible information on a subject, carefully weighs alternatives, and chooses from among them. But Charles Lindblom and David Braybrooke have pointed out that administrative decision making is generally not preceded by the establishment of precise goals, while the pressures of limited time and a large volume of information prevent the administrator from attending to all the facts and choices available.[10] The administrator must simplify the relevant data to make it comprehensible and may often act, in Herbert Simon's word, as a "satisficer," seeking a satisfactory decision rather than the best possible one.[11] He who controls the point at which the administrative process simplifies a complex situation has a determining influence in the making of decisions.

There is no single correct form of organizational structure or pattern of behavior since this is dependent on time, place, economic development, physical size, the technology of the country concerned, the social forces, and the cultural environment. The United States and Sweden, for example, are more apt to use independent boards and agencies or to appoint an official to perform a task than is Britain, which acts mainly through governmental departments. Nor are there any universal principles of organization or "proverbs of administration." If Western European countries have placed great stress on the differentiation of administrative levels, the United States has emphasized the difference between line authority—the authority possessed by those in a chain of command—and staff authority, possessed by those who engage in research and provide advice but who have no power to command.

The administrator's approach to a problem is conditioned by a number of factors, of which three seem especially significant. The first is the amount of relevant information of which the administrator is aware and can master and the time in which he or she can absorb it. The second is the individual's frame of reference, largely the result of his or her social background, education, training, and professional experience. And affecting all of the administrator's behavior is the accepted working of the organization and the political culture of the system.

The impact of political culture might be shown by the difference between the operation of the German and Italian bureaucracies. The former not only is highly professional, often rigid in behavior, incorruptible, and efficient, but also benefits from the communal regard for legalism and is supported by the great prestige that bureaucratic office has enjoyed in Germany. In Italy, with its deeper cultural, religious, and political divisions, its more cynical attitude to government and greater willingness to use corruption, its public service dominated by people of south Italian origin, and its prominent Communist party, there is less respect for a bureaucracy, which is often more responsive to political influence and which is involved in politics.

The views of administrators on their function is also normally dependent on the political environment. In a comparison of Soviet and Western administrative behavior, John Armstrong has argued that Soviet administrators place a lower priority on welfare administration than do their Western counterparts, since the more capable officials prefer technical activities to involvement in a politicized administration.[12] At the same time, the engineering training of many Soviet administrators leads, consciously or not, to an "engineering" and somewhat callous approach to human problems.

As a contrast with both European democracies and the Soviet regime, in the United States with its egalitarian social atmosphere, the development of an elite corps, and to some degree of a career service in government, was checked. The nonaristocratic ethos has allowed scientists and professionals to occupy some of the senior positions in the administrative hierarchy.

Administrators and Specialists

Conflict is always acute between the administrators and the professional experts. Differences result partly from the nature of the activity of the two groups, the first concerned with the orderly and continuing processes of government, and the second with the use of techniques to provide needed services. Administrators in a given system adhere to professional standards and share a knowledge of techniques by which public policies are formulated and implemented. The administrator is concerned with economy and efficiency. The expert is somewhat suspicious of bureaucratic deliberation or negativism, which he or she tends to see as imposing checks on imaginative programs. This difference between the generalist and the specialist may be widened by the different perception each has of the other's social status, administrators tending to rank themselves higher than professional experts.

In Britain there has always been a tendency for specialists to be regarded as subordinate to the administrative civil servants, and usually a division has existed between specialist and administrative officials who have been placed in separate hierarchies. But in recent years the work of government agencies has become increasingly technical and the role of specialists has increased so that they now have responsibilities and duties previously reserved for administrative officials. It is evident that there has been no transfer of duties from specialists to administrative officials.

A similar argument has been made by Don Price in *The Scientific Estate* in his review of the four broad functions performed in governmental and public affairs: the scientific, the professional, the administrative, and the political. At one end of the spectrum, science is concerned with the advancement of knowledge free from any utilitarian considerations; at the other end politics is concerned with purpose, policy, and action. But the professionals and the scientists have been playing an increasing role in the formulation of purpose and policy and in the initiation of action, while politicians act in a setting largely constructed by science. By 1958 almost half the bureau chiefs in the United States were professionals and scientists, and their influence has been strengthened by their frequent alliance with congressional committees, sometimes against the political executive.

Non-Western Administrations

Students of the newer nations have indicated that the admirable characteristics of administrative systems in Western societies are not necessarily desirable in developing countries. The introduction of a merit system may interfere with the manner in which tribal authorities control their peoples. Fred Riggs has argued that in the new nations a merit system may prevent the growth of a spoils system, which may be needed to aid the development of party organization, and that a career bureaucracy without correspondingly strong political institutions does not necessarily result in administrative efficiency.[13] Too rapid an expansion of the bureaucracy may delay political development. Indeed, Ralph Braibanti in his study of Pakistan has suggested that a less hierarchical and status-ridden bureaucracy might have reduced its prestige and that a preference for the specialist rather than the generalist civil service might have lessened the possibility of stability.[14] Bureaucracy in some of the newer nations is not always modeled on Weber's legal-rational type since it may be lacking in skilled personnel, may have unclear organizational lines, and may be concerned above all with rapid economic development. Economic development may benefit more from civil servants who are more adventurous than from those who adhere closely to accepted procedures. Moreover, in developing countries bureaucracies need to serve both the cause of development and the traditional features of the society that remain.

Morroe Berger in *Bureaucracy and Society in Modern Egypt*, a study of 249 civil servants, argued that there seemed to be no positive correlation between the degree of professionalism and the Weber model of bureaucracy that in the Western countries was also accompanied by the development of a monied economy, the emergence of the modern nation-state, and a capitalist economy. Weber's model may therefore be of limited utility in the non-Western world. In some of the newer countries the bureaucratic function may even be performed by the military, as in Burma, or in collaboration with the military, as in Egypt and Turkey.

Students of the newer countries have recently tried to formulate more appropriate models of non-Western administrative behavior. The most interesting studies have been the work of Fred Riggs who suggested at first an apposition between two model types, Agraria and Industria.[15] They are differentiated by their economic basis — either rural or industrial — their social structure — depending on the relative significance of primary organizations, such as the family, tribe, or clan, and secondary associations such as unions, schools, and clubs — and by their ideology — either sacred and subjective or secular and objective. In spite of the somewhat forbidding abstract nature of these generalizations, Riggs' models have been useful in illustrating different administrative methods. In Agraria, a relatively static and immobile society, inherited status is more important than achievement, there is deference toward superiors, and officials who possess a high status constitute a powerful class. Legal rules are not applied equally to all but differ according to the individual concerned. In the more mobile systems of Industria achievement is more highly regarded, the reputation of business is high, while the status of officials is relatively low.

A second formulation of the subject by Riggs, in a rather private language of his own in *Administration in Developing Countries,* led him to postulate three types of bureaucratic activity, depending on whether the society was "fused," "diffracted or refracted," or "prismatic." He sees bureaucracy as concerned not simply with the application of rules, but also with "aggregating" interests, with articulating the interests of itself as a group, and with participation in the whole political process. As countries developed they might move from fused to diffracted societies as a result of forces such as political factors, the need for money, increased armies, better communication, the growth of markets and of a money agriculture, the growth of population, the spread of science, and increased industrialization. Through these models Riggs suggests comparisons between bureaucracy in diffracted societies, which are essentially the Anglo-American types, and fused and prismatic societies. The last type possesses a combination of characteristics present in the other two types and is typical of developing nations, in which bureaucracy may be marked by traditional status, elite recruitment, corruption, inefficient budgeting and accounting, a gap between income and expenditure, a lack of enforcement of rules, and an independence of political control.

Useful though Riggs' typology may be in differentiating administrative behavior in the newer from that in the older nations, abstract concepts of this nature are not necessarily congruent with political reality. Lucian Pye in his study of Burmese politics and administration has warned that, far from being unduly influenced by personal relationships as an observer might logically expect to be the case in an undeveloped society, the Burmese have tried to solve problems by "finding a relevant regulation in an appropriate rule book."[16]

But certainly, administration in the newer nations has been a formidable burden since the colonial powers rarely prepared those countries for independence and self-government. When independence was granted to the Sudan in 1956, the executive and judiciary were completely in the hands of British officials, and Sudan, like other countries such as Burma, Ceylon, Indonesia, Tunisia, and Morocco, was obliged to obtain foreign officials in order to perform certain services. Only in India was the proportion of natives staffing the higher civil service over 50 percent.

Experience in the newer nations since the former colonial powers have withdrawn their political and administrative organization has illustrated the cruel dilemma facing countries whose society is industrially undeveloped and whose economy cannot yet support a good educational structure; such countries usually contain a largely uneducated people and thus have a small source from which administrators can be drawn. The public services are obliged to compete with industrial, commercial, and educational institutions for skilled individuals from that small source. The dilemma is intensified where the society lacks a common language, as in India, which has 14 main languages and hundreds of regional dialects and for which English, as Nehru said, was a window on the outside world.

The administrative task is complicated even more where internal divisions may prevent coherent government from operating, as in Morocco where some tribes have refused to cooperate with administrators from other tribes, in Ghana where native chiefs have been recalcitrant, or in a number of countries where the administrator is popularly viewed as the tax collector or corrupt official. Even more problems arise from fiscal difficulties because some of the newer countries find difficulty in imposing meaningful taxes on a newly independent nation. There is thus considerable dependence on unpredictable foreign aid for the provision of essential services.

In regimes whose major emphasis has been on the need for national unity, bureaucrats have shown great loyalty not only to the state as such but also to the existing government, which has, in some systems, chosen the civil servants by favoritism or nepotism. Nevertheless, there is often an uneasy relationship between the civil service and the political executive concerning their respective spheres of competence. At the same time the shortage of competent administrative personnel and the poor lines of internal communication have led to excessive centralization in many of the newer states, with consequent delays in decision making, inefficient operation, and deleterious effect on expression of differing opinion.

The Administrative Function

If Woodrow Wilson and Vladimir Lenin had little else in common, they both argued at one time that administration was simple. For Wilson it was the clerical part of government; for Lenin in the future desirable social order "the more and more simplified functions of control and accounting will be performed by each person in turn, will then become a 'habit and will finally die out as special functions of a special stratum of the population."[17]

On the contrary, the administrative task has always been complex and onerous. Historians record that Henry II of England became bowlegged as a result of attending to his administrative chores for too long a period. In medieval Europe, the administrators were the friars, dedicating themselves to the vows of poverty, chastity, and obedience. Though opponents of government action have been eager to suggest this is the case, bureaucracy is not synonymous with either laziness or tyranny, nor does it need only simple talents and skills.

Administrators give effect to political policies and decisions, provide services, and exercise regulatory powers. The administrative task is concerned with five overlapping functions: (1) establishing and maintaining a coherent machinery of government, (2) planning or managing the affairs of economic enterprises, (3) collecting information and data, (4) acting as aides to political ministers, and (5) helping in the formulation of policy.

The first function is the basis of all others because government and power depend on organization. By running the machinery of government the bureaucracy provides the essential physical equipment, the organizational patterns, and the procedural arrangements that allow policy and orders to be implemented. In executing policy the bureaucracy normally adheres to precedent that insures both stability and impartiality and that at best allows the bureaucrat with a sense of historical continuity to provide purpose to administration. But the bureaucracy must also master the intricacies of the corridors of power and be familiar participants in the workings of parliamentary, executive, and advisory committees. In the United States this need has been shown by the increasing degree of liaison with the legislature established by administrative officials. Continuous liaison may exist between members of the two branches who have known each other over a number of years. Similar intimacy may exist between administrators and interest groups whose cooperation may be essential to carry out services such as education, agriculture, and health.

A key factor in running the machinery of government is control over appointments—especially to the top positions in the administrative departments, government agencies, and corporations and concerns in which the government has a financial share—and over the choice of outside experts to be put on the hundreds of advisory committees necessary for government in the modern world. But civil servants also possess in reality a substantial amount of patronage by their power of making recommendations to political ministers. In Britain this power, largely in the hands of Treasury officials, extends not only to other administrative posts but to judicial and some ecclesiastical positions, the poet laureate, the constable of the Tower of London, and the trustees of national museums.

Managing the Economy

In all countries the preparation of the annual budget is now a function of the executive, and the senior financial civil servants have responsibility for framing the major proposals under political guidance. The role of parliamentarians in this process has been sharply reduced in most countries. The bureaucracy is necessarily involved in management of a considerable part of the economy since all modern regimes are engaged to some degree in planning. Developing nations seek above all greater economic development. All developed nations are moving in the same direction of trying to maintain full employment, increasing productivity, exercising some control over prices and wages, determining the level of public investment, establishing priorities for social welfare, housing, and health services, and planning parts, if not the whole, of the economy. In recent years the task of controlling inflationary pressures, which have led in some Western countries to annual price increases of over 20 percent, has been of equal importance to the reduction of unemployment, which was higher in the 1970s than it was for the previous two decades.

Sometimes the market largely dictates what commodities should be produced and at what cost; planning, aided by government investment and budgetary controls, influences the areas in which economic growth should occur, but takes a variety of different forms. Planning in the Netherlands tries to affect aggregate levels of demands and output, while in Sweden and Japan it largely means making economic forecasts and setting general economic objectives. In France private industry participated with government officials in drafting the plans to modernize the economy and in helping execute them. By contrast, in Norway private industry is rarely consulted in the formulating of government programs for the public sector of the economy. In Britain government intervenes directly through the departments or local government and indirectly through the boards of nationalized industry in enterprises accounting for an expenditure of about 60 percent of the gross national product and employing about 25 percent of the working population.

More extreme forms of planning exist in those regimes, such as the Soviet Union, in which the state controls the productive forces, allocates resources, and determines prices and wages. But communist regimes, while emphasizing central planning, may take less extreme forms. The Czechoslovak "socialist market economy" allows central planners to formulate long-term plans, fix basic wage rates, and determine major investment decisions, while individual factory managers have some degree of discretion and independence, though not enough to be a rival power to the Communist party.

In both democratic and undemocratic modernized countries the civil service has been involved in the planning process with differing degrees of success. But in the developing nations planning has been less successful, not only because it has been both ambitious and undertaken with limited economic resources, but also because the administrative officials have often been incompetent, have not possessed adequate data, have worked with a lack of technicians and with an unclear organizational jurisdiction.

Regulation of economic and social matters has necessitated the growth, not only of the civil service and government departments, but also of administrative boards, regulatory commissions, and public corporations that can issue orders and regulations concerned with these matters and can adjudicate differences. The independent commissions are all similar in that they consist of an administrative board, not a single head, appointed for a fixed term. Their members, often experts in the field, are in general free from interference from both the executive head and from the legislature. Independent regulatory commissions are freer of partisan political considerations than are government departments, though they are not removed from political pressures, and they make rules and judicial decisions as well as administer their areas of competence in a more independent and more expert fashion than do the departments. But in an era of positive government, the technical levels of policy making with which the commissions are concerned are closely interrelated with major government policies, and critics have suggested that the commissions exercise power in many areas of life without any substantial control over their activity. Moreover, some of the agencies have been so closely identified with the industries they are regulating that the theory of their operating in the public interest is open to question. The doubt has been increased with the knowledge that many senior officials have later been employed by the regulated industry after leaving the bureaucracy.

Information and Advice

Much of the influence and power of the civil service results from administrative expertise and possession of knowledge and information with which the multiplicity of public issues can be tackled. "Generally speaking," Max Weber argued, "the trained permanent bureaucrat is more likely to get his way in the long run than his nominal superior, the political minister, who is not a specialist." Not only is control the result of knowledge, but also the information received by politicians may often be largely that which the civil service, which serves as a filter, thinks desirable. Even an absolute monarch depends for information on the bureaucracy.

The need for skilled expertise has been amply illustrated by the experience of West Germany where the postwar leadership has been characterized, as Lewis Edinger has pointed out, by those who were ambivalent or neutral to the Nazi regime, being among neither its leaders nor major opponents.[18] The need for skilled officials and both civilian and military leaders led to a somewhat flexible interpretation of Nazi allegiance. Only some 2 percent of the 50,000 German public servants dismissed in the Allied zones of occupation as part of the denazification program after World War II were classified as permanently ineligible for reemployment.

Ministers, in turn, aware of their dependence on officials for knowledge, have tried to acquire information from people outside the departmental hierarchy. This may be done by informal "brain-trust" groups a minister may gather, or more formally by the "cabinet" system of France by which a number of people may act as personal aides and work in the office of a minister, assisting in the collection of information, the preparation of memoranda on issues with which the minister or government may be involved, the carrying on of research, the representation of the minister, and the coordination of departmental activity. But in the decade after 1945, about 75 percent of the members of these cabinets were civil servants; in the Fifth Republic the proportion has increased to about 90 percent. Since 1970 in Britain some political aides, usually academics or party officials, have been appointed as temporary civil servants. The Central Policy Review Staff, a think tank of 20 civil servants, half career officials and half from outside the service, has been located in the Cabinet Office to help the cabinet formulate overall government strategy.

As aides to the political ministers, bureaucrats ideally act in neutral fashion, not only providing material for ministers and keeping them informed, but also trying to protect them from committing political errors through lack of information or understanding. Bureaucrats are advised by and enter into negotiations with interest groups on lines thought desirable to government policy. They advise ministers on the probable reactions of the interest groups to proposed courses of action.

In spite of the fears of left-wing writers such as Harold Laski that the higher civil service would try to emasculate proposals of social governments,[19] there is no evidence in the recent politics of Western Europe that it has attempted to do this or has not faithfully attempted to follow the general direction of electoral decisions. Neutrality implies working honestly for the policies of all governments, no matter what their political affiliation, and an avoidance of identification with a particular government or minister.

But neutrality does not mean an acquiescence in the status quo nor a lack of initiative, either in the older or newer nations. Bureaucrats, acting in the interest of the whole society, may engage in planning or help formulate policies. Their neutrality reflects the differentiation of function in the political system. They are reluctant to be seen as policy makers and willing to be regarded as implementers of the policies of the ruling political groups.

Political systems have been anxious to prevent political extremists from occupying significant positions in the civil service. Since 1972 new applicants in the West German civil service have been checked for their loyalty to the democratic system; between 1973 and 1975, 235 of 454,000 applicants were rejected on these grounds.

Statesmen in Disguise?

The civil service supposedly acts as the servant of political leaders who issue the guidelines to be followed in the implementation of their policy and who are responsible for ministerial decisions. Perhaps this view was valid when the activities of the state were limited. But the multitude and complexity of the activities of modern government have meant that ministers cannot personally control all the work of their ministries and much departmental activity escapes their attention. In any case their tenure in a particular office is usually short: the average time of a Cabinet member in one of the top 11 posts in Britain in recent years was 26 months. Ministers are rarely specialists or particularly knowledgeable about the work in their departments. In all

systems the administration plays a larger role than simply the execution of orders. In many ways the senior civil service can be seen as really a part of the executive apparatus, and it is always a major actor in
the political process even if it does not totally control the operation of
the state as some have suggested.

The political role of the senior civil service is evident in both internal and external affairs. A study of the British budgetary process has
shown that the 200 or so civil servants involved in the process engage
in a complex compromise with ministers.[20] In his study of the Cuban
missile crisis,[21] Graham Allison has argued that a foreign policy is
partly explainable by conflicting pressures of internal bureaucratic
politics and the routine application of normal procedures, and that
bureaucrats perceive the strength of their organization as vital to the
national interest.

The bureaucracy plays a major role not only by the gathering of information and data, but also by the initiation of policy proposals, preliminary planning, its presence in ministerial cabinets, the possibility
of occupying a governmental position, the exercise of delegated legislative authority, and the control over appointments. In both developed and developing systems the bureaucracy has been a key instrument in preventing chaos and in providing stability and
permanence.

The experience of the newer nations has shown very clearly that
the differentiation made by Woodrow Wilson[22] between politics,
"which sets the task for administration," and administration, which is
concerned with particular applications of general law, is hardly tenable, since bureaucrats in those countries often perform political
functions and determine objectives, cannot easily be controlled by the
ordinary political institutions, and sometimes may be the most significant power group in the system.

One of the most influential criticisms of the theory of separation of
powers is that made by Frank Goodnow in *Politics and Administration*.
For him the whole concept was a mistake since there are not three
powers, but really only two functions: policy, which is the expression
of the will of the state, and administration, which is its execution. The
administrative function includes at least five categories: (1) the adjudication of disputes, (2) the execution of general rules, (3) statistical and
research functions, (4) positive and technical intervention by government, and (5) quasi-judical decision making. All except the first, which
is the function of courts of law, are performed by administrators.

The supposed dichotomy of function between the political executive formulating policy and a civil servant administering it pays scant heed to reality. Policy may result from the programs of successful political parties, but it often evolves out of the needs of changing mores or patterns of behavior, economic conditions, pressure of events, or accidental forces. In these cases it may be the civil service that suggests the need for change and helps initiate policy proposals or legislation. Policy and administration are interrelated since the formulation of policy is a joint effort of constant interaction between civil servants and political ministers, who provide guidance and direction but who also depend on and benefit from departmental experience and the alternatives presented by their civil servants. The task of the administrators, as Wallace Sayre has argued in *Goals for Americans,* is to convert "the synthesis of risks and opportunities into innovative yet realistic recommendations, the process of bargaining and accommodations which transform proposals into accepted policies" as well as to execute plans and programs.

The reality of modern political life is that most laws are drafted by civil servants, that many of those laws have originated with the bureaucrats, that most laws allow the civil servants great powers of making delegated legislation, and that there is a constant interaction between administrators, political actors, and interest groups. A great deal of work concerned with preliminary planning takes place within departments unknown to political ministers, and it is this lack of participation in the long discussion preceding the formation of policy that sometimes has made ministers virtual prisoners of their civil servants.

Power, as Norton Long once said, is the most overlooked factor in public administration.[23] Bureaucrats inevitably seek support from those groups that possess political strength or from the public in general. The bureaucracy tries to accommodate demands made by individuals or groups as well as help determine the order of political priorities. The bureaucracy far from being the source of tyranny, may be regarded as more representative of the people's wishes than is the legislature, since its members are often likely to be seen as the providers of desired services. Officials are not merely subordinates of the political executive; they also respond to the groups and individuals whom they serve. But their view of the needs of these groups and individuals depends on a number of factors, such as their level of responsibility and the nature of their job, the kind of services provided, the degree of their career orientation, and their concern with the general welfare or that of particular groups.

The exercise of discretion is inherent in the administrative function and can take a variety of forms, ranging from the use of common sense to implement a minor function, the use of judgment to act quickly in an emergency where the public health and safety may be concerned, the use of knowledge and experience to decide on what basis licenses should be awarded or if inspected premises satisfy required minimum standards, to the use of political skill and diplomacy to amplify general legislative phrases such as "fair," "necessary," "adequate," or "reasonable."

Sometimes the civil service enters more directly into politics. In Finland a government composed of senior civil servants has been appointed when a political crisis has made a coalition government of politicians difficult. In both Greece and Holland civil servants have occasionally been appointed as caretaker prime ministers. In Switzerland the civil service makes its position known in the initiative and referendum process. The French Fifth Republic has been marked by the presence of bureaucrats or technocrats as political ministers. In Sweden, with its system of functional decentralization, it is the central boards rather than the ministers that are the real administrative bodies. Postwar Japan also has illustrated the entrance of civil service into political roles. After the Meiji restoration the samurai caste, constituting about 5 percent of the population, had supplied the largest number of members in the bureaucracy and other public services since it was the only group with specialized knowledge. Since World War II about two-thirds of the newly chosen governors in Japan have been civil servants who have supplied some of the chief political figures of the new regime including prime ministers.

The Problem of Administrative Law

The greater role played by the civil service in framing delegated legislation and in making judicial or quasi-judicial decisions has led to considerable criticism, especially by those who fear that the rule of law may have been subverted. In his *Introduction to the Study of the Law of the Constitution*, A. V. Dicey provided a classic definition of the supremacy of law: "no man is punishable or can lawfully be made to suffer in body or goods except for a distinct breach of law established in the ordinary legal manner before the ordinary courts of the land." In this view, other methods of making decisions, such as by administrative law in France, belonged to an alien culture in which government officials had rights and privileges that other citizens did not possess, and these privileges were granted on principles other than those determining the legal rights of citizens.

But just as it is clear that civil servants have always exercised specialized powers dealing with matters such as health, housing, police, and education as well as possessing a general discretionary power, it is also clear that they now exercise a considerable amount of judicial power. The criticism of lawyers on this development has focused on the absence of formal procedures—such as the right to be heard, the right to adequate notice, adherence to the rules of evidence, ability to cross-examine, the recording and explanation of decisions, and the right of appeal—traditionally associated with the operation of common law courts. It is certainly true that not all these formal procedures are followed in the judicial activities of administrative officials and that there is great reliance on informal procedures, interviews, inspections, and correspondence rather than adversary hearings. But it is also true that the common law courts, which are suitable to handle disputes between private litigants, are not really adequate to deal with relationships between citizens and governments, with the exercise of government prerogative, or with the multitude of official actions. Moreover, the maxim "ignorance of the law is no defense," which can barely be applied with equity to common law today, is hardly applicable to the volume of delegated legislation made by civil servants, and the consequent ignorance of citizens must be treated with discretion. The case for the existence of administrative tribunals and for administrative officials making judicial decisions is based on the desire to escape from the purely legalistic approach in the making of decisions, the need for informed discretion rather than the application of a law, and the advantage of speed. Administrative officials are better able to frame rules and to apply them in specific cases than are the ordinary courts, which lack both time and competence.

The most renowned of administrative tribunals, and the object of Dicey's wrath, is the *Conseil d'État* in France, which from its inception has performed the triple functions of collaborating with the government in the drafting of bills and regulations, being a reservoir of officials from which senior civil servants would be drawn to perform a number of functions in government departments or agencies, and acting as a tribunal to decide on the behavior of officials. The pressure of work in recent years has somewhat transformed its function as a tribunal so that, since 1953, the *Conseil d'État* has ceased to be a court of general original jurisdiction in administrative matters. This jurisdiction is now exercised by regional administrative tribunals, while the *Conseil d'État* acts as a court of appeal from them.

The major advantage of this French system is to allow any person or group that feels aggrieved by an administrative decision to argue that it be revoked on the grounds of an absence or authority, impropriety of form, contravention of a statute or general rule of law, and a misuse of power. The fact that troubled Dicey and many others is that decisions on administrative activity are made by individuals who are not magistrates, who are not specialists in those subjects under litigation, and who may also act as administrative officials and government advisers as well as in a judicial capacity. But in the case of France this has not led to arbitrary behavior on the part of the bureaucracy. The *Conseil d'État*, in its judicial capacity, has tried to protect the individual against unlawful administrative action and has tried to restrict the degree of administrative discretion.

Control over Bureaucracy

The prominence of the civil service in many aspects of the public service has led to the growing belief that there is insufficient control over it. Control over administrative behavior is sometimes sought by formal mechanisms. In the United States fear of abuse of power led to the 1946 Administrative Procedures Act, which stated the need for providing notice of proposed rules, for allowing all interested to have an opportunity to participate, and for protecting those involved in judicial proceedings.

Frequently, however, legislative and judicial controls seem to be limited in effectiveness. In France neither the plans for modernization and equipment nor the problem of nationalized industries were ever seriously discussed in the legislature. The Western countries have found it difficult to control the spending of the public sector: in 1974–1975 Britain spent about £5 billion more than intended. The permanent status of the civil service, its syndicalization and powers of self-government make it difficult for the executive to control. The difficulty is increased when the common social background and training of the senior civil service and its sense of its own intellectual distinction produces a group mentality and a spirit of camaraderie, heightened by a similar education as in the British public schools or Oxford and Cambridge universities or in the French Ecole Nationale d'Administration or Ecole Polytechnique.

Yet the civil service is not a monolithic entity whose senior members are devoted to the insidious pursuit of power. Individual bureaucrats try to maximize their own share of the total budget, because their activity will depend on the amount allocated. Those concerned with technical matters may be opposed to those involved in political and juridical decisions. "Spending" departments may war with "savings" departments, and central organizations be opposed by local and regional agencies. Agencies engaged in formulating programs may find they are checked by general review agencies such as the Treasury in Britain or the Bureau of the Budget in the United States. Bureaucracy may check bureaucracy as in West Germany where the veto of the Bundesrat (and therefore of the bureacrats of the Länder who are the real force in it) prevents the encroachment of the federal government, while the federal civil service supervises the land civil services in the execution of federal laws. Unity in the United States has been limited not only by the divisions between departments, but also by an understandable lack of agreement and intimacy between the changing group of top civil servants and the stable permanent administrators, by the virtual autonomy of some bureaus in government departments, by the competition of bureaus for the resources of departments, and by alliances made between congressional committees and pressure groups and some favored bureaus.

Civil servants are in general responsive to the wishes of their superiors or to the needs of society and are accountable for their actions or behavior. Control over the behavior of bureaucrats may be internal or external. Internal controls exist when bureaucrats accept the ethic of their profession and the agreed rules and due processes that impose restraints on the use of power and do not allow personal considerations to influence their behavior. External controls may be imposed by the discipline of the profession, ranging from reprimand or dismissal to reduction of salary or failure to promote. They may be judicial impositions resulting from the breaking of civil and criminal laws. They may result from investigations by legislative committees into bureacratic behavior or from the control over appropriations to government departments. They may stem from party policies or electoral decisions, which may reflect criticism of certain administrative actions. They may be enforced by specific outside bodies, such as the *Conseil d'Etat* in France, the *Consiglio di Stato* in Italy, and the office of ombudsman in the Scandinavian countries, all of which are given the function of controlling the legality of administrative actions.

The middle- or upper-class status or social background of senior civil servants has frequently led to criticism that they are incapable of perceiving the needs of modern society. Demands that the bureacracy be made more responsive normally implies that its members should be drawn from wider social backgrounds and experiences and that their professional training should include a knowledge of economic and social matters. Though schools of public administration that help train civil servants have fostered conceptions of positive government and dealt with economic problems, the selection process by which civil servants are chosen has not yet been able in most countries to alter substantially the type of candidates who are successful. In an age of strong government the old maxim *quis custodiet ipsos custodes* (who shall guard the guardians) is still appropriate.

Notes

[1] W. H. Willoughby, *Principles of Legislative Organization and Administration* (Washington, D.C.: The Brookings Institution, 1934).

[2] L. H. Gulick, ed., *Papers on the Science of Administration* (New York: Columbia University Press, 1937).

[3] Herbert Simon, *Administrative Behavior* (New York: Free Press, 1957), pp. 147–149; and Chester Barnard, *The Functions of the Executive* (Cambridge, Mass.: Harvard University Press, 1938), p. 77.

[4] Max Weber, *From Max Weber,* H. H. Gerth and C. Wright Mills, eds. (New York: Oxford University Press, 1946).

[5] Robert Merton, *Social Theory and Social Structure* (New York: Free Press, 1949).

[6] Robert D. Putnam, "The Political Attitudes of Senior Civil Servants in Britain, Germany, and Italy," in Mattei Dogan, ed., *The Mandarins of Western Europe* (New York: Wiley, 1975), pp. 87–123.

[7] Samuel J. Eldersveld et al., "Elite Perceptions of the Political Process in the Netherlands," in Dogan, ibid., pp. 129–159.

[8] Bruce W. Headey, "A Typology of Ministers," in Dogan, ibid., pp. 63–84.

[9] Mattei Dogan, "The Political Power of the Western Mandarins," in Dogan, ibid., pp. 3–21.

[10] Charles Lindblom and David Braybrooke, *A Strategy of Decision* (New York: Free Press, 1963).

[11] Simon, op. cit., p. xxv.

[12] John Armstrong, "Sources of Administrative Behavior: Some Soviet and Western European Comparisons," *American Political Science Review* (September 1965), pp. 643–655.

[13] Fred Riggs, "Bureaucrats and Political Developments: A Paradoxical View," in Joseph La Palombara, ed., *Bureaucracy and Political Development* (Princeton University Press, 1967), pp. 128–129.

[14] Ralph Braibanti, *Research on the Bureaucracy of Pakistan* (Durham, N.C.: Duke University Press, 1966).

[15] Fred Riggs, "Agraria and Industria," in W. J. Siffin, ed., *Toward the Comparative Study of Public Administration* (Bloomington: Indiana University Press, 1957), pp. 23–116.

[16] Lucian Pye, *"The Spirit of Burmese Politics* (Cambridge, Mass.: M.I.T. Press, 1959).

[17] V. I. Lenin, *The State and Revolution* (New York: International Publishers, 1932).

[18] Lewis Edinger, "Post-Totalitarian Leadership: Elites in the German Federal Republic," *American Political Science Review* (March 1960), p. 72.

[19] Harold Laski, *Parliamentary Government in England* (New York: Viking Press, 1938).

[20] Hugh Heclo and Aaron Wildavsky, *The Private Government of Public Money* (Berkeley: University of California Press, 1974).

[21] Graham Allison, *Essence of Decision* (Boston: Little, Brown, 1971).

[22] Woodrow Wilson, "The Study of Aministration," *Political Science Quarterly* (June 1887), pp. 197–222.

[23] Norton Long, *The Polity* (Skokie, Ill.: Rand McNally, 1962).

Selected
Bibliography

The Study of Comparative Government and Politics

ALMOND, G., and J. S. COLEMAN, eds., *The Politics of the Developing Areas.* Princeton University Press, 1960.

ALMOND, G., and G. B. POWELL, *Comparative Politics: A Developmental Approach.* Boston: Little, Brown, 1966.

BEER, S., *et al., Patterns of Government.* 2nd ed., New York: Random House, 1962.

CRICK, B., *The American Science of Politics.* Berkeley: University of California Press, 1959.

CURTIS, M., ed., *The Nature of Politics.* New York: Avon Books, 1962.

DAHL, R., *Modern Political Analysis.* Englewood Cliffs, N.J.: Prentice-Hall, 1963.

EASTON, D., *The Political System.* New York: Knopf, 1953.

ECKSTEIN, H., and D. APTER, eds. *Comparative Politics: A Reader.* New York: Free Press, 1963.

EULAU, H., *The Behavioral Persuasion in Politics.* New York: Random House, 1963.

FARRELL, R. B., ed., *Approaches to Comparative and International Politics.* Evanston, Ill.: Northwestern University Press, 1966.

HOLT, R. T., and J. E. TURNER, eds., *The Methodology of Comparative Research.* New York: Free Press, 1970.

KUHN, T. S., *The Structure of Scientific Revolutions.* 2nd ed. University of Chicago Press, 1970.

MACRIDIS, R., *The Study of Comparative Government.* New York: Random House, 1955.

RUNCIMAN, W. G., *Social Science and Political Theory.* New York: Cambridge University Press, 1969.

SORAUF, F., *Perspective on Political Science.* Columbus, Ohio: Merrill, 1965.

STORING, H., *et al., Essays on the Scientific Study of Politics.* New York: Holt, Rinehart and Winston, 1962.

VAN DYKE, V., *Political Science: A Philosophical Analysis.* Stanford University Press, 1960.

WINCH, P., *The Idea of a Social Science.* Boston: Routledge & Kegan Paul, 1958.

YOUNG, O., *Systems of Political Science.* Englewood Cliffs, N.J.: Prentice-Hall, 1968.

YOUNG, R., ed., *Approaches to the Study of Politics*. Evanston, Ill.: Northwestern University Press, 1958.

Society and the State

ALMOND, G., and S. VERBA, *The Civic Culture*. Boston: Little, Brown, 1965.

BARKER, E., *Principles of Social and Political Theory*. New York: Oxford University Press, 1951.

BEARD, C., *The Economic Basis of Politics*. New York: Random House (Vintage Books), 1957.

BELL, D., *The Coming of Post-Industrial Society*. New York: Basic Books, 1973.

BOTTOMORE, T., *Elites and Society*. New York: Basic Books, 1964.

CASSINELLI, C. W., *The Politics of Freedom*. Seattle: University of Washington Press, 1961.

CASSIRER, E., *The Myth of the State*. New Haven, Conn.: Yale University Press, 1946.

DENNIS, J., ed. *Socialization to Politics*. New York: Wiley, 1973.

DOWNS, A., *An Economic Theory of Democracy*. New York: Harper & Row, 1957.

EDELMAN, M., *The Symbolic Uses of Politics*. Urbana: University of Illinois Press, 1964.

GREENSTEIN, F., *Personality and Politics*. Chicago, Il.: Markham, 1969.

HYMAN, H. H., *Political Socialization*. New York: Free Press, 1959.

JOHNSON, C., *Revolutionary Change*. Boston: Little, Brown, 1966.

KORNHAUSER, W., *The Politics of Mass Society*. New York: Free Press, 1959.

LINDSAY, A. D., *The Modern Democratic State*. New York: Oxford University Press, 1943.

LIPSET, S. M., *Political Man*. Garden City, N.Y.: Doubleday, 1960.

MACIVER, R., *The Web of Government*. New York: Macmillan, 1947.

MANUEL, F. E., *Shapes of Philosophic History*. Stanford University Press, 1965.

MERTON, R. K., *Social Theory and Social Structure*. New York: Free Press, 1949.

MOORE, B., JR., *The Social Origins of Dictatorship and Democracy*. Boston: Beacon Press, 1966.

PYE, L., and S. VERBA, eds., *Political Culture and Political Development*. Princeton University Press, 1965.

SARTORI, G., *Democratic Theory*. New York: Praeger, 1965.

SCHUMPETER, J., *Capitalism, Socialism and Democracy*. New York: Harper & Row, 1942.

SHONFELD, A., *Modern Capitalism*. New York: Oxford University Press, 1965.

SOLOMON, R., *Mao's Revolution and Chinese Political Culture*. Berkeley: University of California Press, 1971.

SPITZ, D., *Democracy and the Challenge of Power*. New York: Columbia University Press, 1958.

STRAUSS, L., *Natural Rights and History*. University of Chicago Press, 1953.

THORSON, T. L., *The Logic of Democracy*. New York: Holt, Rinehart and Winston, 1962.

TUSSMAN, J., *Obligation and the Body Politic*. New York: Oxford University Press, 1960.

WALLAS, G., *Human Nature in Politics*. New York: Knopt, 1921.

The Classification of Political Systems

ARENDT, H., *The Origins of Totalitarianism*. Rev. ed., New York: Harcourt Brace Jovanovich, 1966.

ARISTOTLE, *The Politics*. Edited by E. Barker. New York: Oxford University Press, 1946.

BARBU, Z., *Democracy and Dictatorship*. New York: Grove Press, 1956.

BINDER, L. et al., *Crises in Political Development*. Princeton University Press, 1972.

BLACK, C. E., *The Dynamics of Modernization*. New York: Harper & Row, 1966.

BRYCE, J., *Studies in History and Jurisprudence*. 2 vols., New York: Oxford University Press, 1901.

BRYCE, J., *Modern Democracies*. New York: Macmillan, 1921.

BRZEZINSKI, Z. K. and S. HUNTINGTON. *Political Power, USA/USSR*. New York: Viking Press, 1964.

CARTER, G. M., ed., *National Unity and Regionalism in Eight African States*. Ithaca, N.Y.: Cornell University Press, 1966.

COLEMAN, J. S., ed., *Studies in Political Development*. Princeton University Press, 1965.

DEAN, V. M., *The Nature of the Non-Western World*. New York: New American Library, 1963.

DJILAS, M. *The New Class*. New York: Praeger, 1957.

ELAZAR, D., *American Federalism*. New York: Crowell, 1966.

FINER, S., *The Man on Horseback*. London: Pall Mall, 1962.

FRIEDLAND, W. H. and C. G. ROSBERG, JR., eds., *African Socialism*. Stanford University Press, 1964.

FRIEDRICH, C., ed., *Totalitarianism*. Cambridge, Mass.: Harvard University Press, 1954.

FRIEDRICH, C., and Z. K. BRZEZINSKI. *Totalitarian Dictatorship and Autocracy*. 2nd ed., New York: Praeger, 1966.

FRIEDRICH, C., M. CURTIS, and B. BARBER, *Totalitarianism in Perspective*. New York: Praeger, 1970.

HOLT, R. T., and J. E. TURNER, *The Political Basis of Economic Development*. New York: Van Nostrand, 1966.

HUNTINGTON, S. P., *Political Order in Changing Societies*. New Haven, Conn.: Yale University Press, 1968.

KAUTSKY, J., *The Political Consequences of Modernization*. New York: Wiley, 1972.

LACQUEUR, W., ed., *Polycentrism*. New York: Praeger, 1962.

LIVINGSTON, W., *Federalism and Constitutional Change*. New York: Oxford University Press (Clarendon Press), 1956.

MCCORD, W., *The Springtime of Freedom*. New York: Oxford University Press, 1965.

MCMAHON, A., ed., *Federalism, Mature and Emergent*. Garden City, N.Y.: Doubleday, 1955.

MILLER, J. D. B., *The Politics of the Third World*. New York: Oxford University Press, 1967.

NOLTE, E., *Three Faces of Fascism*. New York: Holt, Rinehart and Winston, 1966.

PAYNE, S. G., *Politics and the Military in Modern Spain*. Stanford University Press, 1967.

PYE, L., *Aspects of Political Development*. Boston: Little, Brown, 1966.

ROSTOW, W. W., *The Stages of Economic Growth*. New York: Cambridge University Press, 1960.

SCHAPERA, I., *Government and Politics in Tribal Societies*. London: Watts, 1956.

SIGMUND, P., ed., *The Ideologies of the Developing Nations*. New York: Praeger, 1963.

TALMON, J., *The Origins of Totalitarian Democracy*. New York: Praeger, 1960.

WEBER, M., *From Max Weber.* Edited by H. H. Gerth and C. W. Mills. New York: Oxford University Press, 1946.
WHEARE, K. C., *Federal Government.* 4th ed., New York: Oxford University Press, 1964.

The Fundamental Rules of Regimes:
Constitutions, Conventions, and Law

ABRAHAM, H. J., *Freedom and the Court.* New York: Oxford University Press, 1967.
ABRAHAM, H. J., *The Judicial Process.* New York: Oxford University Press, 1962.
BERMAN, H. J., *Justice in the USSR.* Rev. ed., Cambridge, Mass.: Harvard University Press, 1963.
CARDOZO, B., *The Nature of the Judicial Process.* New Haven, Conn.: Yale University Press, 1921.
CURTIS, M., ed., *The Great Political Theories.* 2 vols., New York: Avon Books, 1961–1962.
FRIEDRICH, C., ed., *Justice.* New York: Atherton, 1963.
JACKSON, R. M., *The Machinery of Justice in England.* New York: Macmillan, 1960.
KIRCHHEIMER, O., *Political Justice.* Princeton University Press, 1961.
MCILWAIN, C. H., *Constitutionalism: Ancient and Modern.* Ithica, N.Y.: Cornell University Press, 1947.
MILL, J. S., *On Liberty.* New York: Oxford University Press, 1954.
MURPHY, W. and C. H. PRITCHETT, eds., *Courts, Judges and Politics.* New York: Random House, 1961.
NEUMANN, F., *The Democratic and the Authoritarian State.* New York: Free Press, 1956.
OPPENHEIM, F., *Dimensions of Freedom.* New York: St. Martin's Press, 1961.
ROSENBLUM, V., *Law as a Political Instrument.* Garden City, N.Y.: Doubleday, 1955.
SCHWARTZ, B., ed., *The Code Napoleon and the Common Law World.* New York University Press, 1954.
VANDERBILT, A. T., *The Doctrine of the Separation of Powers.* Lincoln: University of Nebraska Press, 1953.
WHEARE, K. C., *Modern Constitutions.* New York: Oxford University Press, 1963.
WORMUTH, F. D., *The Origins of Modern Constitutionalism.* New York: Harper & Row, 1949.

Representation and Voting

BERELSON, B., *et al., Voting.* University of Chicago Press, 1954.
BLONDEL, J., *Voters, Parties and Leaders.* Baltimore: Penguin Books, 1963.
BONE, H. A., and A. RANNEY, *Politics and Voters.* New York: McGraw-Hill, 1963.
BONHAM, J., *The Middle Class Vote.* London: Faber & Faber, 1954.
BURNS, J. M., *The Deadlock of Democracy.* Englewood Cliffs, N.J.: Prentice-Hall, 1963.
BUTLER, D., *The Electoral System in Britain, 1918–1951.* New York: Oxford University Press (Clarendon Press), 1954.
CAMPBELL, A., *et al., The American Voter.* New York: Wiley, 1960.
CAMPBELL, A., et al., *Elections and the Political Order.* New York: Wiley, 1966.
DAVIES, J. C., *Human Nature in Politics.* New York: Wiley, 1963.

EMDEN, C. S., *The People and the Constitution.* 2nd ed., New York: Oxford University Press, 1956.

HERMENS, F., *Europe Between Democracy and Anarchy.* University of Notre Dame, 1951.

KEY, V. O., JR., *Public Opinion and American Democracy.* New York: Knopf, 1961.

KITZINGER, U., *German Electoral Politics.* New York: Oxford University Press, 1960.

LAKEMAN, E., and J. D. LAMBERT, *Voting in Democracies.* London: Faber & Faber, 1959.

MACKENZIE, W. J. M., *Free Elections.* New York: Holt, Rinehart and Winston, 1958.

MILL, J. S., *Representative Government.* New York: Oxford University Press, 1946.

NORDLINGER, E. A., *The Working-Class Tories.* Berkeley: University of California Press, 1967.

PITKIN, H. F., *The Concept of Representation.* Berkeley: University of California Press, 1968.

RAE, D., *The Political Consequence of Electoral Laws.* New Haven, Conn: Yale University Press, 1967.

RANNEY, A., *Pathways to Parliament.* Madison: University of Wisconsin Press, 1965.

ROSE, R., *Influencing Voters.* London: Faber & Faber, 1967.

ROSS, J. F. S., *Elections and Electors.* London: Eyre and Spottiswoode, 1955.

SCHATTSCHNEIDER, E., *The Semisovereign People.* New York: Holt, Rinehart and Winston, 1961.

TRUMAN, D., *The Governmental Process.* New York: Knopf, 1951.

TUCKER, R. C., *The Soviet Political Mind.* New York: Praeger, 1963.

WILSON, F. G., *A Theory of Public Opinion.* Chicago: Regnery, 1962.

Interests, Political Parties, and Party Systems

ALFORD, R., *Party and Society.* Skokie, Ill.: Rand McNally, 1964.

BOSWORTH, W., *Catholicism and Crisis in Modern France.* Princeton University Press, 1962.

CARTER, G. M., ed., *African One-Party States.* Ithaca, N.Y.: Cornell University Press, 1962.

CHRISTOPH, J. B., *Capital Punishment and British Politics.* University of Chicago Press, 1962.

COLEMAN, J. S., and C. G. ROSBERG, JR., eds., *Political Parties and National Integration in Tropical Africa.* Berkeley: University of California Press, 1964.

DUVERGER, M., *Political Parties.* 2nd ed., New York: Wiley, 1959.

ECKSTEIN, H., *Pressure Group Politics.* Stanford University Press, 1960.

EHRMANN, H. W., ed., *Interest Groups on Four Continents.* University of Pittsburgh Press, 1958.

EPSTEIN, L. D., *Political Parties in Western Democracies.* New York: Praeger, 1967.

HODGKIN, T., *African Political Parties.* Baltimore: Penguin Books, 1961.

HUNTINGTON, S., and C. H. MOORE, eds., *Authoritarian Politics in Modern Society.* New York: Basic Books, 1970.

JENNINGS, W. I., *Party Politics.* 3 vols., New York: Cambridge University Press, 1960.

KEY, V. O., JR., *Parties, Politics, and Pressure Groups.* 5th ed., New York: Crowell, 1964.

LA PALOMBARA, J., and M. WEINER, eds., *Political Parties and Political Development.* Princeton University Press, 1966.

LA PALOMBARA, J., *Interest Groups in Italian Politics.* Princeton University Press, 1964.

LEISERSON, A., *Parties and Politics.* New York: Knopf, 1958.

LIPSET, S. M., and S. ROKKAN, eds., *Party Systems and Voter Alignments.* New York: Free Press, 1967.

MACKENZIE, R. T., *British Political Parties.* 2nd ed., New York: St. Martin's Press, 1963.

MICHELS, R., *Political Parties.* New York: Dover, 1959.

NEUMANN, S., ed., *Modern Political Parties.* University of Chicago Press, 1956.

OSTROGORSKI, M. I., *Democracy and the Organization of Political Parties.* Garden City, N.Y.: Doubleday (Anchor Books), 1964.

POTTER, A., *Organized Groups in British National Politics.* London: Faber & Faber, 1961.

ROSSITER, C., *Parties and Politics in America.* Ithaca, N.Y.: Cornell University Press, 1960.

RUSTOW, D. A., *The Politics of Compromise.* Princeton University Press, 1955.

SARTORI, G., *Parties and Party Systems.* New York: Harper & Row, 1969.

SINDLER, A., *Political Parties in the United States.* New York: St. Martin's Press, 1966.

SKILLING, H. G., and F. GRIFFITHS, *Interest Groups in Soviet Politics.* Princeton University Press, 1971.

WILLIAMS, P., *Crisis and Compromise.* Garden City, N.Y.: Doubleday (Anchor Books), 1966.

WILSON, H. H., *Pressure Group.* New Brunswick, N.J.: Rutgers University Press, 1961.

WOOTON, G., *Interest Groups.* Englewood Cliffs, N.J.: Prentice-Hall, 1970.

ZOLBERG, A., *Creating Political Order.* Skokie, Ill.: Rand McNally, 1967.

Assemblies and Rule Making

BAILEY, S. K., *Congress Makes a Law.* New York: Columbia University Press, 1950.

BARBER, J. D., *The Lawmakers.* New Haven, Conn.: Yale University Press, 1965.

BAYLEY, D. H., *Public Liberties in the New States.* Skokie, Ill.: Rand McNally, 1967.

BLONDEL, J., *Comparative Legislatures.* Englewood Cliffs, N.J.: Prentice-Hall, 1972.

CRICK, B., *The Reform of Parliament.* London: Weidenfeld and Nicolson, 1964.

DAHL, R. A., ed. *Political Oppositions in Western Democracies.* New Haven, Conn.: Yale University Press, 1966.

FROMAN, L. A., JR., *The Congressional Process.* Boston, Little, Brown, 1966.

GROSS, B. M., *The Legislative Struggle.* New York: McGraw-Hill, 1953.

HANSON, A. H., and H. WISEMAN. London: *Parliament at Work.* Stevens, 1962.

HIRSCH, H., and M. D. HANCOCK, eds., *Comparative Legislative Systems.* New York: Free Press, 1971.

JENNINGS, W. I., *Parliament.* 2nd ed. New York: Cambridge University Press, 1957.

LEITES, N., *On the Game of Politics in France.* Stanford University Press, 1959.

LOEWENBERG, G., *Parliament in the German Political System.* Ithaca, N.Y.: Cornell University Press, 1967.

LOEWENBERG, G., ed. *Modern Parliments: Change or Decline.* New York: Atherton, 1971.

MACKENZIE, K. R., *The English Parliament.* Baltimore: Penguin Books, 1950.

MACRAE, D., JR., *Parliament, Parties and Society in France 1946–1958.* New York: St. Martin's Press, 1967.

MATTHEWS, D., *U. S. Senators and Their World.* Chapel Hill: University of North Carolina Press, 1960.

ROWAT, D. C., ed. *The Ombudsman.* London: Allen and Unwin, 1965.

WAHLKE, J. C., et al., *The Legislative System.* London: Wiley, 1962.

WAHLKE, J. C., and H. EULAU, eds., *Legislative Behavior.* New York: Free Press, 1959.

WHEARE, K. C., *Legislatures.* New York: Oxford University Press, 1963.

YOUNG, R., *The British Parliament.* London: Faber & Faber, 1962.

The Political Executive

BARNARD, C., *The Functions of the Executive.* Cambridge, Mass.: Harvard University Press, 1938.

CARTER, B., *The Office of Prime Minister.* Princeton University Press, 1956.

EDINGER, L. J., ed., *Political Leadership in Industrialized Societies.* New York: Wiley, 1967.

GRANICK, D., *The Red Executive.* Garden City, N.Y.: Doubleday, 1960.

HEIDENHEIMER, A., *Adenauer and the C.D.U.* Nijhoff, 1960.

HOFFMAN, S., ed., *In Search of France.* Cambridge, Mass.: Harvard University Press, 1963.

JENNINGS, W. I. *Cabinet Government.* 3rd ed. New York: Cambridge University Press, 1959.

KING, A. *The British Prime Minister.* New York: Macmillan, 1969.

KOENIG, L., *The Chief Executive.* New York: Harcourt Brace Jovanovich, 1964.

LOEWENSTEIN, K., *British Cabinet Government.* New York: Oxford University Press, 1967.

MACKINTOSH, J., *The British Cabinet.* University of Toronto Press, 1962.

MORRISON, H., *Government and Parliament.* 2nd ed., Oxford University Press, 1959.

NEUSTADT, R., *Presidential Power.* New York: Wiley, 1960.

ROSSITER, C., *The American Presidency.* 2nd ed. New York: Harcourt Brace Jovanovich, 1960.

WALKER, P. G., *The Cabinet: Political Authority in Britain.* New York: Basic Books, 1970.

WILLIAMS, P., and M. HARRISON. *De Gaulle's Republic.* New York: McKay, 1960.

WISEMAN, H. V., *The Cabinet in the Commonwealth.* London: Stevens, 1958.

Administrative Systems

ALLEN, C. K., *Law and Orders.* London: Stevens, 1950.

ARMSTRONG, J. A., *The European Administrative Elite.* Princeton University Press, 1973.

BAKER, R. J. S., *Administrative Theory and Public Administration.* London: Hutchinson, 1972.

BROWN, R., *The Administrative Process in Britain.* London: Methuen, 1970.

CHAPMAN, B., *The Profession of Government.* Allen and Unwin, 1961.

CROZIER, M., *The Bureaucratic Phenomenon.* University of Chicago Press, 1964.

DE SAINTONGE, R., *Public Administration in Germany.* London: Weidenfeld and Nicolson, 1961.

EISENSTADT, S. N., *The Political Systems of Empires.* New York: Free Press, 1963.

FREEDEMAN, C. A., *The Conseil d'Etatin Modern France.* New York: Columbia University Press, 1961.

GROVE, J. W., *Government and Industry in Britain.* New York: McKay, 1962.

KAUFMAN, H., *Politics and Policies in State and Local Governments.* Englewood Cliffs, N.J.: Prentice-Hall, 1963.

KINGSLEY, J. D., *Representative Bureaucracy.* Yellow Springs: Antioch Press, 1944.

LA PALOMBARA, J., ed., *Bureaucracy and Political Development.* Princeton University Press, 1963.

MACKENZIE, W., and J. GROVE. *Central Administration in Britain.* New York: McKay, 1957.

NORMANTON, E. L., *The Accountability and Audit of Governments.* New York: Praeger, 1966.

RIGGS, F. W., *Administration in Developing Countries.* Boston: Houghton Mifflin, 1964.

ROBSON, W. A., *Justice and Administrative Law.* 3rd ed. London: Stevens, 1951.

ROURKE, F. E., ed., *Bureaucratic Power in National Politics.* Boston: Little, Brown, 1965.

SIFFIN, W., ed., *Toward the Comparative Study of Public Administration.* Bloomington: Indiana University Press, 1957.

SIMON, H. A., *Administrative Behavior.* 2nd ed. New York: Macmillan, 1957.

SNOW, C. P., *Science and Government.* Cambridge, Mass.: Harvard University Press, 1961.

STRAUSS, E., *The Ruling Servants.* New York: Praeger, 1965.

WALDO, D., *The Administrative State.* New York: Ronald Press, 1948.

Index

285